Azure Adventures with C#

First Steps for C# Developers into Azure Cloud

Michał Świtalik

Apress®

Azure Adventures with C#: First Steps for C# Developers into Azure Cloud

Michał Świtalik
Zabrze, Poland

ISBN-13 (pbk): 979-8-8688-0423-6 ISBN-13 (electronic): 979-8-8688-0424-3
https://doi.org/10.1007/979-8-8688-0424-3

Managing Director, Apress Media LLC: Welmoed Spahr
Acquisitions Editor: Smriti Srivastava
Development Editor: Laura Berendson
Editorial Project Manager: Kripa Joseph

Cover designed by eStudioCalamar

Cover image designed by Freepik (www.freepik.com)

Distributed to the book trade worldwide by Springer Science+Business Media New York, 1 New York Plaza, Suite 4600, New York, NY 10004-1562, USA. Phone 1-800-SPRINGER, fax (201) 348-4505, e-mail orders-ny@springer-sbm.com, or visit www.springeronline.com. Apress Media, LLC is a California LLC and the sole member (owner) is Springer Science + Business Media Finance Inc (SSBM Finance Inc). SSBM Finance Inc is a **Delaware** corporation.

For information on translations, please e-mail booktranslations@springernature.com; for reprint, paperback, or audio rights, please e-mail bookpermissions@springernature.com.

Apress titles may be purchased in bulk for academic, corporate, or promotional use. eBook versions and licenses are also available for most titles. For more information, reference our Print and eBook Bulk Sales web page at http://www.apress.com/bulk-sales.

Any source code or other supplementary material referenced by the author in this book is available to readers on GitHub. For more detailed information, please visit https://www.apress.com/gp/services/source-code.

If disposing of this product, please recycle the paper

I want to dedicate this book to my wife, who has always supported me in my career and encouraged me to never stop learning and growing. Even if my ideas are crazy, she always believes in me and inspires me to follow my dreams.

Table of Contents

About the Author

Michał Świtalik is a Software Engineer with over eight years of experience. Since the beginning of his journey, he always loved to share his knowledge with others. He shares his knowledge through lectures inside his company, for students, or through blog posts and by being a mentor for trainees. Michał has diverse knowledge across Azure, SharePoint, and Microsoft 365 environments. He always loves to develop himself and doesn't avoid hard and complex solutions for his clients.

Currently working as a Principal Software Engineer at Volvo, Michał's main responsibilities are to provide secure and stable solutions for his company. He watches other team members to have the same standards in their projects. Additionally, he brings new technologies or ideas and improves ways of working to stay up to date.

Michał's Microsoft certifications include Azure Solutions Architect Expert and Azure Developer Associate.

About the Technical Reviewers

 As a seasoned Full-Stack Engineer at Microsoft with over 12 years of industry experience, **Vamsi Krishna Devulapalli** brings a wealth of expertise in .NET development, Azure PaaS services, and front-end frameworks such as Angular and Vue.js. His current exploration into the latest GenAI technologies reflects his commitment to staying at the forefront of technological advancements.

Vamsi is also an avid technical book reviewer specializing in Azure PaaS services. His reviews are informed by hands-on experience and a deep understanding of cloud architecture and application development. He enjoys distilling complex technical concepts into accessible insights for fellow engineers and enthusiasts.

Beyond his professional endeavors, Vamsi indulges in travel and culinary adventures, finding inspiration in exploring new cultures and cuisines. This diverse set of interests enriches his perspective as a technical reviewer, allowing him to offer holistic evaluations that consider both technical depth and practical application.

Vamsi presents his insights into Azure and C# with a comprehensive review that delves into their practical relevance, technical rigor, and applicability in real-world scenarios.

Kasam Shaikh is a prominent figure in India's artificial intelligence landscape, holding the distinction of being one of the country's first four Microsoft Most Valuable Professionals (MVPs) in AI. Currently serving as a Senior Architect, Kasam boasts an impressive track record as an author, having authored five best-selling books dedicated to Azure and AI technologies. Beyond his writing endeavors, Kasam is recognized as a Microsoft Certified Trainer (MCT) and influential tech YouTuber (@mekasamshaikh). He also leads the largest online Azure AI community, known as DearAzure | Azure INDIA, and is a globally renowned AI speaker. His commitment to knowledge sharing extends to contributions to Microsoft Learn, where he plays a pivotal role.

Within the realm of AI, Kasam is a respected subject matter expert (SME) in generative AI for the cloud, complementing his role as a Senior Cloud Architect. He actively promotes the adoption of No-Code and Azure OpenAI solutions and possesses a strong foundation in hybrid and cross-cloud practices. Kasam Shaikh's versatility and expertise make him an invaluable asset in the rapidly evolving landscape of technology, contributing significantly to the advancement of Azure and AI.

In summary, Kasam Shaikh is a multifaceted professional who excels in both technical expertise and knowledge dissemination. His contributions span writing, training, community leadership, public speaking, and architecture, establishing him as a true luminary in the world of Azure and AI. Kasam was recently recognized as a LinkedIn Top Voice in AI, making him the sole exclusive Indian professional acknowledged by both Microsoft and LinkedIn for his contributions to the world of artificial intelligence!

Introduction

Being only a C# developer limits your opportunities in the job market. It is important to expand your skill set and knowledge in order to stay competitive. In this book, we will learn what Azure is and how to use it to enhance your development skills and open up new possibilities for your career.

I like to learn by looking at specific examples and seeing the results of my work in action without building a big project to see how to do it. In this book, you will find step-by-step instructions and a code.

I have also tried to give examples of the usage of all the components mentioned in the book so that you can easily apply the concepts to your own projects. You will be able to build an API, secure it, and deploy infrastructure. At the beginning of each chapter, I have tried to give a brief overview of what you would learn in that chapter. It is helpful for developers, architects, and project managers to understand the purpose and value of each concept before diving into the technical details.

Chapter 1 is an introduction to the Azure cloud platform and covers key concepts and benefits.

Chapter 2 shows how to build an API using Azure Functions with example scenarios.

Chapter 3 shows monitoring for your Azure environment using Application Insights.

Chapter 4 demonstrates how to work with Azure Storage and implement advanced features like blob storage, table storage, and file storage.

Chapter 5 shows how to use Event Grid to build event-driven applications and automate workflows.

Chapter 6 shows how to use Service Bus to build reliable messaging solutions and integrate applications across different services.

In Chapter 7, we will use SQL Server with Azure Functions.

In Chapter 8, we will use the Key Vault service to securely store and manage sensitive information and keys.

In Chapter 9, we will use Managed Identity to authenticate and authorize our applications to access Azure resources securely. We will also define some basic roles for the services and define their permissions and access levels accordingly using RBAC.

Chapter 10 shows how to integrate a virtual network into our Azure resources for increased security and isolation.

I am sure that after reading this book, you will be a better developer and can take full advantage of Azure's capabilities.

CHAPTER 1

Introduction to Azure

Cloud computing is a concept used to describe the distribution of computing services over the Internet, including networking, software, storage, databases, analytics, and artificial intelligence. Cloud computing can be chosen over on-premise solutions for several reasons, depending on the needs and goals of the organization. In this chapter, the main advantages of using cloud computing will be described.

One of the major benefits of cloud computing is that it eliminates the hardware maintenance overhead for individual organizations. Unlike on-premise solutions, where the organization has to purchase, install, and manage its own servers, storage devices, and network equipment, cloud computing allows the organization to access these resources as a service from a cloud provider. This means that the cloud provider is responsible for maintaining, upgrading, and securing the hardware, as well as providing technical support and troubleshooting. This can save the organization time, money, and resources, as well as reduce the risk of hardware failure or downtime. It also helps to mitigate the impact of both natural and man-made disasters, such as fires, earthquakes, deliberate equipment destruction, or theft.

Another advantage of cloud computing is that it enables the organization to create a data copy in different places, not only different countries but also different continents. This is also known as data redundancy or backup. Data redundancy is important for ensuring data availability and reliability, as well as protecting data from natural disasters, cyberattacks, or human errors. By using cloud computing, the organization

© Michał Świtalik 2024
M. Świtalik, *Azure Adventures with C#*, https://doi.org/10.1007/979-8-8688-0424-3_1

can store its data in multiple locations across the globe and access it from any device or location. This can also improve the performance and speed of data access, as well as comply with data regulations and laws in different regions.

A third advantage of cloud computing is that it offers easily scalable services. Scalability refers to the ability of a system to adapt to increasing or decreasing demand for resources. Cloud computing provides scalability by allowing the organization to adjust its resource usage according to its needs. For example, if the organization experiences a spike in traffic or workload, it can easily increase its cloud capacity by adding more servers, storage, or bandwidth. Conversely, if the organization experiences a drop in demand, it can reduce its cloud usage and save costs. This way, cloud computing can help the organization optimize its performance and efficiency, as well as avoid overprovisioning or underutilization of resources. Developers and architects need to be vigilant on the scaling of cloud resources and ensure that only the required amount of resources is provisioned to avoid unnecessary costs.

SaaS, PaaS, IaaS

It is worth knowing that there are three different layers in cloud computing. Some of the layers may require more work to maintain and develop a complex solution. This depends on the requirements for the solution; it will increase or decrease the amount of job and price required to create software for the business. So it is crucial to choose the correct layer for the specific solution. There are three layers: Software as a Service (SaaS), Platform as a Service (PaaS), and Infrastructure as a Service (IaaS).

With the Software as a Service (SaaS) delivery model, customers can access cloud-hosted apps online. SaaS applications are usually subscription based or pay per use and do not require installation or maintenance by the users. Examples of SaaS applications are Microsoft 365 applications (which include Teams, Word, and SharePoint), Dynamics 365, and Power BI.

Developers can create, test, deploy, and manage applications on a platform provided by PaaS (Platform as a Service) in the cloud without worrying about the cloud hardware. PaaS offers tools and frameworks for various programming languages, databases, and web servers. Examples of PaaS services are Azure App Service, Azure Functions, Event Grid, Service Bus, and Azure SQL Database.

IaaS is a cloud layer that provides basic computing resources, such as servers, storage, network, and virtualization. IaaS allows users to have full control and flexibility over their infrastructure, but also requires more responsibility for security, backup, and maintenance. Examples of IaaS services are Azure Virtual Machines, Azure Storage, and Azure Virtual Network.

The amount of work required to maintain or create an application or solution in each layer depends on the level of abstraction and customization. SaaS offers the highest level of abstraction and the lowest level of customization, meaning that users do not have to worry about the infrastructure or the platform, but also have limited options to modify the application. PaaS offers a balance between abstraction and customization, meaning that users can focus on the application logic and features, but also have some control over the platform configuration. IaaS offers the lowest level of abstraction and the highest level of customization, meaning that users have to manage everything from the infrastructure to the application, but also have the most freedom to customize their solution.

Azure Portal

The Azure Portal is a web-based application that allows users to access and manage various Azure services and resources. Users can create, configure, monitor, and troubleshoot cloud applications and infrastructure using either a command-line interface (CLI) or a graphical user interface (GUI). Some of the tasks that can be done in the Azure Portal include

- Creating and deploying virtual machines, containers, web apps, databases, and other cloud services

- Managing subscriptions, billing, and resource groups

- Setting up identity and access management (IAM), role-based access control (RBAC), and security policies

- Checking up on the availability, performance, and health of cloud apps and resources

- Troubleshooting issues using diagnostics tools, logs, and alerts

- Integrating with other Azure services and third-party tools

The Azure Dashboard from Figure 1-1 is a highly adaptable interface that enables users to generate and oversee diverse lists and visual representations of their resources, including resource groups and functions. The dashboard may be accessed by users using the Azure Portal, enabling them to customize its settings and configurations based on their individual tastes and requirements. The dashboard has the capability to present information from the monitor as well as other statistical measures, including metrics, alarms, logs, and health status. Through the utilization of the dashboard, individuals can obtain a concise summary of their resources and effectively track their performance and accessibility.

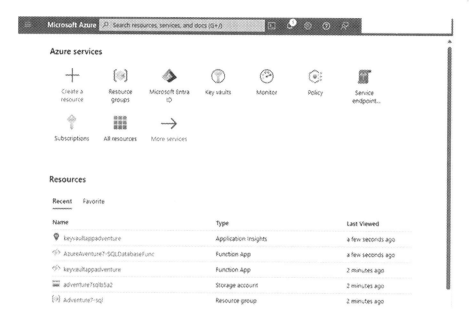

Figure 1-1. *Azure Portal*

The dashboard has been intentionally built to possess a high degree of flexibility and user-friendliness, allowing users to personalize it by incorporating various widgets, layouts, filters, and themes. Individuals have the ability to incorporate widgets into their interface by either selecting from a preexisting collection or generating their own using JSON or ARM templates. Widgets have the capability to exhibit several forms of data, including charts, tables, maps, photos, or text. Users have the ability to modify the size, position, or removal of widgets according to their preferences. The dashboard possesses the capability to accommodate many tabs, hence enabling users to systematically categorize their widgets into various groupings or situations. Additionally, users have the capability to distribute their dashboards to other users or convert them into PDF format.

5

The Azure Portal also provides the availability to open Cloud Shell. In order to run it, you will need to create or use any existing Account Storage. It can run any of the Azure CLI command in order to manage, create, or delete resources or permissions. More about the Azure CLI will be described later in this chapter.

Azure Resources

Azure is a cloud computing platform that offers a variety of services and solutions for different needs. One of the key concepts to understand when working with Azure is how its resources are structured and organized. In this section, we will explain the four main levels of the Azure resource hierarchy: management groups, subscriptions, resource groups, and resources. The relation is shown in Figure 1-2.

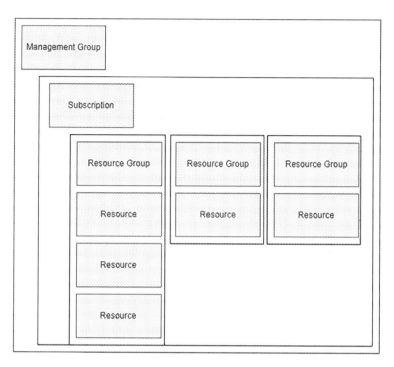

Figure 1-2. *Microsoft Azure resource hierarchy*

Management groups in Azure have the highest level of scope above subscriptions. They are containers that help organize subscriptions and resources into hierarchies, allowing for more efficient management of access, policies, and compliance across multiple subscriptions. With the management groups, you can apply policies and access controls across multiple subscriptions simultaneously. This structure is particularly useful for large organizations with complex resource arrangements, as it simplifies governance and provides a clear hierarchy for managing various subscriptions and resources. For instance, you can assign different levels of access and permissions to different teams or departments within the organization or limit regions of resources based on compliance requirements. A subscription is the second level of the Azure resource hierarchy. It is a logical container that holds all the Azure services, data, and applications that you use. A subscription is associated with a billing account, which determines how you pay for the Azure services you consume. You can have multiple subscriptions under one billing account, and you can use them to separate different environments, projects, or teams.

A resource group is the second level of the Azure resource hierarchy. It helps to logically place the resources together that are similar in terms of life cycle, access, and policies. It can contain resources from different Azure services, such as virtual machines, databases, storage accounts, web apps, etc. A resource group helps you manage, monitor, and deploy your resources as a unit. You can have multiple resource groups under one subscription, and you can use them to organize your resources by function, location, or any other criteria.

A resource is the lowest level of the Azure resource hierarchy. It is an individual instance of an Azure service or application that you create and use. For example, a virtual machine, a database, a network interface, etc., are all resources. A resource has a unique name and ID within its resource group, and it has properties and settings that you can configure and modify. You can have multiple resources under one resource group, and you can use them to perform specific tasks or functions.

How to Create Resources

You can use Bicep, Azure Portal, Azure CLI, or another library to build a resource in the Azure cloud. These are the widely utilized methods in modern solutions for creating and managing all resources. Bicep and Azure CLI are easy to use and can be easily integrated with continuous deployment pipelines to create or update many environments and resources at once.

In order to create a resource group, follow these steps:

- Go to `www.portal.azure.com`.

- Log in, if you have to – start with a new subscription.

- Click the Create a resource tile.

- A Marketplace will open up with all available resources.

- Search for Resource Group and click Create.

- Decide which subscription to choose, enter a new resource group name, select Region, then click the Review + create button.

- Click the Create button, and you can go now to your newly created resource group.

After these steps, you will have created a resource group. Inside it, you can create many resources like Azure Function, SQL Server, Storage Account, and many, many more resources. Microsoft is expanding its cloud with more features every year. You can easily find a suitable resource for your solution and create, configure, and manage it in the future.

Pricing

It is always difficult to estimate the total cost of resources that your solution will require in order to comply with all required and gathered business requirements. You can estimate the Azure pricing with the following options:

- Use the pricing calculator to find out how much cost the Azure services would incur on an hourly or monthly basis. You can customize the parameters, choose the services you require, and view the anticipated cost. Additionally, you may export your estimate as a PDF file and compare costs with those of different cloud providers.

- Acquire knowledge pertaining to the several procurement alternatives available for Microsoft Azure. There are two payment options available: pay-as-you-go and prepayment for reserved instances. The pay-as-you-go option allows users to pay solely for the resources they utilize. On the other hand, prepaying for reserved instances entails committing to a specific duration of usage, either one or three years, in exchange for discounted rates. Individuals can also derive advantages from exclusive promotions, incentives, and initiatives that have the potential to reduce their expenses.

- Please evaluate the cost information pertaining to each Azure service and its corresponding features. The pricing table for each service can be located on either its respective product page or the Pricing Details page. The pricing table displays the unit price for each service, denoted by metrics such as hourly rates, gigabyte charges, or per-request fees. The pricing structure is subject to variation based on factors such as geographical location, service tier, and performance level.

- The utilization and expenditure of resources can be effectively tracked and managed through the utilization of Azure Cost Management and Billing capabilities. Users have the ability to access their billing account, where they may monitor invoices and payments, evaluate expenses based on specific services or resource groups, establish budgets and alerts, and optimize expenditure through the utilization of recommendations.

- This tool aims to investigate the sophisticated methodologies for cost estimation utilizing Azure tools and resources. The Total Cost of Ownership (TCO) Calculator can be utilized to do a comparative analysis of the expenses associated with operating applications either on-premises or on other cloud platforms, such as AWS or Google Cloud. The Azure Pricing API can be utilized to programmatically retrieve the most up-to-date pricing data for all Azure services. The Azure retail price sheet can be downloaded to get the pricing information for all Azure regions and currencies.

In Figure 1-3, the screenshot displays the pricing calculator that Microsoft offers to its customers in order to provide an estimate of the future expenses of Azure resources. It is possible to select a number of resources all at once, and those resources may be altered and adjusted according to the needs of the solution. You can also find many configuration examples for Azure cloud in the next tab. These examples will show you the various types of configurations that are available.

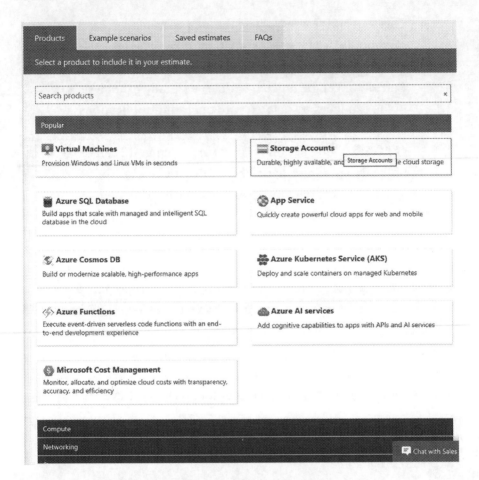

Figure 1-3. *Total Cost of Ownership screenshot*

During selection, it might be strange that some resources can be displayed with high cost at the beginning, for example, the default Azure SQL Database with vCore, which can cost up to $375, as shown in Figure 1-4. However, most small projects do not need such big size and fast data center. If the solution is being used by limited users, it is worth considering the appropriate Database Transaction Unit (DTU) model and choose 100 or even 10 DTUs.

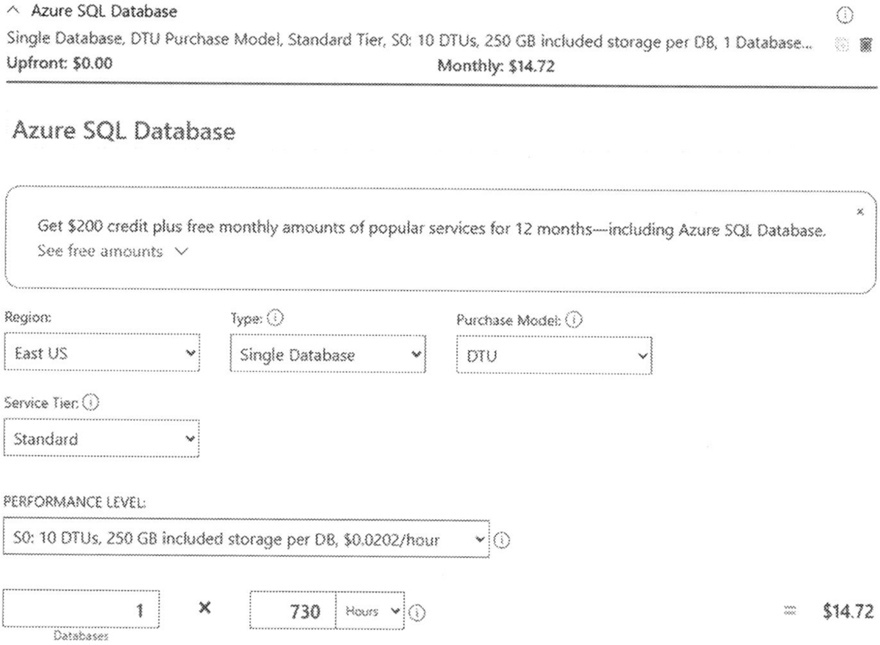

∧ Azure SQL Database

Single Database, DTU Purchase Model, Standard Tier, S0: 10 DTUs, 250 GB included storage per DB, 1 Database...

Upfront: $0.00   Monthly: $14.72

Azure SQL Database

Get $200 credit plus free monthly amounts of popular services for 12 months—including Azure SQL Database.

See free amounts ∨

Region: Type: ⓘ   Purchase Model: ⓘ

East US   ∨   Single Database   ∨   DTU   ∨

Service Tier: ⓘ

Standard   ∨

PERFORMANCE LEVEL:

S0: 10 DTUs, 250 GB included storage per DB, $0.0202/hour   ∨ ⓘ

1   ✕   730   Hours ∨ ⓘ   ⁝ $14.72

Databases

Figure 1-4. *Azure SQL Database price example*

The price also depends on the region, so it is worth checking other regions as well, if it is not critical or required to create them in this specific data center.

For a small project example, we may select using Account Storage to store files, we assume we use only 100GB for data retrieval and index, and we do around 10,000 operations in a month; it may cost only $32. Example costs are shown in Figure 1-5.

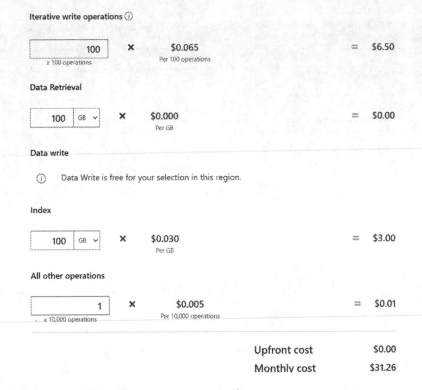

Figure 1-5. *Azure Storage cost example*

Then we add the Azure Function with the Consumption tier. We assume we won't have more than 1,000,000 requests to the API per month – it might be free. On the other hand, hosting the Azure Function on the Standard tier of the App Service plan may cost $73, as shown in Figure 1-6. It is worth noting that the Premium tiers have more features for more complex and advanced solutions. The App Service plan can host many applications.

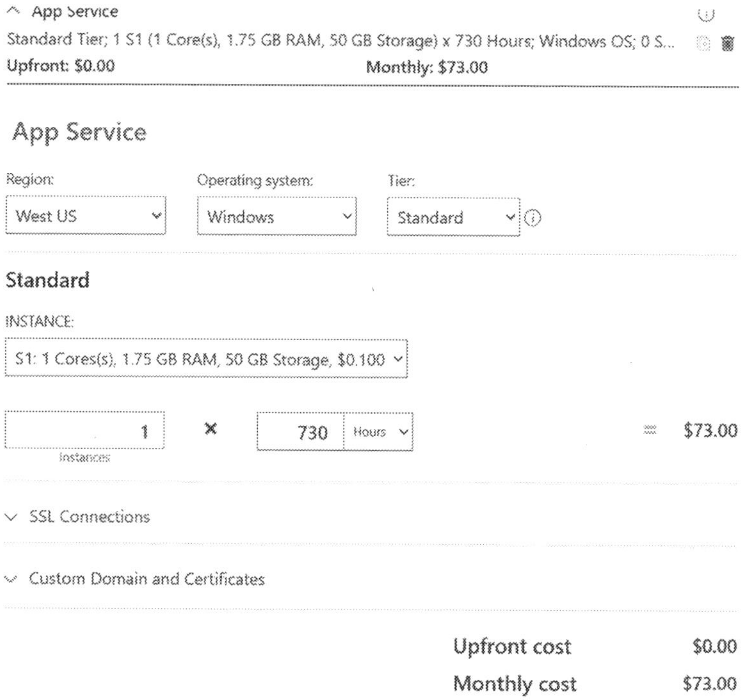

Figure 1-6. *App Service cost example*

Last but not least, the cost of selecting a SQL Database instance that has only 20 DTU units could be close to $30. The total amount that will be spent each month on the project comes to approximately $134. Naturally, this is just one possible outcome for a straightforward and not complex project. The Azure platform pricing calculator can be found at this URL: `https://azure.microsoft.com/en-us/pricing/calculator/`.

Azure CLI

In addition to the website, a command-line tool can also be used to manage Azure resources. This can be useful for developers or administrators to automate daily tasks, perform operations, or manage resources. You can create and manage Azure resources using the Azure CLI, which is a set of commands. It may be accessed via Docker, Windows, macOS, Linux, and Azure Cloud Shell. You can install Azure CLI by following instructions for your operating system from this link: `https://learn.microsoft.com/en-us/cli/azure/install-azure-cli`. To use Azure CLI, you need to sign in with your Azure account credentials using the command az login.

Azure CLI has many modules that correspond to different Azure services. You can list all the available modules using the command az --help. Some of the modules that are useful for this book are as follows:

- az functionapp – This module is allowing to create, manage, and deploy Azure functions, which are serverless applications that run on demand in response to events.

- az network – This module is allowing to create, manage, and configure Azure virtual networks (vnets), which are isolated networks that connect your Azure resources and provide secure communication.

- az keyvault – This module is allowing to create, manage, and access Azure key vaults, which are secure storage for your secrets, keys, and certificates.

- az group – This module is allowing to create, manage, and delete Azure resource groups, which are logical containers for your Azure resources that help you organize and manage them.

- az bicep – This module is allowing to create, build, and deploy Azure Resource Manager (ARM) templates using Bicep language, which is a declarative syntax for describing your Azure resources.

16

- az role – This module is allowing to create, manage, and assign Azure roles and permissions, which control the access level of users and groups to your Azure resources.

- az storage – This module is allowing to create, manage, and access Azure storage accounts, which provide scalable and durable cloud storage for your data.

Bicep

A declarative language for Azure resource deployment is called Bicep. It is designed to simplify the authoring and management of infrastructure as code. Over Azure Resource Manager (ARM) templates, Bicep provides a clear abstraction, which means that anything that can be done with an ARM template can also be done with Bicep.

To deploy a Bicep file, you need to have the Azure CLI installed and the Bicep extension enabled. Bicep files can be built, deployed, and decompiled using the az bicep command. The build command converts into an ARM template from a Bicep file, which can then be deployed using the az deployment command. The decompile command converts an ARM template into a Bicep file, which can be useful for migrating existing templates to Bicep.

A Bicep file consists of one or more resources that define the Azure resources to be deployed. Each resource has a type, a name, an API version, and a group of properties. For example, the code in Listing 1-1 defines a storage account.

Listing 1-1. Bicep for Storage Account

```
resource stg 'Microsoft.Storage/storageAccounts@2023-01-01' = {
  name: 'mystorageaccount'
  location: resourceGroup().location
  sku: {
    name: 'Standard_LRS'
  }
  kind: 'StorageV2'
}
```

Bicep supports variables and parameters to make the code more reusable and configurable. Variables are values that are defined within the Bicep file and can be referenced by other elements in the file. Parameters are values that are passed to the Bicep file from outside, such as from the command line or a parameter file. For example, the code in Listing 1-2 is using a parameter and a variable with a definition of the storage account name and location.

Listing 1-2. Bicep with variables

```
param storageName string = 'mystorageaccount'
var location string = resourceGroup().location

resource stg 'Microsoft.Storage/storageAccounts@2023-01-01' = {
  name: storageName
  location: location
  ...
}
```

Bicep also supports modularization, which means that you can split your code into multiple files and reference them from a main file. This can help organize your code and avoid duplication. To reference another Bicep file, you need to use the module keyword and provide the path to the file and the parameters to pass to it. For example, the module in Listing 1-3 references a bicep file that defines a virtual network.

Listing 1-3. Bicep using module

```
module vnet './vnet.bicep' = {
  name: 'vnetModule'
  params: {
    vnetName: 'myvnet'
    addressSpace: '10.0.0.0/16'
  }
}
```

In order to deploy, you can use Azure CLI command az deployment. It requires properties to provide like --template-file with the path to the Bicep file. You can deploy Bicep on different levels of resource – from tenant to subscription to resource group. Example of the full Bicep file, that includes Azure Function and resource group, will be in the second chapter. There will be also instructions how to deploy a file.

Security

The splitting of security responsibilities is shared between the customer and the cloud provider. The concept being referred to is commonly known as the shared responsibility paradigm. The allocation of duties may differ depending on the specific service type, such as SaaS, PaaS, and IaaS.

In a broad sense, Microsoft assumes the responsibility for ensuring the security of the cloud environment. This entails safeguarding the foundational components of the infrastructure, including the hardware, software, and facilities that serve as the hosting platform for Azure services.

Microsoft provides a wide range of tools and features that are intended to help customers protect their data and apps in cloud environments.

The responsibility for ensuring security in the cloud lies with customers, who are tasked with safeguarding their own data, identities, devices, and applications utilized or implemented on the Azure platform. In addition to their data and workloads, customers are also required to adhere to any legal or regulatory obligations that are applicable.

In Figure 1-7, the table summarizes the main areas of responsibility for each type of service. We are focusing on the PaaS layer, where customers need to take care of security for their application, data, and authentication if it's required. The OS, Internet connection, and physical infrastructure security are taken care of by the host provider.

Area	SaaS	PaaS	IaaS	On-Prem
Data	X	X	X	X
Application		X	X	X
Virtual Network		X	X	X
OS			X	X
Network/Inter net				X
Physical Infrastructure				X

Figure 1-7. *IaaS, PaaS, and SaaS examples*

In this book, we will cover the PaaS layer. The main advantages are that we don't need to take care of the OS, which includes system updates, installation, choosing the right version, licenses, etc. We can focus only on the development of the application, the storage of our data, and managing access. Furthermore, PaaS offers scalability and flexibility, allowing us to easily scale our application as needed and adapt to changing business requirements. It also provides a collaborative and efficient development environment, enabling teams to work together seamlessly and streamline the development process. Additionally, PaaS offers built-in security features, ensuring the protection of our data and reducing the risk of security breaches. Overall, the PaaS layer simplifies the development and deployment of applications, freeing up valuable time and resources for organizations to focus on their core competencies.

Azure Entra ID (also known as Azure Active Directory, AAD) provides functions such as identity and access management. It can enable such features as single sign-on and multifactor authentication using either SMS, an application, or a phone call. Additionally, this component enables the use of conditional access policies for the purpose of regulating access to resources, contingent upon specific variables such as geographical location, device type, or user affiliation. This facilitates the enhancement of security protocols within businesses, thereby mitigating the potential for unwanted access.

Furthermore, Azure Entra ID provides comprehensive auditing and monitoring functionalities called identity protection, enabling enterprises to effectively monitor user actions and promptly identify any potentially illegal activity. By utilizing these security measures, enterprises may effectively reduce the likelihood of security breaches and guarantee the authenticity and reliability of their apps and data. The enhancement of identity protection for Azure resources is achieved by the utilization of Azure Entra ID. This functionality enables enterprises to manage the authorization of user access to their Azure resources, thereby guaranteeing that only authorized individuals will be able to access confidential data and applications.

The Privileged Identity Management (PIM) service is a functionality integrated into the Azure platform designed to augment the protection of identities. Privileged Identity Management (PIM) enables enterprises to efficiently manage privileged access to their Azure resources through the implementation of just-in-time access, time-bound access, and approval workflows. This measure mitigates the potential for unauthorized access and serves as a deterrent against security breaches. Furthermore, PIM offers comprehensive audit logs and reporting functionalities, enabling enterprises to effectively monitor and trace privileged access activities in order to ensure compliance to required standards.

The Key Vault service allows developers and architects to safely operate and save cryptographic keys and secrets used in cloud applications. This service eliminates the need for developers to hardcode these sensitive credentials within their code, reducing the risk of exposure in case of a security breach. Furthermore, Key Vault provides seamless integration with Azure Active Directory and offers strong access controls, allowing developers to restrict access to only authorized individuals or services. Overall, Key Vault enhances the security posture of cloud applications and ensures the confidentiality and integrity of sensitive information.

Data Backup

Data backup is the process of creating and storing copies of data that can be used to restore the original data in the case of corrupted or lost data. Data backup is a crucial component of every organization's data protection strategy, as it ensures business continuity and decreases the probability of data loss.

In the PaaS layer, we have the SQL Database, Storage Account, and other data services. The SQL Database can be replicated to other data centers within the same zone or in another geographic region. Three categories of storage backup choices exist:

- Locally redundant storage (LRS) – This is a type of data storage replication strategy used by cloud service providers. It involves storing multiple copies of data within a single data center. This redundancy ensures that even if one copy of the data becomes unavailable, it can be easily accessed from another copy within the same data center. LRS is a cost-effective option for businesses that prioritize data availability and durability within a localized region.

- Zone-redundant storage (ZRS) – This is a similar data storage replication strategy used by cloud service providers. However, instead of storing multiple copies of data within a single data center, ZRS distributes the copies across multiple data centers within the same geographic region. This provides an added layer of protection against localized disasters or outages. ZRS is a more robust option for businesses that require higher levels of data resilience and availability.

- Geo-redundant storage – On the other hand, this takes data replication a step further by storing copies of data in multiple geographic regions. This ensures that even if an entire data center or a specific region experiences a disaster or outage, the data can still be accessed and restored from another location. This level of redundancy provides businesses with the highest level of data protection and availability, making it the perfect option for business owners that cannot afford any interruptions or data loss.

Policies

One tool that can support you in enforcing organizational standards and defining compliance for your Azure resources is Azure Policy. Azure Policy can be used to create rules that govern how resources are deployed and configured in your cloud environment.

With Azure Policy, you can manage and prevent IT issues by applying policy definitions to your resources. Policy definitions are JSON files that describe the conditions and effects for your rules. You can assign policy definitions to any scope of resources, including individual resources, subscriptions, resource groups, and management groups.

Azure Policy can help you implement governance for various scenarios, such as cost, management, security, compliance with regulations, and resource consistency. Azure provides built-in policy definitions for these common use cases, or you can create your own custom policy definitions to suit your specific needs.

Azure Policy additionally supports you to use organizing principles to bring your resources up to compliance. You can remediate existing resources in bulk or automatically remediate new resources as they are created. The Azure Policy compliance dashboard allows you to keep an eye on the compliance status of your resources.

Here are some examples of usage of the policies:

- A policy can be employed to set limitations on the allowed locations for the creation of Azure Function apps, Azure Storage accounts, and SQL Database servers. This can aid in compliance to data sovereignty requirements and reduce latency.

- One can apply a policy to investigate or restrict the creation of Azure Function applications, Azure Storage accounts, and SQL Database servers that lack encryption measures for data at rest or during transmission. Through introducing these protections in place, you can effectively protect your data from unauthorized access and guarantee that established security protocols are followed.

- One can use a policy to set restrictions on the utilization of SKUs or tiers for Azure Function apps, Azure Storage accounts, and SQL Database servers. This approach may improve cost management and enhance operational efficiency.

- One has the ability to apply a policy in order to assign metadata, such as owner, department, project, or environment, to Azure Function apps, Azure Storage accounts, and SQL Database servers. This tool facilitates the organization of resources and automates the processes of billing and reporting.

Install Required Components for Development Environment

Before going further, let's install some Azure components for Visual Studio. Follow these steps to install the required libraries:

- Run the installer of Visual Studio.

- Select the Modify option.

- Check the Programming for Azure platform component and click Close.

- Go to the Components tab and ensure that the .Net 8 Runtime is checked.

- Click the Install button.

This will install the SDK and runtime required by Azure applications. It will also provide templates for Azure Functions or Azure Resource Manager. It will be necessary to create a new solution with a default code and configuration to start the programming in the Azure platform.

Azurite is a local emulator for Azure Storage that can be used for development and testing purposes. It supports Blob, Queue, and Table services. It can be installed as a stand-alone application. Azurite is not installed with Visual Studio 2022 or with the solution. It can be added as a dependency using the NuGet package manager, then the correct values must be added to the appsettings.json file. It can be added as well during solution creation by checking the "Use Azurite for runtime storage account" option.

It is worth installing the Azure Storage Explorer as well. This program is a powerful tool that enables easy and convenient management and manipulation of Azure Storage resources. It provides a graphical interface for browsing and managing various types of storage accounts, including Blob, Queue, and Table services. With Azure Storage Explorer, users can easily upload, download, and delete files, as well as view and edit properties of storage resources. It also supports advanced capabilities such as creating and managing shared access signatures and generating SAS tokens.

Summary

In this chapter, I have introduced the cloud terminology, how it works, what the layers of cloud computing are, how Azure works, what the hierarchy is, and how to calculate the pricing of usage of future services. The required tools for developing were mentioned in this chapter and how to install them. There were also mentioned some important or event critical in some cases like security and backup of the data and application in the cloud. The chapter also discussed how the security is divided between the cloud providers and the customer.

CHAPTER 2

Azure Function

When we need an API, we traditionally create an ASP.NET service that contains controllers. However, even if it is a simple service with a few controllers, it turns out to be a large and complex solution that requires a dedicated server with appropriate settings. Therefore, in this book, we will not describe this approach, but we will describe Azure Functions, which are a serverless solution.

Azure Functions are a serverless solution that allows us to create an API without the need for a dedicated server or complex controllers. Some of the benefits of Azure Functions are as follows:

- They are scalable and can handle variable loads of requests.

- They are cost-effective and only charge for the time and resources used.

- They are easy to develop and deploy using various tools and languages.

- They have good integrations with third-party apps and other Azure services.

In this book, we are going to focus on the Platform as a Service (PaaS) level of creating solutions. The Azure Function is a great example of such resource which is widely used and has multiple options. Thanks to the PaaS approach, we can be productive from the beginning as it allows us to deploy and execute code without having to worry on the server

© Michał Świtalik 2024
M. Świtalik, *Azure Adventures with C#*, https://doi.org/10.1007/979-8-8688-0424-3_2

infrastructure maintenance, web server configurations, system updates, etc. In this chapter, we will cover the basic and more advanced feature of Azure Functions. Because it is being continuously improved and many additional capabilities are being added every year, this chapter helps you get started with Azure Functions and guide you in building your first solution.

Scenarios for Using Functions

Before starting to implement the application, it is worth knowing cases when the Azure Function can be used. These are some examples of using Azure Functions in the solution.

- Event processing

    Scenario: You have an application that needs to process events or messages in response to certain triggers. Event processing is crucial for real-time applications that require quick and automated responses to specific triggers. By efficiently analyzing and handling incoming events or messages, the application can perform actions such as updating a database, sending notifications, or triggering other processes. Implementing event processing ensures that time-sensitive tasks are executed promptly, leading to an enhanced user experience and seamless system functioning.

    Example: Use Azure Functions to process messages from a Service Bus queue, Event Grid, or Account Storage Queue events. This could be useful for order processing system. It can add a task to a queue, then it will be handled by Azure Functions asynchronously for processing notifications, delivery, or payments. Additionally, event processing can be used to analyze real-time data streams, enabling businesses to make faster and more informed decisions. By leveraging event processing, organizations can automate repetitive tasks, reduce manual intervention, and improve overall efficiency. Furthermore, event processing allows for the integration of disparate systems, enabling seamless communication and data transfer between different applications and services.

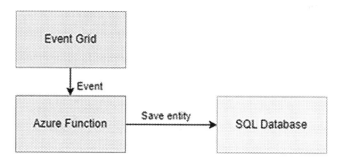

Figure 2-1. *Event processing diagram*

In Figure 2-1, the diagram shows the flow beginning with an event from the external source which is captured by the Event Grid, then it triggers an Azure Function. The Azure Function saves an entity to the SQL database.

- Scheduled tasks

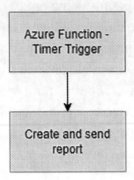

Figure 2-2. *Scheduled task diagram*

Scenario: Your application requires periodic, scheduled tasks. Using Azure Functions, you can easily automate these tasks by triggering specific events at predetermined intervals. This eliminates the need for manual intervention and ensures that these tasks are executed consistently and on time.

Example: Implement scheduled Azure Functions to perform tasks like data cleanup, sending regular reports, or triggering maintenance activities at specified intervals. Azure Functions allows you to schedule daily, weekly, or monthly tasks. This automates data retention, backup, and system updates without user intervention.

In Figure 2-2, the diagram illustrates an automated workflow where an Azure Function, triggered by a timer, generates and dispatches a report.

- REST API endpoints

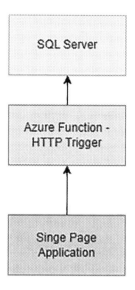

Figure 2-3. *REST API diagram*

Scenario: Extend your C# application by adding lightweight RESTful API endpoints. These endpoints can be accessed by other applications or services to retrieve or manipulate data. With REST API endpoints, it is possible to easily integrate your C# application with the front-end single-page application (SPA).

Example: Create Azure Functions to handle specific HTTP requests, allowing your application to expose API endpoints for specific functionalities. This is especially useful for microservices architectures. This allows for better scalability, maintainability, and independent deployment of different parts of your application.

31

In Figure 2-3, the diagram shows an SPA that triggers an HTTP Azure function trigger type, and then it can save the data to the SQL Server.

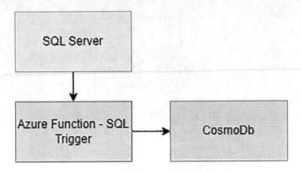

Figure 2-4. *Data processing and transformation diagram*

- Data processing and transformation

  Scenario: Your application needs to process and transform data. REST API endpoints can be used to send data to external systems or receive data from them for processing and transformation. You can utilize REST API endpoints to retrieve data from a database, perform calculations or transformations on the data, and then send the processed data to another system or service. This allows for seamless integration with various data processing tools or services, enhancing the capabilities and efficiency of your application.

  Example: Use Azure Functions to process data from Azure Storage, Cosmos DB, or other sources. For instance, you might transform and aggregate data for reporting purposes or convert data into a different format.

In Figure 2-4, the diagram shows a SQL Server that triggers changes and sends them to the Azure Function, then it may save them to another Cosmos DB for the integration process or to send a notification about the changes if it is required.

- Real-time data stream processing

    Scenario: Deal with real-time data streams. Azure Stream Analytics processes real-time data streams. This technology lets you handle and analyze streaming data to make quick decisions or take rapid actions. This is important for real-time monitoring, fraud detection, and IoT applications that require fast and accurate data processing.

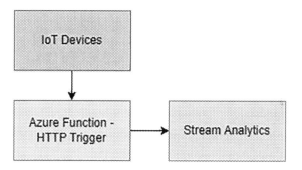

Figure 2-5. *Real-time data stream processing diagram*

Example: Utilize Azure Functions to process and analyze real-time data from Azure Event Hubs or IoT Hub. This can be beneficial for applications requiring real-time insights, such as monitoring and analytics. Another way to leverage the power of Stream Analytics is by integrating it with

33

Power BI. This allows users to create interactive dashboards and visualizations that provide real-time insights into the streaming data.

In Figure 2-5, the diagram shows the IoT devices that send data to the Azure Function. It can be a telemetry data or notifications. Then it can relay the data further to the database or Stream Analytics service for further investigation and statistics.

- Integration with external services

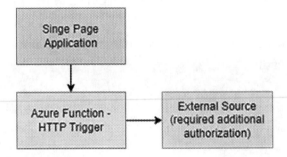

Figure 2-6. *Integration with external service diagram*

Scenario: Integrate your application with external services or APIs.

Example: Use Azure Functions to handle interactions with third-party APIs, process the results, and update your application accordingly. This is helpful for scenarios like integrating with payment gateways or social media platforms.

In Figure 2-6, the diagram shows that the system can be easily integrated. In this example, the SPA application is triggering an HTTP function. After completing its business logic, like saving to the database, sending notifications, etc., it can send the data to another, external system for further processing.

- Asynchronous processing

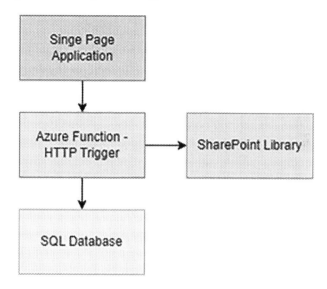

Figure 2-7. *Asynchronous processing diagram*

Scenario: Perform tasks asynchronously to improve application responsiveness.

Example: Move time-consuming tasks, like sending emails or processing large datasets, into Azure Functions. This allows your main application to remain responsive while these tasks are offloaded to serverless functions. This can be critical if the application is supposed to work fast and efficiently while generating big data reports and sending notifications to other users or systems. This will enhance the user experience in the single-page application or desktop program.

In Figure 2-7, the diagram shows another SPA application that sends a request to the Azure Function. In response to the call, it only sends the information that the request is accepted; this can be a 202 HTTP status code. The user does not see the results immediately. The function can send the information to the Azure Queue Storage, and then another function can pick it up and process the information, in this example storing it in a SQL Database and to the SharePoint Library.

First Function

The Azure Function can be created through Visual Studio (either on a Windows or Mac OS system). The first project will be an HTTP trigger function. It is triggered on the request from a browser or other tools. They can be configured to be triggered on POST, GET, DELETE, and other types of methods.

Follow these steps to create a solution with an example of the Azure Function:

- Run Visual Studio.

- Select the Cloud category.

- Search and select the Azure Functions template and click Next.

- Enter your project and solution name and change other fields if it's necessary and click Next.

- Choose HTTP Trigger from the Function templates.

- Choose Anonymous from the Authorization level. Figure 2-8 shows the final page with the selected options.

- Choose the location of your new solution and click Create.

Figure 2-8. *Visual Studio 2022 – selecting Azure Function as the template*

There are two types of Azure Functions – isolated and in-progress. Isolated solutions are those that are self-contained and do not depend on other components or systems. In-progress solutions are those that are part of a larger project and require integration with other elements. The in-progress model will reach the end of support on November 10, 2026, and it is recommended to migrate the apps to the isolated model.

The main difference between isolated and in-progress solutions is the level of complexity and risk involved. Isolated solutions are usually simpler and easier to test, debug, and deploy. In-progress solutions can be more complex to deploy and require more coordination and communication with other developers and administrators. They also have higher chances of encountering errors, conflicts, or compatibility issues.

The solution will be created with a few files:

- host.json – This file contains settings for the application like the logging level or route prefix.

- local.settings.json – This file contains local settings to be loaded when running from Visual Studio, for example, Azure Storage can be set up for the local Azurite emulator.

- Function.cs – This file contains the code of the function.

Listing 2-1. Hello world of the default Azure Function HTTP trigger

```
[Function("Function1")]
public HttpResponseData Run([HttpTrigger(AuthorizationLevel.
Anonymous, "get", "post")] HttpRequestData req)
{
    _logger.LogInformation("C# HTTP trigger function processed
    a request.");

    var response = req.CreateResponse(HttpStatusCode.OK);
    response.Headers.Add("Content-Type",
    "text/plain; charset=utf-8");

    response.WriteString("Welcome to Azure Functions!");

    return response;
}
```

Listing 2-1 depicts a simple HttpTrigger function. In the code snippet, the "Function" attribute sets the method as a starting point for function execution. The string passed in the Function attribute defines the name of the function, in this case, "Function1".

The Run method signature can have the following sections: Triggers, Bindings, Execution context, and Cancellation token. Triggers define how a function is called. And they have associated data called the payload of the function. The HttpTrigger attribute has the following parameters: AuthLevel, HTTP Methods, and Route. Bindings are used to define the methods, parameters, and return types. In our example, we have the HttpRequestData parameter, which contains the raw HTTP request. In the body of the function, the logger has logged information which is saying that the HTTP trigger has been triggered. Then the code is creating an object response with the HTTP status code as OK. Then a content type is added a text/plane to the header of the response. Then a string is writing to the response and is returning to the browser.

In order to run the project, press F5. A new command-line window will show. This terminal will contain such information as initial loading logs, loaded Azure Function triggers (in this case, it is only the default HTTP trigger with the address to request it), console output from the program, and exception or other traces.

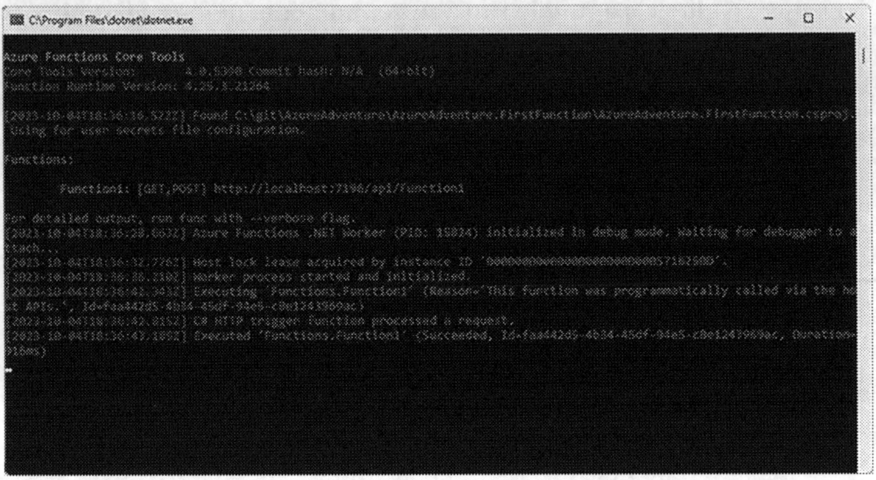

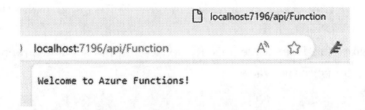

Figure 2-9. *Terminal – execution of the Azure Function HTTP trigger*

When you copy the URL from the terminal named Function1 and paste it to the browser, you should see the following result in the browser like in Figure 2-10.

localhost:7196/api/Function

localhost:7196/api/Function

Welcome to Azure Functions!

Figure 2-10. *Screenshot of the Azure Function result in the browser*

In the terminal (shown in Figure 2-9), you should see logs about the triggering Azure Function (the message starts with C# HTTP trigger...) and its end of execution (the message starts with Executed...).

Program Class

By default, the project will have added the Program.cs file. This file is very important. This is where you can add your services to inject them into classes, set up a custom middleware, or add a custom logging.

Listing 2-2. Code inside the default Program.cs file

```
using Microsoft.Azure.Functions.Worker;
using Microsoft.Extensions.DependencyInjection;
using Microsoft.Extensions.Hosting;

var host = new HostBuilder()
    .ConfigureFunctionsWorkerDefaults()
    .ConfigureServices(services =>
    {
        services.AddApplicationInsightsTelemetryWorker
        Service();
        services.ConfigureFunctionsApplicationInsights();
    })
    .Build();

host.Run();
```

The code in Listing 2-2 is the default setup during the creation of the Azure Function. In the ConfigureFunctionsWorkerDefaults program, set up the default configuration like adding environment variables to the IConfiguration interface, integration with Azure Function logging, and others. In the ConfigurationServices, you can set up your services to inject them as dependencies in a different class using the Scope, Singleton, or Transient life cycle. The HTTP client can also be added there or other hosted services.

A service can be injected with the following methods:

- AddScope/TryAddScope – A single instance will be shared in the same request or timer run.

- AddSingleton/TryAddSingleton – A single instance of the service will be shared between different classes.

- AddTransient/TryAddTransient – A single instance will be created for each request or timer run.

Deploying Azure Resources

Before deploying your application to the Azure cloud, first the resource needs to be created. Create a resource group for your resources; it is described in the first chapter of this book. Then use the script to create automatically all the required resources or create them manually in the Azure Portal.

The following bicep script from the Listing 2-3 will create the required resources that are needed to deploy and then launch the Azure function on the Azure platform. Save it as function1.bicep. Change the appName variable to your own, unique name. This variable will be part of the URL.

Listing 2-3. Bicep file with the Azure Function, Storage Account, and service app plan

```
param appName string = 'azure-function-2'
param location string = resourceGroup().location

var functionAppName = appName
var hostingPlanName = appName
var storageAccountName = replace('sa2${appName}', '-', '')
```

```
resource storageAccount 'Microsoft.Storage/
storageAccounts@2023-01-01' = {
  name: storageAccountName
  location: location
  sku: {
    name: 'Standard_LRS'
  }
  kind: 'Storage'
  properties: {
    supportsHttpsTrafficOnly: true
  }
}

resource hostingPlan 'Microsoft.Web/serverfarms@2022-09-01' = {
  name: hostingPlanName
  location: location
  sku: {
    name: 'Y1'
    tier: 'Dynamic'
  }
  properties: {}
}

resource functionApp 'Microsoft.Web/sites@2022-09-01' = {
  name: functionAppName
  location: location
  kind: 'functionapp'
  identity: {
    type: 'SystemAssigned'
  }
  properties: {
    serverFarmId: hostingPlan.id
    siteConfig: {
```

```
appSettings: [
  {
    name: 'AzureWebJobsStorage'
    value: 'DefaultEndpointsProtocol=https;Account
    Name=${storageAccountName};EndpointSuffix=
    ${environment().suffixes.storage};AccountKey=
    ${storageAccount.listKeys().keys[0].value}'
  }
  {

    name: 'WEBSITE_CONTENTAZUREFILECONNECTIONSTRING'
    value: 'DefaultEndpointsProtocol=https;AccountName=
    ${storageAccountName};EndpointSuffix=
    ${environment().suffixes.storage};AccountKey=
    ${storageAccount.listKeys().keys[0].value}'
  }
  {
    name: 'WEBSITE_CONTENTSHARE'
    value: toLower(functionAppName)
  }
  {
    name: 'FUNCTIONS_EXTENSION_VERSION'
    value: '~4'
  }
  {
    name: 'FUNCTIONS_WORKER_RUNTIME'
    value: 'dotnet-isolated'
  }
]
ftpsState: 'FtpsOnly'
minTlsVersion: '1.2'
}
```

```
    httpsOnly: true
  }
}
```

Now you can run the commands in Listing 2-4 to create resources.

Listing 2-4. Command to deploy the bicep file

```
az group create --name Azure-Function-1 --location westeurope
az deployment group create --resource-group Azure-Function-1
--template-file function1.bicep
```

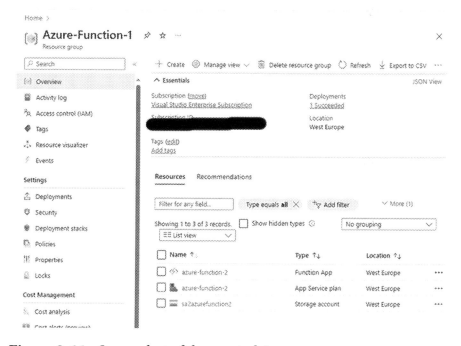

Figure 2-11. *Screenshot of the created Azure resource group*

In Figure 2-11, the screenshot shows a new resource group provisioned with the resources that are listed in the bicep file. On the left, there are sections to manage this resource security and permissions and view the history of deployments or changes.

The function files are saved in the Storage Account resource when it is deployed. The AzureWebJobsStorage and WEBSITE_ CONTENTAZUREFILECONNECTIONSTRING parameters are required for deployment purposes and permissions to load and run the application. The WEBSITE_CONTENTSHARE parameters target folder for the files to store during the deployment. This is by default for the Standard and Premium tiers of the Azure Function plan. The Storage Account is extended in the third chapter. These are some benefits of using the File Stream to store the runtime files for Azure Functions:

- It allows for more flexibility and scalability of the function app, as the runtime files can be accessed from different instances and regions.

- It reduces the risk of losing or corrupting the runtime files due to hardware failures or accidental deletions on the function host.

- It enables faster deployments and updates of the function app, as the runtime files can be synchronized across multiple instances and regions without requiring a restart of the function host.

- It simplifies the management and monitoring of the function app, as the runtime files can be accessed and modified from a centralized location for multiple applications.

The free or dev tiers of plans can be stored in the Azure Function instance. To do this, you have to remove WEBSITE_ CONTENTAZUREFILECONNECTIONSTRING and WEBSITE_ CONTENTSHARE variables from the arm and application configuration; you can as well remove the Account Storage from the arm template. Then the application must be deployed again. It will reduce the cost of the app (there is no need for Account Storage) and increase the security, because it will be isolated from other resources.

The code with the hostingPlan resource variable specifies the name, location, sku, and properties of the hosting plan. The name is a parameter that can be set by the user. The location of the Azure resource is where the function and other services will be deployed. The sku is the pricing tier and size of the resource. In this case, the code chooses the "Y1" sku, which is a dynamic plan that scales automatically based on the number of requests. The properties are optional and can be used to configure additional settings for the resource.

Deploying Azure Function

After creating the application and the resources on the Azure platform, you can now deploy your application to the host. In order to deploy and test the function on the Azure, follow these steps to deploy the application:

- Right-click the project, then select Publish.
- Choose Azure and click the Next button.
- Choose Azure Function App (Windows) and click the Next button.
- Sign in to your Azure subscription.
- Select the previously created resource group and service app plan.
- Click the Publish button.
- Test it!

Your URL can be found in the URL property of the function resource Overview section. Go to the browser and type the URL to test the Azure function (replace the hostname with yours):

```
www.hostname.azurewebsites.com/api/Function1
```

Request Object

The request object (HttpRequestData class called req variable by default) contains information sent by the requestor, such as

- Body

- Headers

- Claims

- Requested URL

- Method

- Parameters

- Query

Reading Parameters

In order to receive the JSON object from the request, the body must be read as string, then it can be converted into a class and passed to another method. To read a string from the body of the request, you can use ReadAsString (Listing 2-5).

Listing 2-5. How to use the ReadAsString method

```
var requestBody = req.ReadAsString();
```

After installing the Newtonsoft NuGet package, you can convert a string into a C# class with the example usage of the DeserializeObject method. The usage of this method is in the Listing 2-6.

Listing 2-6. How to use the Newtonsoft package to deserialize an object

```
var models = JsonConvert.DeserializeObject<PostModel>(req.
ReadAsString());
```

The reading parameters from the path can be done by adding a name of the variable in the braces to the URL of the function, and then the variable can be added to the method parameters. Listing 2-7 shows how it can be done.

Listing 2-7. HTTP trigger method with the reading name parameter

```
[Function("ReadingFromRequest")]
public HttpResponseData Run([HttpTrigger(AuthorizationLevel.
Anonymous, "get", "post", Route = "ReadingFromRequest/{name}")]
HttpRequestData req, string name)
{
    _logger.LogInformation("C# HTTP trigger function processed
    a request.");

    _logger.LogInformation(name);

    var response = req.CreateResponse(HttpStatusCode.OK);
    response.Headers.Add("Content-Type",
    "text/plain; charset=utf-8");

    response.WriteString("Welcome to Azure Functions!");

    return response;
}
```

Enter in the browser with the following URL (or different if you changed the route): localhost:7196/api/ReadingFromRequest/Rhonin. Then you should see an output in the terminal, like in Figure 2-12.

Figure 2-12. *Screenshot of the executed Azure Function with logging*

To read the parameters from the query, after the question mark you access through the HttpRequestData class using the Query property. The code Listing 2-8 is an example how to read a value from the query with a 'name' index.

Listing 2-8. Reading parameter from the query

```
var name = req.Query["name"];
```

This property has also other methods and properties:

- AllKeys/Keys – They will return all available keys in the Query.

- GetValues – This will return all values for the requested keys.

Response Object

The HttpResponseData class collects output values that will be sent back to the requestor. It has the following properties:

- Headers
- Body
- Status Code
- Cookies

The response may contain not only a string but also an object (serialized) or a file. To include a string or class object can be done using the code in Listing 2-9.

Listing 2-9. Code with object response

```
[Function("ReturningObjectAsString")]
public HttpResponseData Run([HttpTrigger(AuthorizationLevel.
Anonymous, "get", "post")] HttpRequestData req)
{
    var response = req.CreateResponse(HttpStatusCode.OK);
    response.Headers.Add("Content-Type", "application/
    json");

    var objectModel = new ObjectViewModel
    {
        Name = "New post"
    };
    response.WriteString(JsonConvert.SerializeObject
    (objectModel));

    return response;
}
```

In Listing 2-9, we create a simple ObjectViewModel variable with a Name property. In the line of code where the WriteString method is used, the object is firstly serialized into a string, then it is added to the response object. Then, a script or other APIs can read it from the content property of the response.

Routing

If there is a need to change the route of the function, it can be done via the Route property in the HttpTrigger attribute. It accepts a string as a parameter, and it will be a new route of the method. The code in Listing 2-10 shows how to use it.

Listing 2-10. Code with routing in the HttpTrigger

```
public HttpResponseData Run([HttpTrigger(Authorization
Level.Anonymous, "get", "post", Route = "anotherUrl")]
HttpRequestData req)
```

The code in Listing 2-11 shows how you can specify a different route prefix. The default prefix is "api" string. In order to change this, go to the host.json file and add an http object; inside it, you can add a routePrefix property and assign any other string or leave it empty to remove the prefix.

Listing 2-11. host.json file with an empty routePrefix property

```
{
    "version": "2.0",
    "http": {
        "routePrefix": ""
    }
}
```

Timer Trigger

The timer-triggered function enables you to run the code at specified time intervals. They are based on CRON expressions. This expression is provided in the timer trigger attribute in the code. Listing 2-12 is an example of such a function.

Listing 2-12. Timer trigger code

```
[Function("TimerFunction")]
public void Run([TimerTrigger("0 0 7 * * 1")] MyInfo myTimer)
{
    _logger.LogInformation($"Timer trigger function");
}
```

CRON is an expression of the time precision to the seconds. The following formula is read by the function: second minute hour day month day-of-week.

Here are some commonly used Azure CRON expression examples:

- Once a week at 7 a.m.: 0 0 7 * * 1

- Once a day at 3 a.m.: 0 0 3 * * *

- Every hour: 0 0 * * * *

- Every Friday at 22 a.m.: 0 0 22 ? * FRI

There are special characters used like the asterisks that represent all possible values. The question mark symbol is used to say there is no specific value. In this specific example, it's indicating there is no specific day of the month.

Sometimes, it may happen that you need to change your CRON expression on different environments or to just test something, and you want to run it earlier or other cases. So instead of deploying all the applications once again, the special reference added to the configuration variables can be used.

The code in Listing 2-13 is an example of reading the value from the configuration variables using the references.

Listing 2-13. Timer trigger code

```
public void Run([TimerTrigger("%TimerFunctionCRON%")] MyInfo
myTimer)
```

The variable in the appsettings.json configuration file will look like

"TimerFunctionCRON": "0 0 7 * * 1"

The CRON variable can also be inserted into the Azure Function Configuration section in the Azure Portal, as shown in Figure 2-13.

- Go to the Azure Function resource.

- Go to the Configuration section on the left side.

- Click the New application setting.

- Enter TimerFunctionCRON as name.

- Enter 0 0 7 * * 1 as value.

- Click the OK button.

- Click Save and confirm.

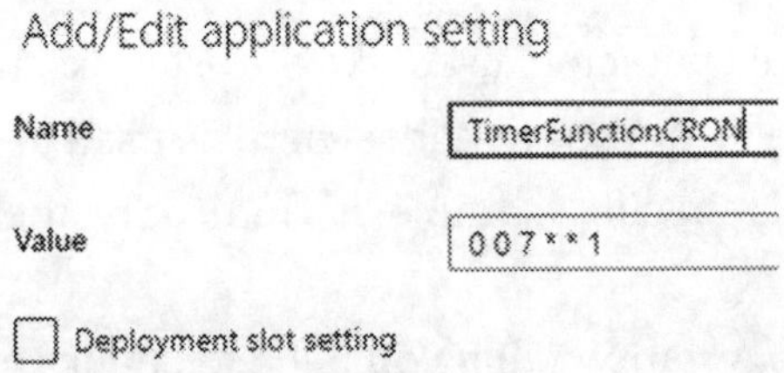

Figure 2-13. *Screenshot of Azure Function Configuration adding a new variable*

Durable Function

Writing state functions in Azure cloud serverless services is made possible by the durable functions, which are an extension of Azure Functions. This extension allows you to define a workflow that has a state. It can be done by writing a function called orchestrator and a stateful entity. They can be used to split tasks among multiple entities in order to multithread tasks. They can also pass results from one entity to another if it requires parameters from the previous task. When dealing with complex processes, the Durable Functions shine.

To create an Azure Durable Function in Visual Studio 2022, follow these steps:

- Open the Visual Studio 2022 program and create a new project; search and select Azure Functions type.

- Enter the project name, solution name, and other required inputs, then click the Next button.

- In the additional information, select the .NET 8.0 Isolated version, check the box to use Azurite, and select Durable Functions Orchestration for the trigger type of the function.

- Click the Create button.

Listing 2-14 is an example class of the default template.

Listing 2-14. Durable Function default code sample

```
using Microsoft.Azure.Functions.Worker;
using Microsoft.Azure.Functions.Worker.Http;
using Microsoft.DurableTask;
using Microsoft.DurableTask.Client;
using Microsoft.Extensions.Logging;
```

```csharp
namespace DurableFunctionApp
{
    public static class Function1
    {
        [Function(nameof(Function1))]
        public static async Task<List<string>> RunOrchestrator(
            [OrchestrationTrigger] TaskOrchestrationContext
            context)
        {
            ILogger logger = context.CreateReplaySafeLogger
            (nameof(Function1));
            logger.LogInformation("Saying hello.");
            var outputs = new List<string>();

            outputs.Add(await context.CallActivityAsync<string>
            (nameof(SayHello), "Tokyo"));
            outputs.Add(await context.CallActivityAsync<string>
            (nameof(SayHello), "Seattle"));
            outputs.Add(await context.CallActivityAsync<string>
            (nameof(SayHello), "London"));

            return outputs;
        }

        [Function(nameof(SayHello))]
        public static string SayHello([ActivityTrigger] string
        name, FunctionContext executionContext)
        {
            ILogger logger = executionContext.
            GetLogger("SayHello");
            logger.LogInformation("Saying hello to {name}.",
            name);
```

```
        return $"Hello {name}!";
    }

    [Function("Function1_HttpStart")]
    public static async Task<HttpResponseData> HttpStart(
        [HttpTrigger(AuthorizationLevel.Anonymous, "get",
        "post")] HttpRequestData req,
        [DurableClient] DurableTaskClient client,
        FunctionContext executionContext)
    {
        ILogger logger = executionContext.GetLogger
        ("Function1_HttpStart");

        string instanceId = await client.ScheduleNew
        OrchestrationInstanceAsync(
            nameof(Function1));

        logger.LogInformation("Started orchestration with
        ID = '{instanceId}'.", instanceId);

        return client.CreateCheckStatusResponse(req,
        instanceId);
    }
  }
}
```

This is the default code of the DurableFunctionApp class, which is used to create function chains in Azure Functions. In this class, there are three methods defined:

- HttpStart – This is a method that is triggered by an HTTP request and is responsible for starting the function orchestrator.

- RunOrchestrator – This is a method that is the orchestrator of the function and coordinates the calls of other functions in the chain.

- SayHello – This is a method that is triggered by the orchestrator and returns a greeting message.

An ActivityTrigger is a binding attribute that enables you to author activity functions in Durable Functions. An activity function is a method that executes a specific task in a workflow, such as calling an API, sending an email, or processing data. An activity function can be invoked by an orchestrator function using the CallActivityAsync method of the TaskOrchestrationContext object. The ActivityTrigger attribute specifies the name of the activity function and the type of the input parameter. The input parameter can be retrieved from the parameter. Using the return statement, an activity function can provide a response to the orchestrator function.

TaskOrchestrationContext is a class in the Microsoft.DurableTask namespace that is used by orchestrators to perform actions such as scheduling tasks, durable timers, waiting for external events, and getting basic information about the current orchestration. It is an abstract class that provides a context object for orchestrators to perform various actions. The TaskOrchestrationContext class is defined in the Microsoft. DurableTask.Abstractions.dll assembly.

The TaskOrchestrationContext class can be used to get the current orchestration time in UTC, the unique ID of the current orchestration instance, and whether the orchestrator is currently replaying a previous execution. It can also be used to create a durable timer that expires at a set date and time or after a specified delay.

The TaskOrchestrationContext class provides several methods, including CallActivityAsync, which asynchronously invokes an activity by name (first parameter) and the specified input value (second parameter). It also provides CallSubOrchestratorAsync, which executes a named sub-orchestrator and returns the result.

An example of using this class is as follows:

- The application sends an HTTP request to the HttpStart method with the name parameter, for example, `https://myfunctionapp.azurewebsites.net/api/Function1_HttpStart`.

- The HttpStart method will start the function orchestrator RunOrchestrator and return a set of properties which includes the unique instance ID and the URL to monitor the orchestration status.

- The function orchestrator RunOrchestrator will call the SayHello method with the string parameter.

- The SayHello method will return a greeting message with the given name, for example, "Hello, Tokyo!"

- The function orchestrator RunOrchestrator will end the orchestration and return the result to the HttpStart method.

- The HttpStart method will return an HTTP response with the orchestration object.

The returned object has the following properties:

- Id – It is a unique GUID of the running orchestration.

- purgeHistoryDeleteUri – A URL that can be used to delete the history of the orchestration.

- sendEventPostUri – A URL to send an Event if it is required by the workflow.

- statusQueryGetUri – A URL to check current orchestration status.

- terminatePostUri – A URL that can be used to cancel running of the orchestration and its tasks.

Get Results and Check Status

Copying and pasting a URL from the statusQueryGetUri return object property to the browser (as shown in Figure 2-14) will show you a new object with the following properties:

- name – The name of the orchestrator.

- instanceId – It is a GUID of a specific instance run.

- runtimeStatus – The status of the orchestrator.

- input – It contains input to the orchestrator.

- customStatus – If provided, it will have a custom status. For example, it can be the name of the current Activity Trigger in progress.

- output – The output of the orchestrator when completed.

- createdTime – The beginning time of the orchestration.

- lastUpdatedTime – The last time when the history was updated.

These are the possible values for the runtimeStatus property:

- Pending – The function is waiting to start.

- Running – The function is actively executing.

- Completed – The function has finished successfully.

- Failed – The function has encountered an error or an unhandled exception.

- Canceled – The function has been canceled by the user or by a timer expiration.

- Terminated – The function has been terminated by the user.

```
localhost:7295/runtime/webhooks/durabletask/instances/ef1a2ece5bb94c1594ce32601749786e?code=_MSaaEuf
```

```
 1  {
 2      "name": "Function1",
 3      "instanceId": "ef1a2ece5bb94c1594ce32601749786e",
 4      "runtimeStatus": "Completed",
 5      "input": null,
 6      "customStatus": null,
 7      "output": [
 8          "Hello Tokyo!",
 9          "Hello Seattle!",
10          "Hello London!"
11      ],
12      "createdTime": "2023-11-28T15:58:21Z",
13      "lastUpdatedTime": "2023-11-28T15:58:23Z"
14  }
```

Figure 2-14. *Getting status and results of the Azure Function*

Durable Function – Chaining Pattern

Function chaining is a series of functions that run in a particular order by applying one function's result to another function's input. This creates a sequence of method calls that can be used in order to apply a different action depending on the previous function results. It can be crucial to some scenarios.

Listing 2-15. Code on how to pass results

```
using Microsoft.Azure.Functions.Worker;
using Microsoft.Azure.Functions.Worker.Http;
using Microsoft.DurableTask;
using Microsoft.DurableTask.Client;
using Microsoft.Extensions.Logging;
using Newtonsoft.Json;
```

```
namespace FunctionAppChaining
{
    public static class Function1
    {
        [Function(nameof(Function1))]
        public static async Task<List<string>> RunOrchestrator(
            [OrchestrationTrigger] TaskOrchestrationContext
            context)
        {
            Ilogger logger = context.CreateReplaySafeLogger(nam
            eof(Function1));
            logger.LogInformation("Starting Orchestrator...");
            var results = new List<string>();
            var inputEntity = context.GetInput<OrderEntity>();

            var entity = await context.CallActivityAsync<OrderE
            ntity>(nameof(SavingDataToDb), inputEntity);

            results.Add(await context.CallActivityAsync<string>
            (nameof(SendingNotification), entity));

            return results;
        }

        [Function(nameof(SavingDataToDb))]
        public static OrderEntity SavingDataToDb([Activ
        ityTrigger] OrderEntity entity, FunctionContext
        executionContext)
        {
            Ilogger logger = executionContext.GetLogger(nameof(
            SavingDataToDb));
            entity.Id = 1;
```

```
    return entity;
}

[Function(nameof(SendingNotification))]
public static string SendingNotification([Activity
Trigger] OrderEntity dbEntity, FunctionContext
executionContext)
{
    Ilogger logger = executionContext.GetLogger(nameof
    (SendingNotification));

    return dbEntity.Id.ToString();
}

[Function("Function1_HttpStart")]
public static async Task<HttpResponseData> HttpStart(
    [HttpTrigger(AuthorizationLevel.Anonymous, "get",
    "post")] HttpRequestData req,
    [DurableClient] DurableTaskClient client,
    FunctionContext executionContext)
{
    Ilogger logger = executionContext.GetLogger
    ("Function1_HttpStart");

    var data = await req.ReadFromJsonAsync<Order
    Entity>();
    string instanceId = await client.ScheduleNew
    OrchestrationInstanceAsync(
        nameof(Function1), data);
    return client.CreateCheckStatusResponse(req,
    instanceId);
}
}
```

```
public class OrderEntity
{
    public int Id { get; set; }
    public int Quantity { get; set; }
    public string ProductName { get; set; }
    public string UserGuid { get; set; }
}
}
```

The code in Listing 2-15 is an example of a Durable Function that simulates a workflow where data is added to a database, then it sends a notification. At first, the HttpStart method must be requested with the Order entity in the body in JSON format. The Order class has simple properties like Id, ProductName, Quantity, and UserGuid. After parsing the JSON data from the request using the ReadFromJsonAsync<OrderEntity>() method, the function then schedules a new orchestration instance using ScheduleNewOrchestrationInstanceAsync().

The name of the orchestration function is Function1, and the data passed to it is the deserialized order entity. Using the GetInput<OrderEntity>() method, it is reading the parameter and casting it to the proper class. When calling the Activity Trigger with the CallAct ivityAsync<OrderEntity>() method, it is passing the model as a second parameter. The generic type provided will be the output of the method.

The SavingDataToDb is simulating the saving model in the database and is adding an ID property. The first parameter is our input; it can be a string, integer, or, in this case, a class. Then the model is sent to the SendingNotification Activity method, and it is simulating sending notifications. Finally, the HttpStart function returns a response using CreateCheckStatusResponse() with the request and the instance ID.

In order to test this Function, it can be requested using the PowerShell script from Listing 2-16.

Listing 2-16. PowerShell script to invoke request on the Azure Function

```
$uri = "http://localhost:7166/api/Function1_HttpStart"
$body = @{
  ProductName = "Book"
  Quantity = 1
  UserGuid = "dbcb2026-e6f4-461d-b329-fde3fa4fcfd6"
}

$response = Invoke-RestMethod -Method Post -Uri $uri
-ContentType "application/json" -Body ($body | ConvertTo-Json)
$response
```

The script has the following variables:

- $uri – The URI of the application

- $body – The order class in JSON format

- $response – Contains a response from the Invoke-RestMethod.

This script is preparing data and the address, then it is invoking a server with the parameters like Method (Post), Content-Type (application/json), Uri ($uri), and Body ($body). In the terminal window (in Figure 2-15), there are logs from the executed methods. They show each method being called, and they can trace that it is being called in sequence with the correct data.

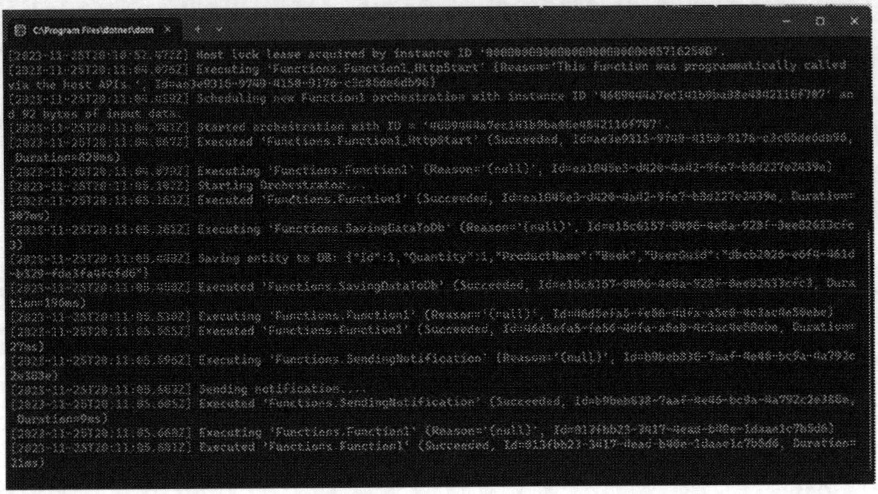

Figure 2-15. *Screenshot of the terminal with logs of the Function*

Durable Function – Fan-Out/Fan-In Pattern

The fan-out/fan-in pattern comes in handy when you have to run several functions simultaneously and then combine the output. The results can be either saved to the Storage Account, sent via email, or returned by the function through the Url result. The fan-out/fan-in pattern allows for parallel execution of multiple functions, which can significantly improve performance and reduce execution time. By distributing the workload across multiple functions, the pattern maximizes resource utilization and ensures efficient utilization of available computing power. Additionally, the pattern facilitates efficient handling of large amounts of data by splitting it into smaller chunks, processing them simultaneously, and then combining the results.

Listing 2-17. Fan-out/fan-in code pattern

```
using Microsoft.Azure.Functions.Worker;
using Microsoft.Azure.Functions.Worker.Http;
using Microsoft.DurableTask;
using Microsoft.DurableTask.Client;
using Microsoft.Extensions.Logging;
using Newtonsoft.Json;

namespace AzureAdveture_2_DurableFanoutFanin
{
    public static class Function
    {
        [Function(nameof(Function))]
        public static async Task<List<string>> RunOrchestrator(
            [OrchestrationTrigger] TaskOrchestrationContext
            context)
        {
            Ilogger logger = context.CreateReplaySafeLogger(nam
            eof(Function));

            var orderModels = context.GetInput<List
            <OrderEntity>>();
            var saveTasks = new List<Task<string>>();

            foreach (var order in orderModels)
            {
                saveTasks.Add(context.CallActivityAsync<string>
                (nameof(SaveMultipleOrders), order));
            }

            await Task.WhenAll(saveTasks);

            return saveTasks.Select(task => task.Result).ToList();
        }
```

```
[Function(nameof(SaveMultipleOrders))]
public static string SaveMultipleOrders([Activity
Trigger] OrderEntity model, FunctionContext
executionContext)
{
    Ilogger logger = executionContext.GetLogger(nameof
    (SaveMultipleOrders));
    model.Id = Guid.NewGuid().ToString();
    logger.LogInformation($"Saving order number:
    {model.Id}");

    return model.Id;
}

[Function("Function_HttpStart")]
public static async Task<HttpResponseData> HttpStart(
    [HttpTrigger(AuthorizationLevel.Anonymous, "get",
    "post")] HttpRequestData req,
    [DurableClient] DurableTaskClient client,
    FunctionContext executionContext)
{

    Ilogger logger = executionContext.GetLogger
    ("Function_HttpStart");

    var orders = req.ReadFromJsonAsync<List<Order
    Entity>>();
    string instanceId = await client.ScheduleNew
    OrchestrationInstanceAsync(
        nameof(Function), orders);

    logger.LogInformation("Started orchestration with
    ID = '{instanceId}'.", instanceId);
```

```
        return client.CreateCheckStatusResponse(req,
        instanceId);
    }

    public class OrderEntity
    {
        public string Id { get; set; }
        public int Quantity { get; set; }
        public string ProductName { get; set; }
        public string UserGuid { get; set; }
    }
  }
}
```

Listing 2-17 is a durable function code which is also simulating the workflow of saving orders to the database. Like in the previous example, we read data from the body request in the HttpStart method. Then the orchestration is started. The orchestration function runs for each order the "SaveMultipleOrders" method, that is an ActivityTrigger type of function. They run in parallel, and their promises are added to the list. Then they are all awaited, until they will be finished to save the data into the database. All functions will return a GUID as string. Then they are all read and returned to the main function and can be gathered by application.

In order to test this Function, it can be requested using the PowerShell script in Listing 2-18.

Listing 2-18. PowerShell script to invoke the Azure Function

```
$uri = "http://localhost:7166/api/Function1_HttpStart"
$body = @(
      @{
        ProductName = "Book"
        Quantity = 1
```

```
      UserGuid = "dbcb2026-e6f4-461d-b329-fde3fa4fcfd6"
   },
   @{
      ProductName = "Pen"
      Quantity = 13
      UserGuid = "2e98e4a2-42d4-45df-9c20-bea2aa5b2750"
   },
   @{
      ProductName = "Notebook"
      Quantity = 22
      UserGuid = "f3fd9053-eb2c-490a-8b13-bc27485c9f1e"
   }
)

$response = Invoke-RestMethod -Method Post -Uri $uri
-ContentType "application/json" -Body ($body | ConvertTo-Json)
$response
```

Durable Function – Monitoring Pattern

The monitoring pattern comes in handy when you need to keep an eye
on the progress of lengthy workflows. It allows you to track the different
stages of the workflow and ensure that tasks are being completed on time.
Additionally, monitoring provides valuable feedback and insights into the
efficiency of the workflow, helping you identify any bottlenecks or areas
for improvement. By being constantly aware of the progress, you can make
timely adjustments to ensure the successful completion of the workflow.

Listing 2-19. Code for the monitoring pattern

```
using Microsoft.Azure.Functions.Worker;
using Microsoft.Azure.Functions.Worker.Http;
using Microsoft.DurableTask;
```

```
using Microsoft.DurableTask.Client;
using Microsoft.Extensions.Logging;

namespace AzureAdventure2_MonitoringPattern
{
    public static class Function1
    {
        [Function(nameof(Function1))]
        public static async Task<string> RunOrchestrator(
            [OrchestrationTrigger] TaskOrchestrationContext
            context)
        {
            Ilogger logger = context.CreateReplaySafeLogger
            (nameof(Function1));

            using var canncelationToken = new Cancellation
            TokenSource();

            var expiryTime = TimeSpan.FromMinutes(20);

            var expiryTask = context.CreateTimer(context.
            CurrentUtcDateTime.Add(expiryTime),
            canncelationToken.Token);
            var resultTask = context.CallActivityAsync<string>
            (nameof(LongRunningTask), "Inputs");
            await Task.WhenAny(resultTask, expiryTask);

            if (resultTask.IsCompletedSuccessfully)
            {
                return "Task completed successfully";
            }

            return "Timeout!";
        }
```

```
[Function(nameof(LongRunningTask))]
public static string LongRunningTask([ActivityTrigger]
string name, FunctionContext executionContext)
{
    Ilogger logger = executionContext.GetLogger(nameof
    (LongRunningTask));

    Task.Delay(TimeSpan.FromMinutes(1));

    return "Completed";
}

[Function("Function1_HttpStart")]
public static async Task<HttpResponseData> HttpStart(
    [HttpTrigger(AuthorizationLevel.Anonymous, "get",
    "post")] HttpRequestData req,
    [DurableClient] DurableTaskClient client,
    FunctionContext executionContext)
{

    Ilogger logger = executionContext.GetLogger
    ("Function1_HttpStart");

    string instanceId = await client.ScheduleNew
    OrchestrationInstanceAsync(
        nameof(Function1));

    logger.LogInformation("Started orchestration with
    ID = '{instanceId}'.", instanceId);

    return client.CreateCheckStatusResponse(req,
    instanceId);
    }
  }
}
```

In Listing 2-19, the LongRunningTask method is delaying for one minute to simulate workload. In the Function1 method, the Cancellation token is created, then the Timer is created, and finally the LongRunningTask is called. The Task.WhenAny is awaiting when of the two tasks are finished faster. Then if the task is completed successfully, the results are returned; if not, it will return "Timeout!" string.

Durable Function – Human Interaction Pattern

When a workflow relies on interaction with a human user, the human interaction pattern comes in handy. It allows the program to pause and wait for user input before proceeding with the next step. This pattern can be implemented by using a combination of timers, events, and user interface controls. By using the human interaction pattern, the program can effectively interact with the user, providing instructions, gathering input, and responding to user actions.

Listing 2-20. Code for the human interaction pattern

```
using Microsoft.Azure.Functions.Worker;
using Microsoft.Azure.Functions.Worker.Http;
using Microsoft.DurableTask;
using Microsoft.DurableTask.Client;
using Microsoft.Extensions.Logging;
using Newtonsoft.Json;

namespace AzureAdventure2_HumanInteraction
{
    public static class Function1
    {
        [Function(nameof(Function1))]
```

```
public static async Task RunOrchestrator(
    [OrchestrationTrigger] TaskOrchestrationContext
    context)
{
    Ilogger logger = context.CreateReplaySafeLogger
    (nameof(Function1));

    var response = await context.WaitForExternalEvent
    <EventResponse>("Approve");

    logger.LogInformation($"User Response:
    {JsonConvert.SerializeObject(response)}");
    // do other required actions, like calling other
    Activity Trigger to save the data into the database
}
```

```
[Function("Function1_HttpStart")]
public static async Task<HttpResponseData> HttpStart(
    [HttpTrigger(AuthorizationLevel.Anonymous, "get",
    "post")] HttpRequestData req,
    [DurableClient] DurableTaskClient client,
    FunctionContext executionContext)
{
    Ilogger logger = executionContext.GetLogger
    ("Function1_HttpStart");

    string instanceId = await client.ScheduleNew
    OrchestrationInstanceAsync(
        nameof(Function1));

    logger.LogInformation("Started orchestration with
    ID = '{instanceId}'.", instanceId);
```

```
        return client.CreateCheckStatusResponse(req,
        instanceId);
    }
}

public class EventResponse
{
    public bool IsApproved { get; set; }
    public string Comments { get; set; }
}
}
```

In Listing 2-20 is an example of how to use Azure Durable Functions to implement human interaction patterns. The code consists of two functions: one is an orchestrator function and the other is an HTTP trigger function.

The orchestrator function, named Function1, is responsible for helping organize the logic of the process. It uses the TaskOrchestrationContext parameter to access the Durable Functions API. The first thing it does is wait for an external event named "Approve," which represents human input or other applications. The external event is sent by a web application or a mobile app that allows the user to approve or reject a request. The orchestrator function receives the event data as an EventResponse object, which contains two properties: IsApproved and Comments. The orchestrator function then logs the user response and may perform other actions, such as calling another activity function to save the data into a database.

This code demonstrates how to use Azure Durable Functions to implement human interaction patterns in a serverless environment. It shows how to use the orchestration trigger and the durable client attributes, how to wait for external events, and how to handle event data.

In order to execute this example, firstly run the project in Visual Studio, then run the PowerShell script from Listing 2-21.

Listing 2-21. PowerShell script to interact with Azure Function

```
$uri = "http://localhost:7039/runtime/webhooks/durabletask/
instances/873f3ac035b2472eb78a9680c09a41b4/raiseEvent/
Approve?code=a_rrOi9qAbO8wk-BKXohgFCblOSwE7RYmJhobr6Xgs3tAzFug7
_96g=="
$body = @{
        IsApproved = $true
        Comments = "Some Comments"
}

$response = Invoke-RestMethod -Method Post -Uri $uri -ContentType
"application/json" -Body ($body | ConvertTo-Json)
$response
```

The code is invoking the URL with the specific object with method type POST. In the screenshot from Figure 2-16, the logger is showing the user response object. The event may be changed and can be a simple string, integer, or Boolean value.

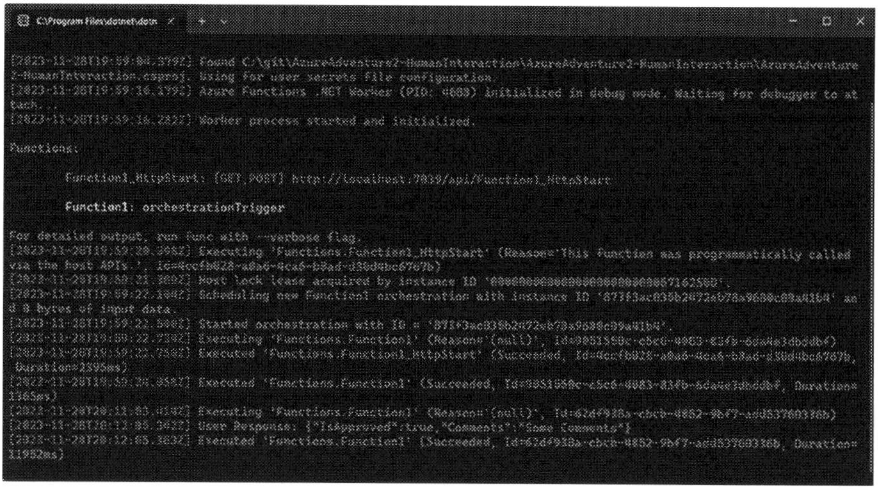

Figure 2-16. *Screenshot of the terminal with the results of running the Azure Durable Function*

Scaling

Azure Function scaling is the process of adjusting the amount of resources allocated to a function app based on the demand or load it receives. Azure Function scaling can be automatic or manual, depending on the hosting plan and configuration of the function app.

Automatic scaling means that the Azure Functions infrastructure adds or removes instances of the function host dynamically, depending on how many events cause the app's functions to activate. For example, if an HTTP request triggers a service, the scale controller monitors the rate of requests per second and scales out the function app accordingly. Similarly, if a queue message triggers a function, the scale controller monitors the queue length and scales out the function app to process the messages faster.

Manual scaling means that the developer or administrator specifies the number of instances of the function host to run at any given time. This option is available for function apps that use a dedicated hosting plan or an App Service Environment (ASE). Manual scaling can provide more control and predictability over the performance and cost of the function app, but it requires more management and monitoring.

An example of Azure Function scaling based on CPU usage is when a function app uses a consumption hosting plan, which scales out automatically based on CPU and memory pressure. If a function app experiences a spike in CPU usage due to intensive computations, the scale controller will add more instances of the function host to distribute the load and maintain optimal performance.

An example of Azure Function scaling based on requests per second, which scales out automatically according to the amount of events per second, is when a function app receives a surge in HTTP requests due to high traffic. In order to handle the requests and prevent delay or timeouts, the scaling controller will create more instances of the function host. In Figure 2-17, the diagram displays what will happen after implementing an autoscale configuration; the function will have added more instances to handle the traffic.

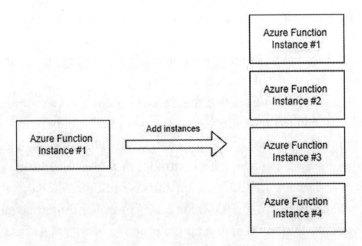

Figure 2-17. *Increasing Azure Function instance diagram*

To add rules using the Azure Portal, you can follow these steps:

- Go to your Azure Function, go to the Scale out (App Service plan) and check the Rules Based option as shown in Figure 2-18.

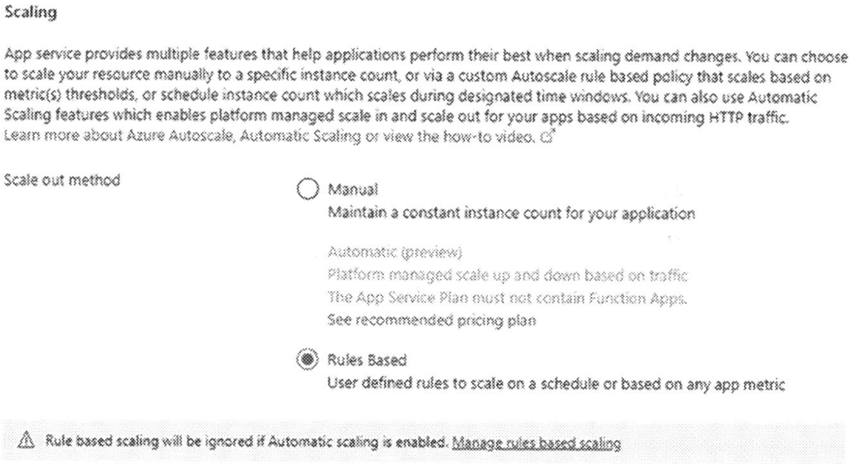

Scaling

App service provides multiple features that help applications perform their best when scaling demand changes. You can choose to scale your resource manually to a specific instance count, or via a custom Autoscale rule based policy that scales based on metric(s) thresholds, or schedule instance count which scales during designated time windows. You can also use Automatic Scaling features which enables platform managed scale in and scale out for your apps based on incoming HTTP traffic. Learn more about Azure Autoscale, Automatic Scaling or view the how-to video.

Scale out method

○ Manual
Maintain a constant instance count for your application

Automatic (preview)
Platform managed scale up and down based on traffic
The App Service Plan must not contain Function Apps.
See recommended pricing plan

◉ Rules Based
User defined rules to scale on a schedule or based on any app metric

⚠ Rule based scaling will be ignored if Automatic scaling is enabled. Manage rules based scaling

Figure 2-18. *Rules Based option for scaling*

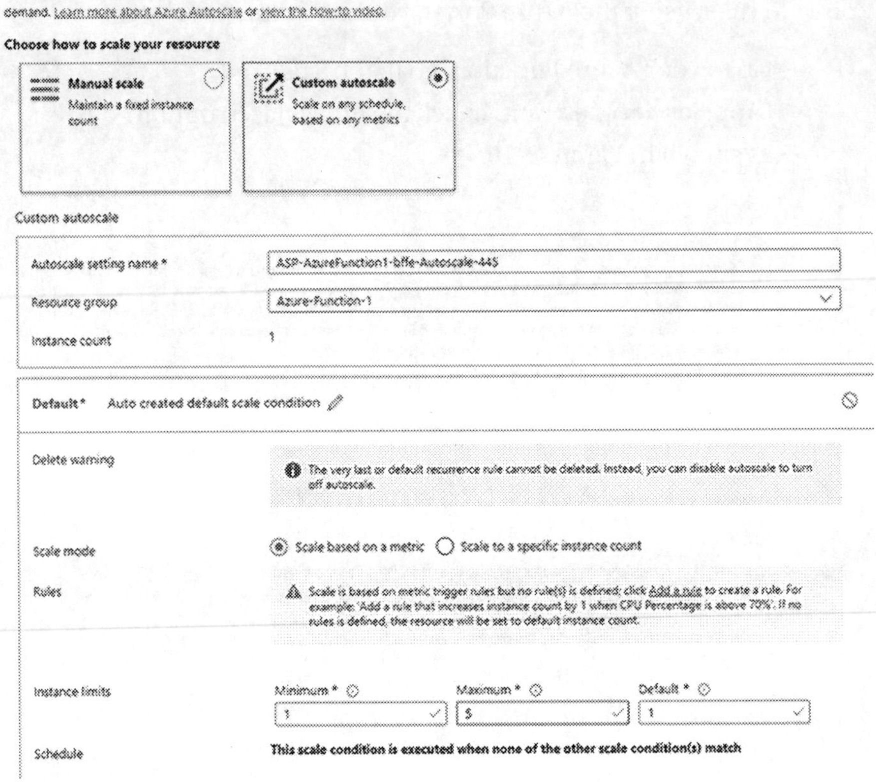

demand. Learn more about Azure Autoscale or view the how-to video.

Choose how to scale your resource

Figure 2-19. Custom autoscale

On the next site, select Custom autoscale, and you should see what is in Figure 2-19. Click the Add rule, and you should see a side panel with configuration; you can set up values like in Figure 2-20. Select Standard metrics as the metric namespace and CPU Percentage as the metric name; in the Operator field, select Greater than, and set the threshold to 70, duration to 10 minutes, increase count to 1, and time gain statistics to Average.

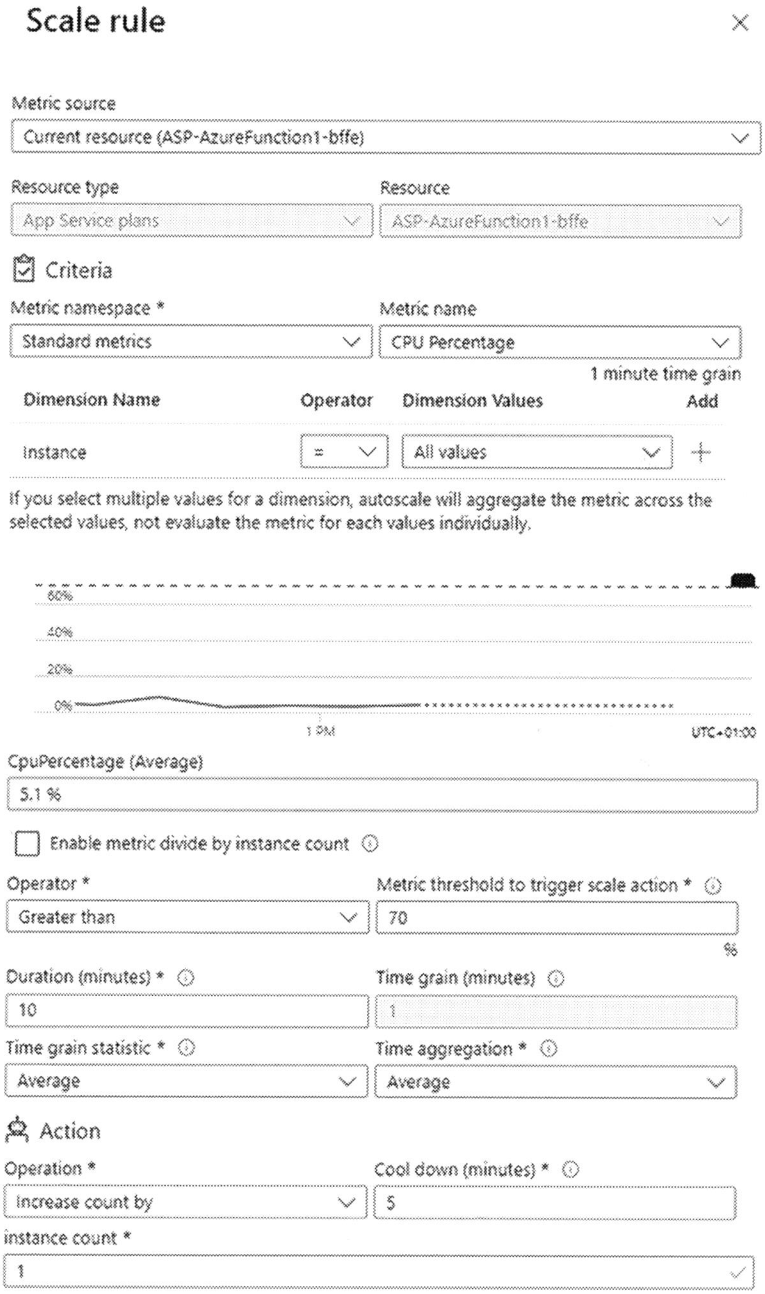

Scale rule   ×

Metric source

Current resource (ASP-AzureFunction1-bffe)   ∨

Resource type   Resource

App Service plans   ∨   ASP-AzureFunction1-bffe   ∨

☑ Criteria

Metric namespace *   Metric name

Standard metrics   ∨   CPU Percentage   ∨

1 minute time grain

Dimension Name	Operator	Dimension Values	Add
Instance	= ∨	All values ∨	+

If you select multiple values for a dimension, autoscale will aggregate the metric across the selected values, not evaluate the metric for each values individually.

CpuPercentage (Average)

5.1 %

☐ Enable metric divide by instance count ⓘ

Operator *   Metric threshold to trigger scale action * ⓘ

Greater than   ∨   70

%

Duration (minutes) * ⓘ   Time grain (minutes) ⓘ

10   1

Time grain statistic * ⓘ   Time aggregation * ⓘ

Average   ∨   Average   ∨

🗙 Action

Operation *   Cool down (minutes) * ⓘ

Increase count by   ∨   5

instance count *

1   ∨

Figure 2-20. *Scale rule to increase instances*

To decrease the count of instances, add another rule, but set the Operation field to Decrease count by, like in Figure 2-21.

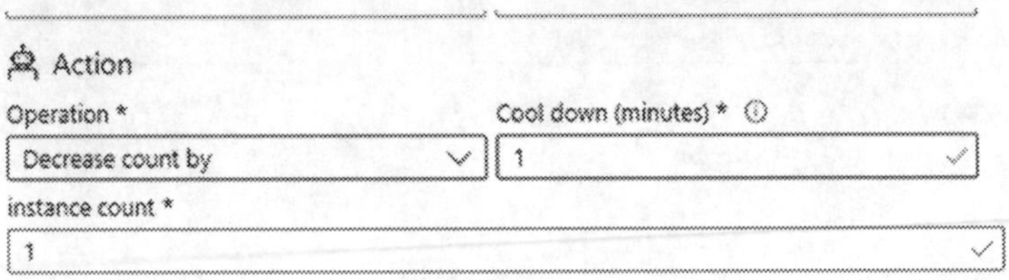

Figure 2-21. *Decreasing instances by 1*

If you prefer to use the command line, you can set up the autoscale rule via the Azure CLI, using Listing 2-22.

Listing 2-22. CLI commands to create the configuration

```
az monitor autoscale create --resource azure-function-1 --
resource-group Azure-Function-1 --name CPUAutoScale --count 1
--min-count 1 --max-count 10
az monitor autoscale rule create -g Azure-Function-1
--autoscale-name CPUAutoScale --scale out 1 --condition
"Percentage CPU > 70 avg 5m"
az monitor autoscale rule create -g Azure-Function-1
--autoscale-name CPUAutoScale --scale in 1 --condition
"Percentage CPU < 30 avg 1m"
```

These commands create an autoscale setting for a resource with the specified ID. The name of the setting is CPUAutoScale, and it specifies that the resource should have one instance by default. The condition for scaling up or down is based on the percentage of CPU usage over a five-minute average. The "min-count" parameter is setting up the minimum. The "max-count" parameter is setting up the maximum quantity of instances that the resource can have. In this example, we can have between one and ten instances.

The same autoscale rule can be applied via Bicep from Listing 2-23.

Listing 2-23. Bicep with the autoscale rule

```
resource myFunction 'Microsoft.Web/sites@2022-09-01' = {
  name: 'myFunction'
  location: resourceGroup().location
  kind: 'functionapp'
  properties: {
    serverFarmId: plan.id
    siteConfig: {
      appSettings: [
        {
          name: 'FUNCTIONS_WORKER_RUNTIME'
          value: 'dotnet'
        }
      ]
    }
  }
}

resource autoscalRule 'Microsoft.Insights/
autoscalesettings@2022-10-01' = {
  name: 'CPUAutoScale'
  location: resourceGroup().location
  properties: {
    profiles: [
      {
        name: 'defaultProfile'
        capacity: {
          minimum: '1'
          maximum: '10'
          default: '10'
        }
```

```
     rules: [
       {
         metricTrigger: {
           metricName: 'Percentage CPU'
           metricResourceUri: myFunction.id
           timeGrain: 'PT1M'
           statistic: 'Average'
           timeWindow: 'PT5M'
           timeAggregation: 'Average'
           operator: 'GreaterThan'
           threshold: 70
         }
         scaleAction: {
           direction: 'Increase'
           type: 'ChangeCount'
           value: '1'
           cooldown: 'PT1M'
         }
       }
     ]
   }
  ]
 }
}
```

The code in Listing 2-24 shows an example command to create autoscale for the Azure Function using the Azure CLI. The command creates an autoscale rule that scales out the number of instances by one when the total number of requests in the last five minutes exceeds 100 and scales in by one when the number of requests falls below 50. The command also sets the maximum number of instances to ten and the minimum to one. The command expects that a resource group, function app, and storage account have already been established.

Listing 2-24. Azure CLI commands to create autoscale rules

```
az monitor autoscale create --resource-group Azure-Function-1
--name RequestsAutoscale --resource-type Microsoft.Web/sites
--resource azure-function-1 --min-count 1 --max-count 10
az monitor autoscale rule create --resource-group Azure-
Function-1 --autoscale-name RequestsAutoscale --scale out 1
--cooldown 1 --condition "requests > 100 avg 5m"
az monitor autoscale rule create --resource-group Azure-
Function-1 --autoscale-name RequestsAutoscale --scale in 1
--cooldown 1 --condition "requests < 50 avg 5m"
```

The same rule is created with the bicep file in Listing 2-25.

Listing 2-25. Bicep file with autoscale rules

```
resource azureFunction 'Microsoft.Web/sites@2022-09-01' = {
  name: 'azureFunction'
  location: resourceGroup().location
  properties: {
    serverFarmId: plan.id
  }
}

resource RequestsAutoscale 'Microsoft.Insights/
autoscalesettings@2022-10-01' = {
  name: 'RequestsAutoscale'
  location: resourceGroup().location
  properties: {
    profiles: [
      {
        name: 'Default'
```

```
    capacity: {
      minimum: '1'
      maximum: '10'
      default: '1'
    }
    rules: [
      {
        metricTrigger: {
          metricName: 'Requests'
          metricResourceUri: azureFunction.id
          timeGrain: 'PT1M'
          statistic: 'Average'
          timeWindow: 'PT5M'
          timeAggregation: 'Average'
          operator: 'GreaterThan'
          threshold: 100
        }
        scaleAction: {
          direction: 'Increase'
          type: 'ChangeCount'
          value: '1'
          cooldown: 'PT1M'
        }
      }
      {
        metricTrigger: {
          metricName: 'Requests'
          metricResourceUri: azureFunction.id
          timeGrain: 'PT1M'
          statistic: 'Average'
          timeWindow: 'PT5M'
          timeAggregation: 'Average'
```

```
        operator: 'LessThan'
        threshold: 50
      }
      scaleAction: {
        direction: 'Decrease'
        type: 'ChangeCount'
        value: '1'
        cooldown: 'PT1M'
      }
    }
  ]
}
]
}
}
```

Always On Feature

The Always On feature in Azure Functions plays an essential role in maintaining optimal performance. The Azure Function application resources will be released after 20 minutes. It will ping the Azure Function in order to make it active. With Always On enabled, the function app will continuously run, ensuring that it is always ready to respond to incoming requests, even during periods of low traffic. This eliminates any potential delay in scaling up instances when there is a sudden increase in demand. By keeping the function app warm, Always On significantly reduces the latency and ensures a seamless experience for users.

The Always On feature can be enabled only on a Dedicated App Service plan, on the Basic, Standard, and Premium tiers. This feature is not available on the Consumption plan. The screenshot in Figure 2-22 is showing you how to change the App Service plan. To change it on the Azure Function resource, you can follow these steps:

- Go to the Azure Function.

- Find and click Change App Service Plan.

- Select Function Premium from the Plan type options.

- Change the name if there is a need; otherwise, it will be a random string.

- Change the Pricing Tier to the application needs and requirements.

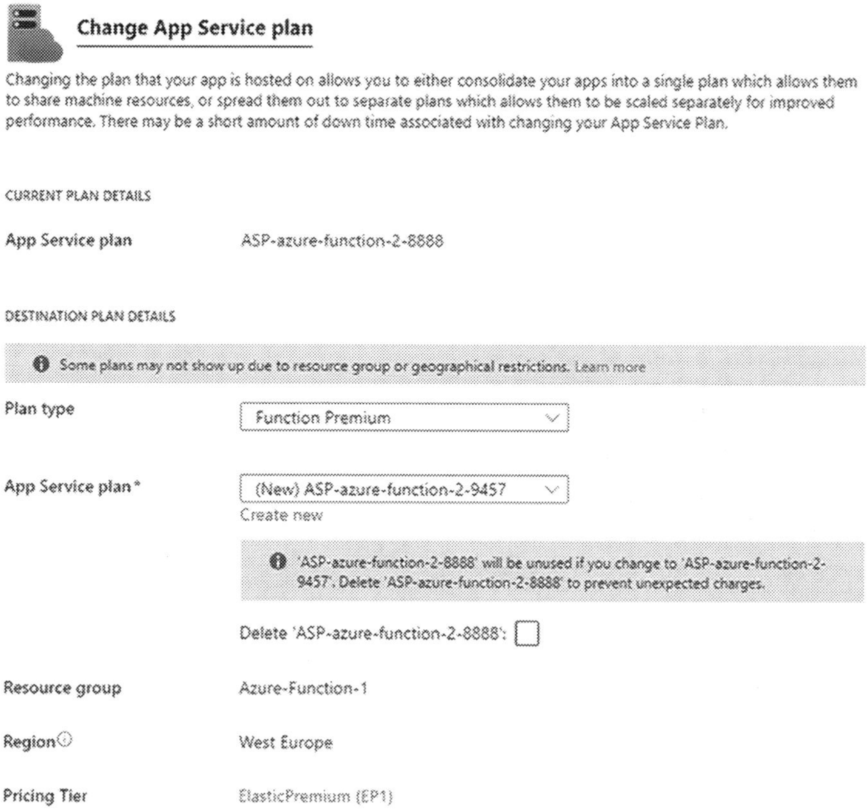

Change App Service plan

Changing the plan that your app is hosted on allows you to either consolidate your apps into a single plan which allows them to share machine resources, or spread them out to separate plans which allows them to be scaled separately for improved performance. There may be a short amount of down time associated with changing your App Service Plan.

CURRENT PLAN DETAILS

App Service plan   ASP-azure-function-2-8888

DESTINATION PLAN DETAILS

> ⓘ Some plans may not show up due to resource group or geographical restrictions. Learn more

Plan type   Function Premium   ∨

App Service plan *   (New) ASP-azure-function-2-9457   ∨
                                Create new

> ⓘ 'ASP-azure-function-2-8888' will be unused if you change to 'ASP-azure-function-2-9457'. Delete 'ASP-azure-function-2-8888' to prevent unexpected charges.

                                Delete 'ASP-azure-function-2-8888': ☐

Resource group   Azure-Function-1

Region ⓘ   West Europe

Pricing Tier   ElasticPremium (EP1)

Figure 2-22. *Screenshot of changing the App Service plan for the Azure Function*

The functionality on the Azure Function with the suitable App Service plan can be enabled in a few different ways.

It can be enabled via the Azure CLI from Listing 2-26.

Listing 2-26. Command to enable Always on feature via Powershell command

```
az functionapp config set -g Function1ResourceGroup -n
Function1 --always-on true
```

To enable it through the Bicep file, insert the alwaysOn with a true value property and set it to true in the siteConfig section, as is shown in the code snippet in Listing 2-27.

Listing 2-27. Bicep script with enabled "Always on" feature

```
resource functionApp 'Microsoft.Web/sites@2022-09-01' = {
  name: functionAppName
  location: location
  kind: 'functionapp'
  identity: {
    type: 'SystemAssigned'
  }
  properties: {
    serverFarmId: hostingPlan.id
    siteConfig: {
      alwaysOn: true
    }
    // the rest of the code has been omitted for clarity
  }
}
```

To enable Always On via Azure Portal Function configuration, as shown in Figure 2-23, follow these steps:

- Go to your Azure Function.

- Search on the left side and click the Configuration section.

- Search for the General settings tab and select it.

- Select the On option on the radio box next to the Always on option, as is shown in the picture.

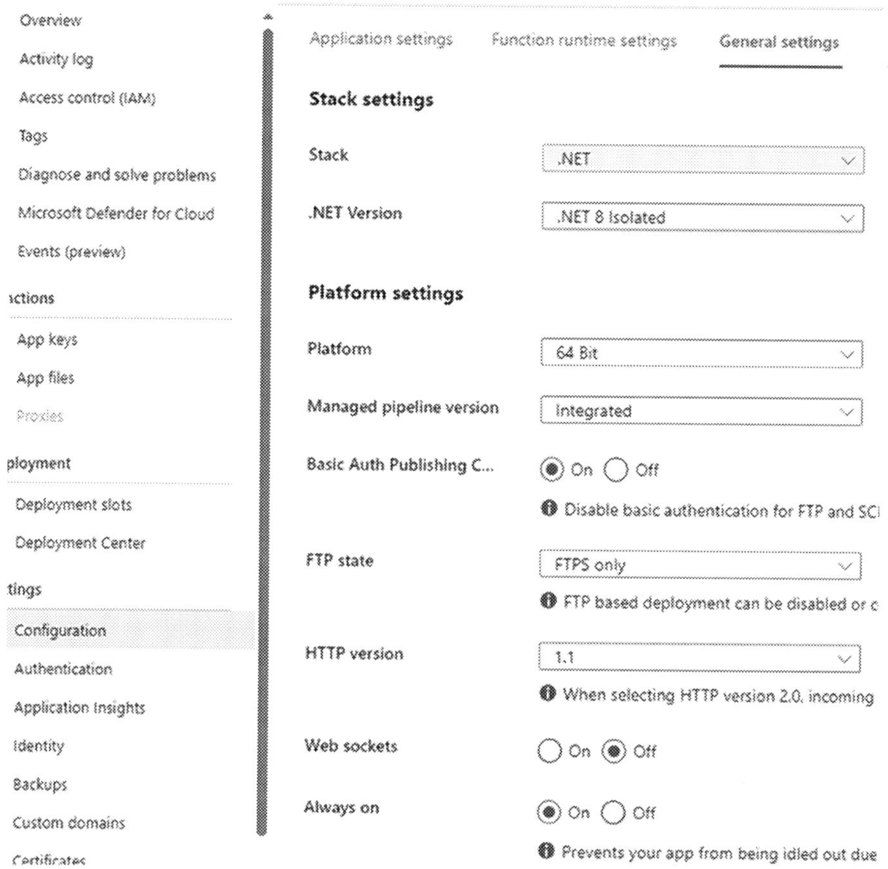

Overview

Activity log

Access control (IAM)

Tags

Diagnose and solve problems

Microsoft Defender for Cloud

Events (preview)

ictions

App keys

App files

Proxies

ployment

Deployment slots

Deployment Center

tings

Configuration

Authentication

Application Insights

Identity

Backups

Custom domains

Certificates

Application settings   Function runtime settings   General settings

Stack settings

Stack | .NET   ∨ |

.NET Version | .NET 8 Isolated   ∨ |

Platform settings

Platform | 64 Bit   ∨ |

Managed pipeline version | Integrated   ∨ |

Basic Auth Publishing C...   ◉ On ○ Off
                               ❶ Disable basic authentication for FTP and SCi

FTP state | FTPS only   ∨ |
                               ❶ FTP based deployment can be disabled or c

HTTP version | 1.1   ∨ |
                               ❶ When selecting HTTP version 2.0, incoming

Web sockets   ○ On ◉ Off

Always on   ◉ On ○ Off
                               ❶ Prevents your app from being idled out due

Figure 2-23. Screenshot of enabling the Always On feature on the Azure Function

Authentication

You can use various authentication methods to secure your functions and control who can access them. Some of the built-in authentication types in Azure Functions are as follows:

- Anonymous – No authentication is required. Anyone can call your function.

- Admin – In this case, calling your function or any other function in the same function app requires a master key. You can see the keys in the same way as the function keys.

- Function – This authentication type requires a function key to access the function. Function keys are specific to individual functions and can be managed independently.

To authenticate using the built-in keys, follow these steps:

- Go to your Azure Function resource through the portal.

- On the left side, choose the App keys section.

- Copy your secret to your request (as shown in Figure 2-24).

- Include a parameter at the end of the requesting URL, ?code={key}, where the {key} placeholder is replaced with the value from the keys.

+ New host key   ○ Refresh

System keys

System keys are automatically managed by the Function runtime. System Keys provide granular access to functions runtime features.

Name	Value

Host keys (all functions)

Use Host keys with your clients to access all your HTTP functions in the app. _master key grants admin access to Functions Runtime APIs.

Name	Value			
_master	••	⧉	◌ Show value	Renew key value
default	••	⧉	◌ Show value	Renew key value ▨

Figure 2-24. *Host key list for the Azure Function*

Authentication Through Azure Portal

In order to set up authentication via the Azure Portal, you must

- Go to your function app in the portal and select Authentication/Authorization under Settings.

Add an identity provider

Choose an identity provider to manage the user identities and authentication flow for your application. Providers include Microsoft, Facebook, Google, and Twitter.

Learn more about identity providers ☐

<kbd>Add identity provider</kbd>

Figure 2-25. *Authentication for the Azure Function*

- Click Add identity provider and select an identity provider from the list as shown in Figures 2-25 and 2-26.

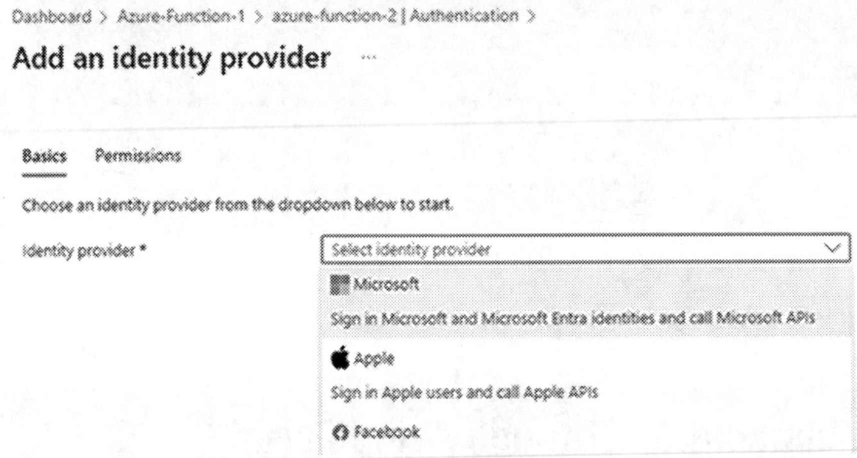

Dashboard > Azure-Function-1 > azure-function-2 | Authentication >

Add an identity provider   ...

Basics   Permissions

Choose an identity provider from the dropdown below to start.

Identity provider *   Select identity provider   ⌄

Microsoft
Sign in Microsoft and Microsoft Entra identities and call Microsoft APIs

 Apple
Sign in Apple users and call Apple APIs

 Facebook

Figure 2-26. *Selecting an identity provider*

- Configure the identity provider settings, such as the client ID, client secret, allowed token audiences, etc., as shown in Figure 2-27.

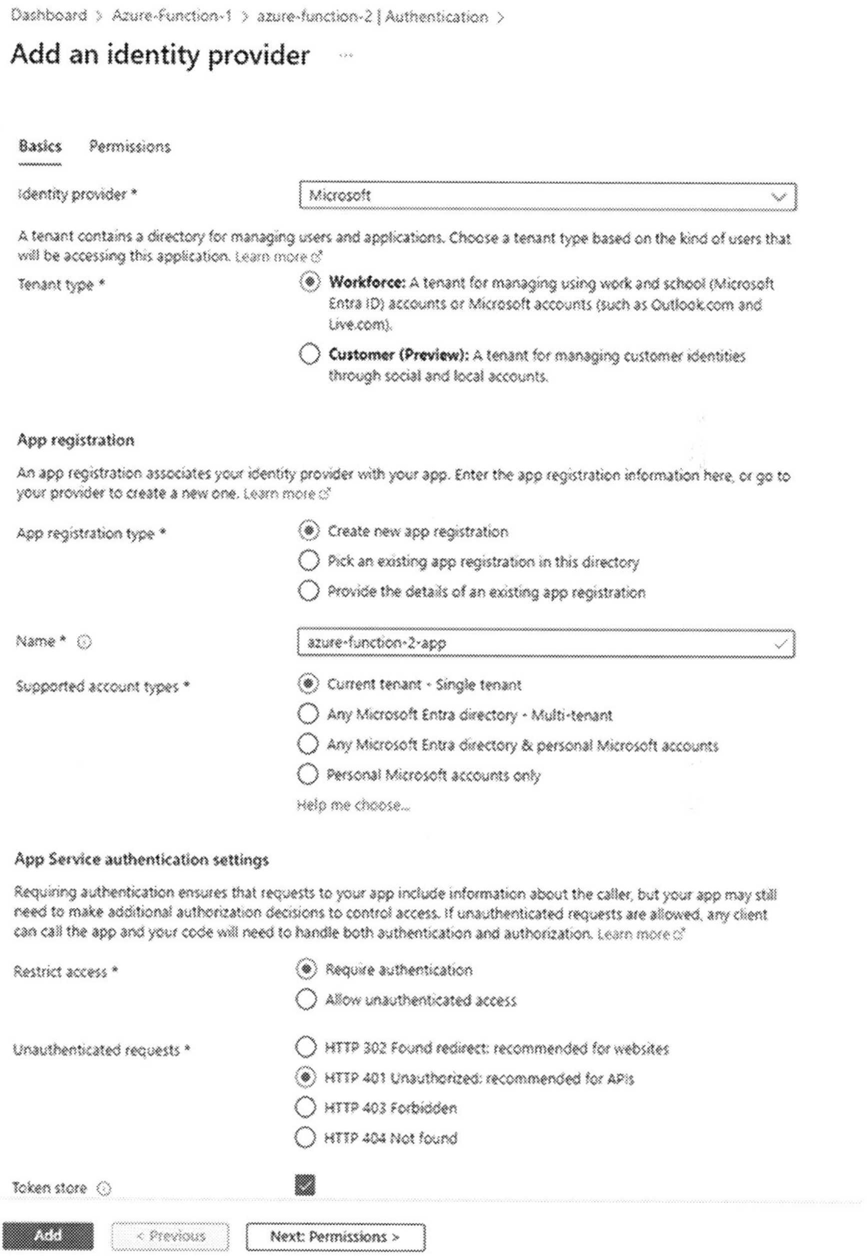

Dashboard > Azure-Function-1 > azure-function-2 | Authentication >

Add an identity provider   ...

Basics   Permissions

Identity provider * | Microsoft   ∨ |

A tenant contains a directory for managing users and applications. Choose a tenant type based on the kind of users that will be accessing this application. Learn more ☐

Tenant type *   ⦿ **Workforce:** A tenant for managing using work and school (Microsoft
                                      Entra ID) accounts or Microsoft accounts (such as Outlook.com and
                                      Live.com).

                                 ○ **Customer (Preview):** A tenant for managing customer identities
                                      through social and local accounts.

App registration

An app registration associates your identity provider with your app. Enter the app registration information here, or go to your provider to create a new one. Learn more ☐

App registration type *   ⦿ Create new app registration

                                 ○ Pick an existing app registration in this directory

                                 ○ Provide the details of an existing app registration

Name * ⓘ | azure-function-2-app   ✓ |

Supported account types *   ⦿ Current tenant - Single tenant

                                 ○ Any Microsoft Entra directory - Multi-tenant

                                 ○ Any Microsoft Entra directory & personal Microsoft accounts

                                 ○ Personal Microsoft accounts only

                                    Help me choose...

App Service authentication settings

Requiring authentication ensures that requests to your app include information about the caller, but your app may still need to make additional authorization decisions to control access. If unauthenticated requests are allowed, any client can call the app and your code will need to handle both authentication and authorization. Learn more ☐

Restrict access *   ⦿ Require authentication

                                 ○ Allow unauthenticated access

Unauthenticated requests *   ○ HTTP 302 Found redirect: recommended for websites

                                 ⦿ HTTP 401 Unauthorized: recommended for APIs

                                 ○ HTTP 403 Forbidden

                                 ○ HTTP 404 Not found

Token store ⓘ   ☑

[**Add**]   [< Previous]   [Next: Permissions >]

Figure 2-27. *Configure identity provider settings*

- Optionally, enable additional settings, such as token store, unauthenticated request handling, etc.

- Save your changes and restart your function app. The results should be with a notification at the top-right corner, as shown in Figure 2-28.

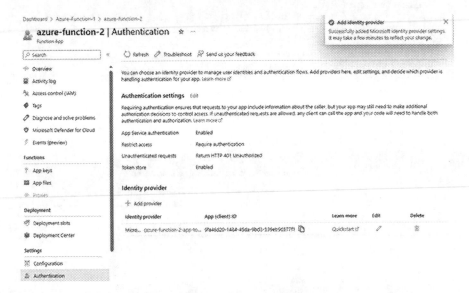

Figure 2-28. *Configured authentication for the Azure Function*

To access the user token in your C# code, you can use the Identities property of the HttpRequestData class. It will return a ClaimIdentity list object that contains information about the authenticated user, such as the name, tenant, email, and many other claims. Listing 2-28 shows how to read properties from the Identity class, using the built-in property and a custom. It is good to remember that the claim can be empty during localhost tests.

Listing 2-28. Reading Identity in the Isolated function

```
[Function("Function1")]
public HttpResponseData Run([HttpTrigger(AuthorizationLevel.
Anonymous, "get", "post")] HttpRequestData req)
{
    var identityName = req.Identities.FirstOrDefault().Name;
    var email = req.Identities.FirstOrDefault().
    FindFirst("Email");

    return req.CreateResponse(HttpStatusCode.OK);
}
```

Creating Middleware

You can create a middleware function that acts as a proxy for your other functions. A middleware function is a normal HTTP-triggered function that receives the request, performs some logic, and then forwards the request to another function using an HTTP client.

Example cases for using middleware are

- Custom authentication

- Modify incoming or outgoing messages

- Validate data

- Additional loggings

Listing 2-29 is an example of a custom middleware for Azure Functions. The code uses the Microsoft.Azure.Functions.Worker namespace, which contains the types and interfaces for the .NET worker. It also uses the Microsoft.Azure.Functions.Worker.Http namespace, which contains the types and interfaces for handling HTTP triggers and bindings. The code defines a class called CustomMiddleware that references to the IFunctionsWorkerMiddleware interface. It requires the class to the implementation of a method called Invoke, which takes two parameters: a FunctionContext object and a FunctionExecutionDelegate object. The FunctionContext object provides access to the function app's configuration, bindings, logger, and other services. The FunctionExecutionDelegate object represents the next middleware or function in the pipeline.

The Invoke method performs several tasks to manipulate the HTTP request and response. First, it reads a parameter from the path of the request using the BindingData property of the BindingContext object. The code uses the TryGetValue method to find the name parameter's value and store it in a variable called name. Then, it gets an instance of the HttpRequestData object using the GetHttpRequestDataAsync extension method on the FunctionContext object. This object represents the HTTP request and response data, such as headers, body, query, status code, etc. The HttpRequestData class is the same class as is used in the HTTP trigger Azure Function. The code then gets a specific header from the request using the Headers property of the HttpRequestData object. The HTTP headers are represented by a set of key-value pairs in this property. The code uses the FirstOrDefault method to get the header with the key "Authorization" and store it in a variable called authorizationHeader. Then, it gets the body of the request using the ReadAsStringAsync method on the HttpRequestData object. The content of the request body is returned as a string by this function. The code stores this string in a variable called body.

The code then gets some parameters from the query string of the request using the Query property of the HttpRequestData object. This property is an instance of QueryCollection, which is a collection of key-value pairs that represent the query parameters. The code uses the GetValues method to get all the values associated with the key id and assign them in the variable with the id1 name. Next, it gets some claims from the identity of the request using the Identities property of the FunctionContext object. This is a collection of ClaimsIdentity class type objects that represent the identities associated with the request. The code uses the FirstOrDefault method to get the first identity and then gets its NameClaimType property, which returns a string that represents the claim type for name claims. The code stores this string in a variable called name2. Finally, it uses the FunctionExecutionDelegate object's Invoke method and passes the FunctionContext object as an argument to call the middleware or function in the pipeline.

Listing 2-29. A custom middleware

```
using Microsoft.Azure.Functions.Worker;
using Microsoft.Azure.Functions.Worker.Http;
using Microsoft.Azure.Functions.Worker.Middleware;

namespace AzureAdventure_Middleware
{
    public class CustomMiddleware : IFunctionsWorkerMiddleware
    {
        public async Task Invoke(FunctionContext context,
        FunctionExecutionDelegate next)
        {
            context.BindingContext.BindingData.
            TryGetValue("name", out var name);

            var data = await context.GetHttpRequestDataAsync();
            // get headers
            var header = data.Headers.FirstOrDefault(h =>
            h.Key.Equals("Authorization"));

            // get body
            var body = await data.ReadAsStringAsync();

            // get parameters from query
            var id1 = data.Query.GetValues("id");
```

```
            // get claims
            var name2 = data.Identities.FirstOrDefault()?.
            NameClaimType;
            await next.Invoke(context);
        }
    }
}
```

Azure Function Portal Overview

After deploying the Bicep file, there are a few resources created. Now we will look closely to the Azure Function resource, what the options are and what can be done through the Azure Portal.

Figure 2-29 is a screenshot of what is the Azure Function management view looks like. There are useful information like the status, Running or Stopped; function address URL, where the function is available to request; tags; and the App Service plan currently used. On the left, there is a side menu. This book will deeply cover some of the following sections:

- Access control (IAM) – Grant access to the current application for other users or resources.

- Tags – Used to group or to find resources with the same purposes or that belong to the same department.

- Activity logs – History of changes on the resource.

- Deployment slots – List of all related slots for the current application. There are usually at least two slots – staging and production. When the application is ready and deployed, it is possible to switch it out for the production slot along the staging slot, and there won't be any service unavailable.

- Configuration – In this section, the environment variables can be inserted, and the language and version of the application language can be selected.

- Authentication – If it is required, a built-in authentication can be used in order to protect the application.

- Application Insights – In this section, you can configure additional logging.

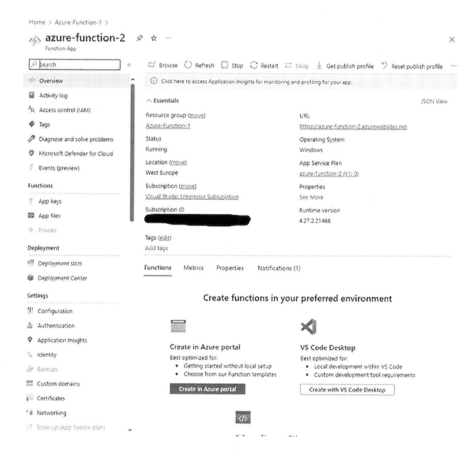

Figure 2-29. *Screenshot of the function app on the Azure site*

101

- Networking – If it is required by the solution, all resources can be connected through an internal virtual network.

- Identity – You can activate this feature in order to allow other applications to connect to this resource without secrets, using only Managed Identity. It will create an application in the Azure Active Directory, and other resources can use it to authorize.

- Advanced tools – Give access to Kudu, a powerful tool to handle environment variables, command console and access to the application files, and many more options.

- CORS – It allows to narrow the address that has access to the application.

- Logs – All logs should be available in this place and can be configured to be saved in the Account Storage.

Tags

Azure Tags are a feature that allows users to assign metadata to their Azure resources, such as resource groups, Azure Functions, Storage Accounts, web apps, and databases. More supported resources can be found on the Microsoft site. Not all resources can use them. Tags can be used for various purposes, such as organizing resources by categories, tracking costs, enforcing policies, and automating tasks.

Business users can use Azure Tags to group resources by business units, projects, environments, or any other criteria that makes sense for their organization. This way, they can easily filter and report on the resources that are relevant to their goals and objectives. For example, a business user can tag resources with the name of the customer they belong to, the stage of the development life cycle they are in, or the budget they are allocated to. By using tags, business users can gain more visibility and control over their Azure resources and optimize their spending.

Administrators can use Azure Tags to enforce policies and governance on their Azure resources. For example, an administrator can create a policy that requires all resources to have a tag with the owner's name and contact information. This way, they can ensure accountability and compliance for their resources. Administrators can also use tags to automate tasks such as backup, recovery, or deletion of resources based on certain conditions. For example, an administrator can create a tag with the expiration date of a resource and use it to trigger a workflow that deletes the resource when the date is reached.

Developers can use Azure Tags to streamline their development and testing processes. For example, a developer can tag resources with the version of the code they are running or the feature they are working on. This way, they can easily identify and isolate the resources they need for their tasks. Developers can also use tags to integrate their Azure resources with other tools and services, such as source control, continuous integration, or monitoring.

To add, edit, or remove tags on any type of resource, go to the Tags section; they are a key-value collection. Figure 2-30 shows tags for the resource group. They can be easily managed. They are not inherently for resources under. To enforce creating tags for other resources, it can be done using policies.

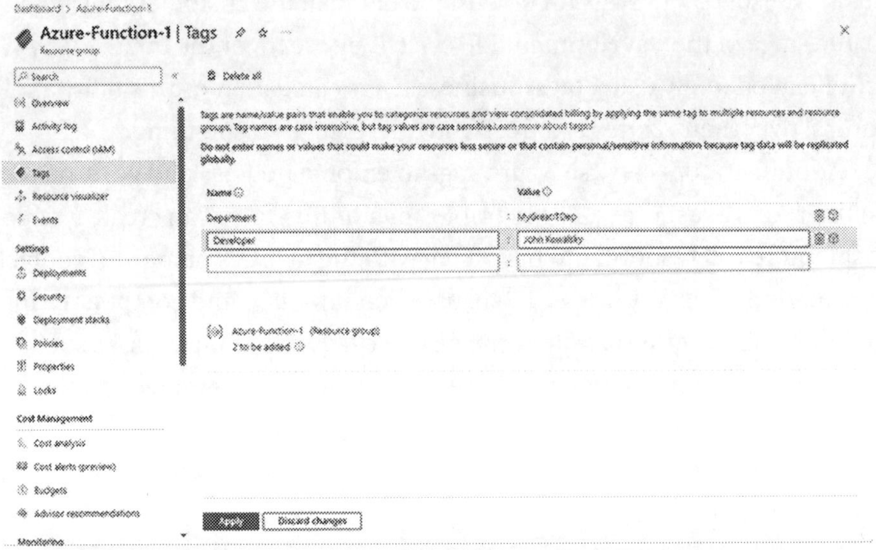

Figure 2-30. *Tags for the Azure Function*

Resource Group – Resource Visualizer

Azure Resource Visualizer is a tool that allows you to view the resources and the relationships between them in an Azure virtual network.

To use Azure Resource Visualizer, you need to go to the resource group you want to visualize. Then, you can click Resource Visualizer under the Monitoring section. You will see a diagram that shows all the resources that are in the same resource group. You can also download the diagram as an editable image file in svg format or export it as a png file. The diagram might help you learn more about your cloud resources and how they are configured, such as IP addresses, network security rules, and routing tables. Figure 2-31 shows an example of such visualizer under the resource group.

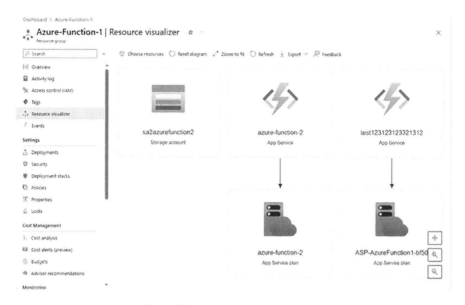

Figure 2-31. *Screenshot of a resource visualizer*

Hosting Plan Tiers

To run serverless code functions on Azure, there is a need to choose a hosting plan for your function app that takes into account the needs of your solution. All hosting plans have different features and configurations. Azure Functions offer three different hosting plans: Consumption, Premium, and Dedicated.

The Consumption plan is the default hosting plan for Azure Functions. The Consumption plan is ideal for scenarios where your functions have unpredictable or sporadic demand, and you want to optimize costs. The Consumption plan has some limitations, such as a maximum execution time of ten minutes per function invocation, and no support for virtual network connectivity.

The Premium plan is an enhanced version of the Consumption plan that provides better performance and more features. It allows you to run your functions on pre-warmed instances, which eliminates cold start delays after idle periods. It also supports larger and more powerful instances, longer execution times (the guaranteed time is up to 60 minutes and is not limited), and virtual network connectivity. The Premium plan is suitable for scenarios where your functions run continuously or frequently, require more CPU or memory options, or need advanced features that are not available on the Consumption plan.

The Dedicated plan is similar to the App Service plan that is used for hosting web apps and other App Service apps. You pay for the compute resources allocated to your App Service plan, regardless of whether your functions are running or not. The Dedicated plan is recommended for scenarios where your functions have long-running or complex workflows that cannot be implemented with Durable Functions or where you need full control over the scaling and configuration of your function app.

Regardless of the chosen plan tier, multiple Azure Functions can always be hosted on a single app service subscription. This is especially useful if there are many Azure Functions for microservices, and they should be connected to a virtual network, and it will be good practice to have them in one service plan.

Summary

In this chapter, you have learned what an Azure Function is; how to program simple triggers, including HTTP and timer; how to read properties from the client post and response; and what an autoscale is and using it to prevent losing availability. Creating middleware is also important for various reasons like additional authentication. We have mentioned authentication topics and durable functions and patterns and how to use them. This chapter is also showing some of the features which has every resource in the Azure, like Tags or they are shortly described without examples. In the next chapter, I will describe Application Insights and how to use them to log or search for problems.

CHAPTER 3

Application Insights

Application Insights for Azure Functions is a function that provides monitoring features for the performance and errors of the Azure Function in the cloud. The Application Insights collects all the data from the function, such as logs, metrics, traces, and events.

This service provides the required tools to analyze and diagnose issues related to the performance, reliability, and quality of the applications. For instance, if an end user raises a ticket related to the degraded application performance or user experience, the technical team will be able to use the Application Insights to trace the end-to-end transaction logs, understand user flows, and easily troubleshoot and identify the root cause. Application Insights has many capabilities which displays the application map, live metrics, transaction search, alerts, logs, workbooks, user flows, sessions, etc.

Deploying Application Insights

Before moving forward with the integration of the Application Insights with the application, we have to deploy the resource to the Azure. In order to do this, we can use the bicep script in Listing 3-1.

Listing 3-1. Bicep with Azure Function and Application Insights

```
param appName string = 'azure-function-2'
param location string = resourceGroup().location

var functionAppName = appName
var hostingPlanName = appName
```

© Michał Świtalik 2024
M. Świtalik, *Azure Adventures with C#*, https://doi.org/10.1007/979-8-8688-0424-3_3

```
resource hostingPlan 'Microsoft.Web/serverfarms@2022-09-01' = {
  name: hostingPlanName
  location: location
  sku: {
    name: 'Y1'
    tier: 'Dynamic'
  }
  properties: {}
}

resource workspace 'Microsoft.OperationalInsights/
workspaces@2022-10-01' = {
  location: location
  name: 'workspace-${appName}'
}

resource applicationInsights 'Microsoft.Insights/
components@2020-02-02' = {
  name: 'application-insights-${appName}'
  location: location
  kind: 'web'
  properties: {
    WorkspaceResourceId: workspace.id
    Application_Type: 'web'
  }
}

resource functionApp 'Microsoft.Web/sites@2022-09-01' = {
  name: functionAppName
  location: location
  kind: 'functionapp'
  identity: {
    type: 'SystemAssigned'
  }
```

```
properties: {
  serverFarmId: hostingPlan.id
  siteConfig: {
    appSettings: [
      {
        name: 'APPINSIGHTS_INSTRUMENTATIONKEY'
        value: applicationInsights.properties.InstrumentationKey
      }
      {
        name: 'APPLICATIONINSIGHTS_CONNECTION_STRING'
        value: 'InstrumentationKey=${applicationInsightsInstr
        umentationKey}'
      {
        name: 'ApplicationInsightsAgent_EXTENSION_VERSION'
        value: '~2'
      }
      {
        name: 'FUNCTIONS_EXTENSION_VERSION'
        value: '~4'
      }
      {
        name: 'FUNCTIONS_WORKER_RUNTIME'
        value: 'dotnet-isolated'
      }
    ]
    ftpsState: 'FtpsOnly'
    minTlsVersion: '1.2'
  }
  httpsOnly: true
}
}
```

You can change the appName variable with a name of your choice, save it, and deploy with the same command. After the command, the following resources will be available in the resource group:

- Application Insights

- Workspace

The variable "workspace" defines a new workspace resource type. It is a container for the data collected by different Application Insights instances. Thanks to this solution, all data from different applications can be viewed in one, single workspace, despite having multiple Application Insights.

The next step is to create Application Insights and assign it to variable applicationInsight. In the property, we provide the required parameters like name and location. We also provide a workspace identifier, where all application logs will be finally sent. Then you can identify logs from a specific application using an Application Insights identifier.

Application Insights Overview

After deploying the Application Insights, go to your resource group. You should see a new resource with the name entered in the bicep file. There are numerous sections located on the left side of the screen. We will cover the following sections:

- Logs – This section helps you to query and analyze the telemetry data from the applications using the Kusto Query Language (KQL).

- Transaction – This section shows an end-to-end view of the application flow, including calling new functions, traces, exceptions, or dependencies.

- Failures – This section displays all failed requests and their details.

- Metrics – In this section, you find existing and ready-to-use metrics to indicate your function performance. You can as well create a new custom metrics for a specific, important code logic to measure.

- Alerts – In this section, you can create alerts for exception or other strange application behaviors. They can be alerted through an email, SMS, or message to a Teams channel.

Figure 3-1 is the screenshot of an example Application Insights instance on the Azure Portal. By default, you have a diagram about failed requests, average response time, count of the server requests, and availability of the application. You can always edit this page and customize it to your needs and business requirements.

Figure 3-1. *Screenshot of the Application Insights resource*

Integration with Existing Project

If you want to continue with the previous project, you can install NuGet packages, make changes to the Program class, and add configuration variables. To insert logs into a new resource from the Azure Function, it needs to be configured and connected with an Instrumentation Key. The first step is to configure variables with a key:

- Log in to the Azure Portal and search for your Application Insights.

- The Instrumentation Key should be on the main view (Overview section).

- Copy it to the configuration variables:

  APPINSIGHTS_INSTRUMENTATIONKEY – Insert only key

  APPLICATIONINSIGHTS_CONNECTION_STRING – Copy Instrumentation Key connection string in format InstrumentationKey={key}

- The next step is to install the following NuGet packages in the project: Microsoft.ApplicationInsights. WorkerService and Microsoft.Azure.Functions.Worker. ApplicationInsights.

- Modify Program.cs and add methods for Application Insights configuration as shown in Listing 3-2.

Listing 3-2. Program class with Application Insights configuration

```
using Microsoft.Extensions.DependencyInjection;
using Microsoft.Extensions.Hosting;

var host = new HostBuilder()
    .ConfigureFunctionsWorkerDefaults()
    .ConfigureServices(services =>
    {
        services.AddApplicationInsightsTelemetryWorkerService();
        services.ConfigureFunctionsApplicationInsights();
    })
    .Build();

host.Run();
```

Now the ILogger interface service can be injected and used as a logger to output information to the Application Insights. For example, create a class and an interface.

Listing 3-3. Service with logging

```
using Microsoft.Extensions.Logging;

namespace AzureAdventure.FirstFunction
{
    public class ResponseService : IResponseService
    {
        private readonly ILogger<ResponseService> _logger;

        public string GetValue()
        {
            _logger.LogTrace("Trace");
            _logger.LogDebug("Debug");
            _logger.LogInformation("Information");
            _logger.LogWarning("Warning");
            _logger.LogError("Error");
            _logger.LogCritical("Critical");
            _logger.LogMetric("Custom Metric", 2.0);
            _logger.LogMetric("Custom Metric", 1.0, new
            Dictionary<string, object>()
            {
                {
                    "CustomProperty", "CustomValue"
                }
            });

            using (_logger.BeginScope("Scope"))
            {
                _logger.LogInformation("Information in scope");
```

```
            _logger.LogInformation("Second information in
            scope");
        }

        return "Hi!";
    }

    public interface IResponseService
    {
        string GetValue();
    }
}
```

The class, from the Listing 3-3, is defining an interface IResponseService with only one public method GetValue, which returns a string value. The ResponseService class is implementing the interface. In the constructor, we inject the ILogger interface type and assign it to a private variable. The logger interface is from the Microsoft.Extensions. Logging namespace. The GetValue is returning a "Hi!" string value and is also calling several logging methods, and their results should be visible in the Application Insights logs.

The logger object is using several methods that can be used to write a message to the logs with different levels of severity. The methods used in this code are as follows:

- LogTrace and LogDebug – These methods send messages which are very useful while debugging and testing. They can help in troubleshooting and tracing the application flow.

- LogInformation – This method should contain messages about the program execution, such as the start or end of actions. They can be used in the production environment to monitor the health of the program and its performance.

- LogWarning – This method can be used to indicate that something unusual happened during the program execution, but it is not affecting the flow of the application. It may require an action in the future and investigation from the software engineer or administrator and provide a possible fix if possible.

- LogError and LogCritical – These methods can be used to indicate a failure, exception, or other unexpected behaviors of the application and that it should be investigated as fast as possible. They should be monitored by the administrators, or there should be automated alerts to be sent when they appear.

- LogMetric – This method can be used to monitor some custom metrics of the application such as the response time, memory usage, or the method run. In this code example, we are using two different executions. In the first call, we only provide the name of the custom metric and its value; it can be a float variable. The second call is also providing the third parameter which is a dictionary, where we can put additional information about the metric. Then these values can be used to monitor and create a graph of how something is changing.

The logger object is also using the BeginScope method to create a logical scope for a related message that is following the scope, until it is disposed. That way, we can associate logs with a specific context or logic in the application. This method is taking one parameter; it can be a string which represents the scope. It will return an IDisposable object which needs to be disposed when it is no longer needed. This object can be used with the using statement. All messages should be associated with the scope and should be easier to filter out later for investigation if needed.

To inject this service, add the following to the Program.cs file in the service builder method as in Listing 3-4.

Listing 3-4. Adding ResponseService

```
services.AddScoped<IResponseService, ResponseService>();
```

Listing 3-5. Injecting service to the Azure Function class

```
using System.Net;
using Microsoft.Azure.Functions.Worker;
using Microsoft.Azure.Functions.Worker.Http;
using Microsoft.Extensions.Logging;

namespace AzureAdventure.FirstFunction
{
    public class Function1
    {
        private readonly ILogger _logger;
        private readonly IResponseService _responseService;

        public Function1(ILoggerFactory loggerFactory,
        IResponseService responseService)
        {
            _logger = loggerFactory.CreateLogger<Function1>();
            _responseService = responseService;
        }

        [Function("Function1")]
        public HttpResponseData Run([HttpTrigger(Authorization
        Level.Anonymous, "get", "post", Route = "helloworld")]
        HttpRequestData req)
        {
```

```
        _logger.LogInformation("C# HTTP trigger function
        processed a request.");

        var response = req.CreateResponse(HttpStatus
        Code.OK);
        response.Headers.Add("Content-Type", "text/plain;
        charset=utf-8");

        response.WriteString(_responseService.GetValue());

        return response;
    }
  }
}
```

Listing 3-5 is injecting the ResponseService class in the constructor and assigning it to the private variable named _responseService. Then the GetValue method is executed in order to get the value to the response object. Finally, the response object is returned to the requestor.

Reading Logs from the Function

There are several ways to read the application logs inside the Azure Portal. To check the live logs during the function execution, go to your Azure Function resource. Find and click your function name. Then go to the Monitor section (as is shown in Figure 3-2). You will see the list of the function execution history in the Invocations tab and the live stream in the Logs tab.

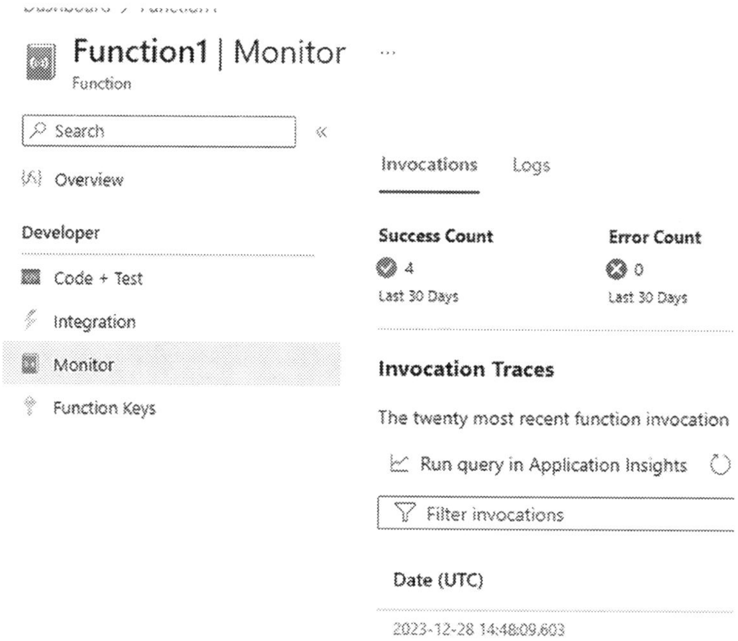

Figure 3-2. *Monitor section for function*

The Logs section is showing the logs with additional data like time and severity. Example messages are shown in Figure 3-3. In the command bar, there are useful commands. Like the source of logs, by default it is set to the App Insights Logs; you can change it into File System Logs. You will receive more logs, except Application Insights. Then you have the Log Level filter to select the severity logs which you want to see, whether you need them for debugging and you can select the information severity or looking for exceptions and you can select the error level.

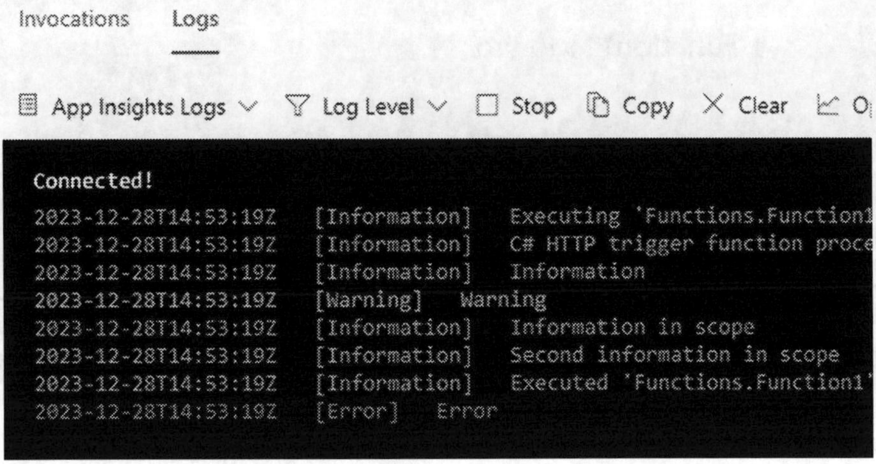

Invocations   Logs

▤ App Insights Logs ∨   ▽ Log Level ∨   ☐ Stop   ⧉ Copy   ✕ Clear   ⌃ O

```
Connected!
2023-12-28T14:53:19Z    [Information]    Executing 'Functions.Function1
2023-12-28T14:53:19Z    [Information]    C# HTTP trigger function proce
2023-12-28T14:53:19Z    [Information]    Information
2023-12-28T14:53:19Z    [Warning]    Warning
2023-12-28T14:53:19Z    [Information]    Information in scope
2023-12-28T14:53:19Z    [Information]    Second information in scope
2023-12-28T14:53:19Z    [Information]    Executed 'Functions.Function1'
2023-12-28T14:53:19Z    [Error]    Error
```

Figure 3-3. *Logs of running function*

When you select any of the history run from the screenshot in
Figure 3-3, you will see similar logs like in Figure 3-4. These logs will
contain a date and a message. You can use the link at the top to go through
the log details.

Invocation Details

⌃ Run query in Application Insights

Timestamp	Message
2023-12-28 14:48:09.611	Executing 'Functions.Function1' (Rea:
2023-12-28 14:48:09.634	Warning
2023-12-28 14:48:09.641	Error
2023-12-28 14:48:09.641	Critical
2023-12-28 14:48:10.065	Executed 'Functions.Function1' (Succ

Figure 3-4. *History of running function*

Searching in Logs

There are cases where you want to search through the logs, whether they were sent by one or more functions in many executions. You can use the KQL language to filter the results, project them, or set the time range.

To use it, follow these steps:

1. Go to the Application Insights resource on your Resource Group.

2. Then select the Logs section.

3. You will have a modal window with some example queries.

4. Close it using the X button on the top-right side.

5. On the top, you should see a text field, where you can enter your query.

All results will be displayed under the query.

KQL is an abbreviation for Kusto Query Language. It is a powerful query language which can help you to filter, aggregate, or sort logs. Put "traces" keyword into the text field, and then choose from the command bar the "Run" button. You should get all the traces from the Application Insights. The results of such action are visible in Figure 3-5.

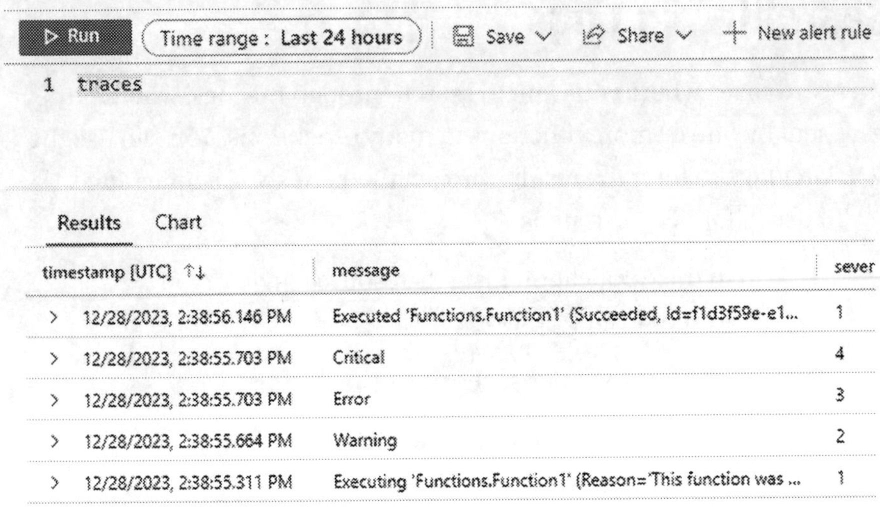

| ▷ Run | Time range : Last 24 hours | 🖫 Save ∨ | 🖄 Share ∨ | + New alert rule |

```
1  traces
```

Results   Chart

timestamp [UTC] ↑↓	message	sever
> 12/28/2023, 2:38:56.146 PM	Executed 'Functions.Function1' (Succeeded, Id=f1d3f59e-e1...	1
> 12/28/2023, 2:38:55.703 PM	Critical	4
> 12/28/2023, 2:38:55.703 PM	Error	3
> 12/28/2023, 2:38:55.664 PM	Warning	2
> 12/28/2023, 2:38:55.311 PM	Executing 'Functions.Function1' (Reason='This function was ...	1

Figure 3-5. *Searching in the Logs section*

To filter out the results, we can use the "where" function, then provide
a logical syntax. For example, we can use the query from Figure 3-6 to get
all logs with error severity. You can also use two other operators:

- Contains – Example syntax: traces | where message
  contains "not delivered". This operator will search for
  any substring that matches the following string.

- Has – Example syntax: traces | where message has
  "not delivered". This operator will search for the exact
  same string.

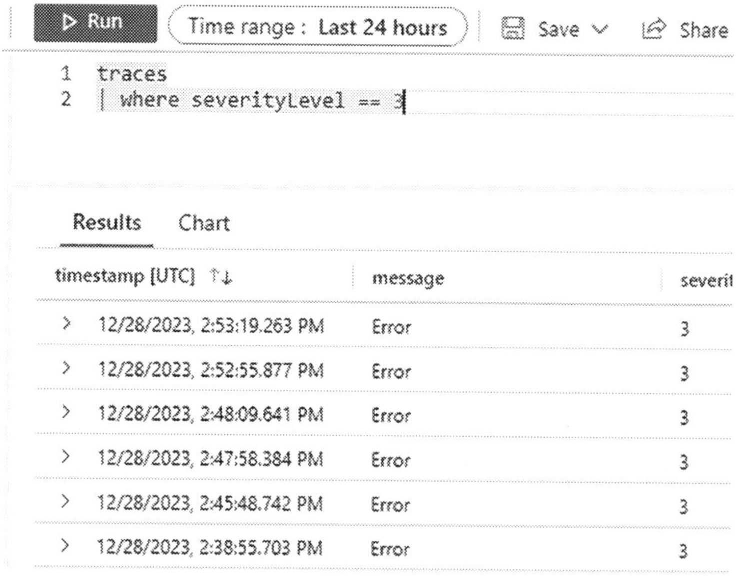

Figure 3-6. *Where query in the App Insights*

Other worth mentioning operators are as follows:

- Take – Syntax: traces | take 10. To limit retrieved logs.

- Distinct – Syntax: traces | distinct columnName.
  This operator will create distinct logs by the
  specified column.

The query from Listing 3-6 shows how to get all traces from the last
48 hours.

Listing 3-6. Query for traces from the last 48 hours

```
traces
| where timestamp > ago(48hr)
| order by timestamp desc
```

The query from Listing 3-7 is summarizing the average time of all
requests since the last 48 hours.

Listing 3-7. Query for the average time of requests from the last 48 hours

```
requests
| where timestamp > ago(48hr)
| order by timestamp desc
| summarize avg(duration)
```

The query from Listing 3-8 shows the average time response for all requests, but they are grouped by user.

Listing 3-8. Query to summarize the average time response for all requests grouped by user

```
requests
| summarize avgDuration = sum(duration) / count() by user_
AccountId
```

Searching in Transaction Section

Transaction search in Azure Application Insights is a feature that allows you to find and explore all traces, exceptions, or other logs from the application. Transaction search helps you to trace and diagnose transactions to identify issues and optimize performance.

To use transaction search, you need to open the Application Insights resource for your web application in the Azure Portal. You can choose the event types that you want to see, such as requests, dependencies, exceptions, or custom events. You can also filter the results by time range, operation name, or other properties. When you select a specific telemetry item, you will be forwarded to a page with details for this item and other logs related to it.

Transaction search is useful for debugging and troubleshooting your web application. You can see the end-to-end transaction details of a request or a page view, including the dependency calls, exceptions, trace logs, and custom events that are part of the same operation.

The screenshot from Figure 3-7 is showing how the transaction looks like. You can enter any string into the text field, and all items will be filtered by them in all columns, and then they will be displayed. The screenshot from Figure 3-8 is showing all logs from the specific transaction with their details when you enter one. All traces, exceptions, logs, and more will be visible there to easily track the flow of the request.

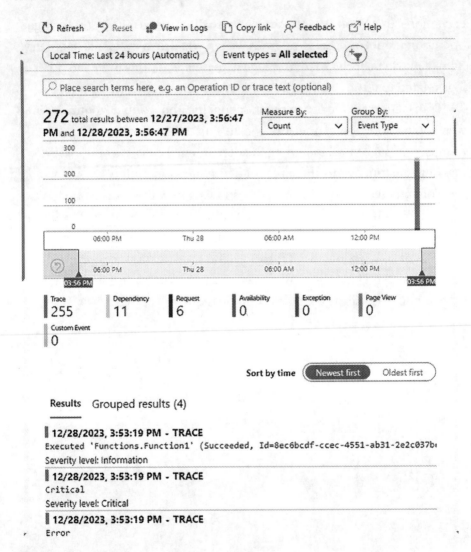

Figure 3-7. Transaction search

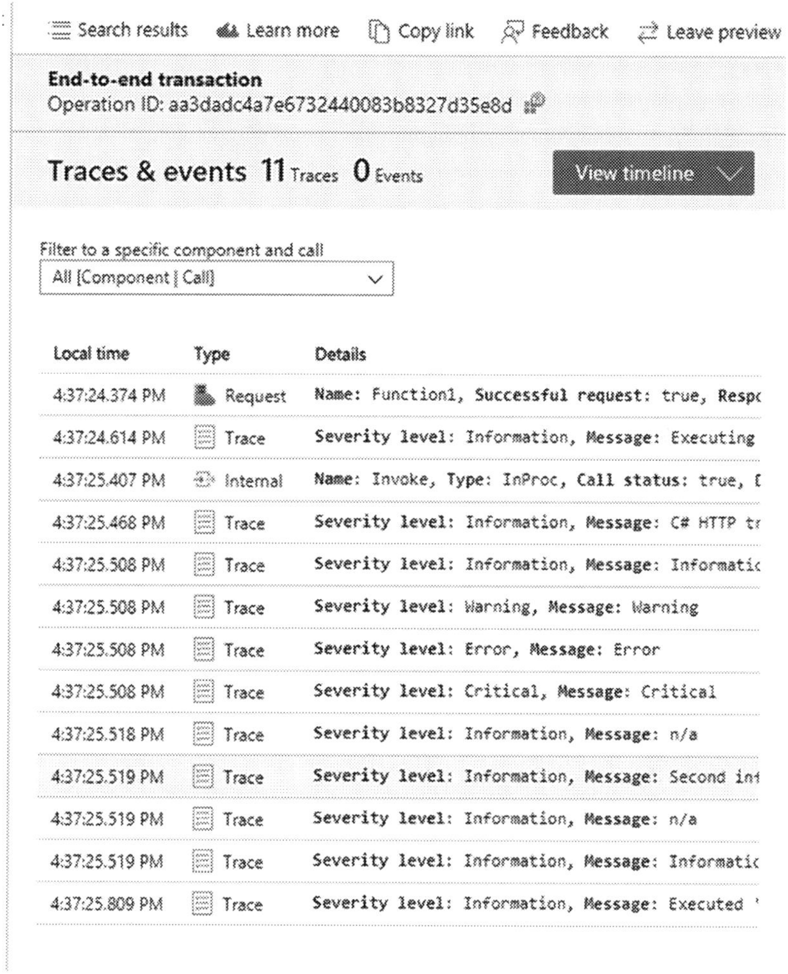

Figure 3-8. *Screenshot of details for a specific item*

Metrics

Metrics are measurable data that indicate the performance or usage of your application. Azure Application Insights collects different types of metrics from your application and the resources it depends on, such as Azure services, web servers, databases, etc. Metrics can be used to track the functionality, availability, and overall health of your application, its components, or a specific piece of code logic with a custom metrics.

The screenshot in Figure 3-9 is showing a simple graph line for custom metrics used in the ResponseService class. You can change the graph to show the average, sum, or count of the provided metrics.

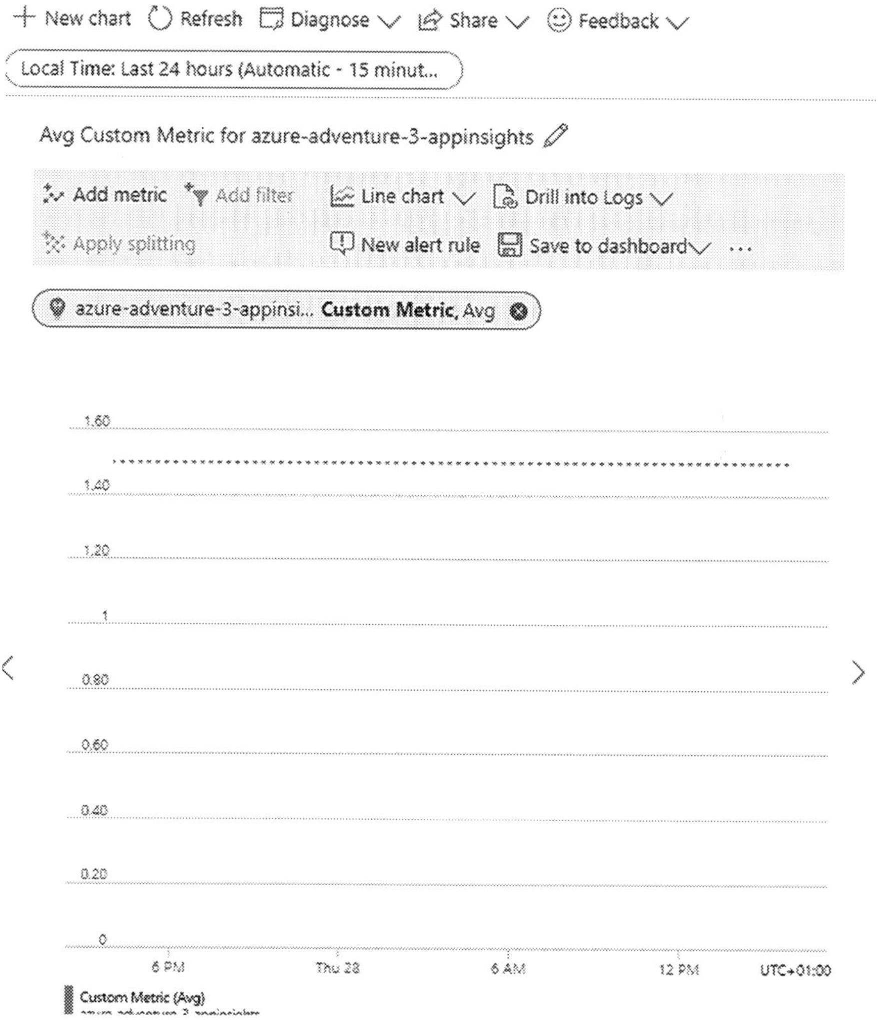

New chart
Refresh
Diagnose
Share
Feedback
Local Time: Last 24 hours (Automatic - 15 minut...
Avg Custom Metric for azure-adventure-3-appinsights
Add metric
Add filter
Line chart
Drill into Logs
Apply splitting
New alert rule
Save to dashboard
azure-adventure-3-appinsi... Custom Metric, Avg
1.60
1.40
1.20
1
0.80
0.60
0.40
0.20
0
6 PM
Thu 28
6 AM
12 PM
UTC+01:00
Custom Metric (Avg)

Figure 3-9. *Screenshot of a custom metrics*

Here are some examples of metrics:

- Availability – It is a percentage of successful web health checks that shows the accessibility of your application from various places.

- Browser page load time – It is the amount of time it takes for a user's browser to load a web page.

- Server response time – It is a duration of time used by your application to send a response after processing a request.

- Dependency duration – It is the time it takes for your application to call an external service or resource, such as a database or an API.

- Performance counters – System-level metrics that show the resource consumption of your application, such as disk I/O, memory usage, and CPU usage.

Failures

In searching for failed requests to your API function, you can go to the Failures section. The screenshot in Figure 3-10 is showing an example failing of the Azure Function called Function1. There will be a display of all failing functions with the number of times when it is failing. In the screenshot in Figure 3-11, you will see how in the details it will be displayed when you click the failing function.

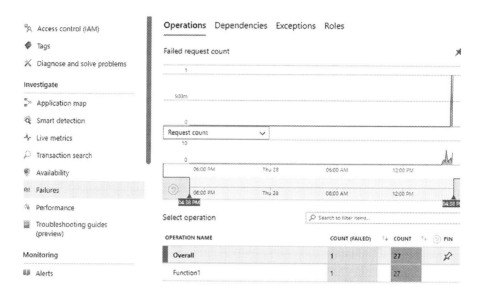

Figure 3-10. *Screenshot of failing function*

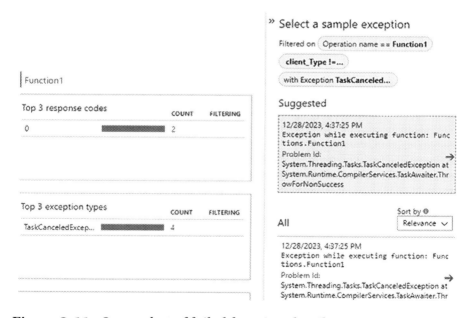

Figure 3-11. *Screenshot of failed function details*

You can scroll through the failing functions or search them. When you select one of the sample exceptions in the pane, you will be redirected to a new site which will look similar to Figure 3-7.

Workbook

Azure workbooks are useful for visualizing and analyzing data in a centralized location, making it easier to gain insights and make informed decisions. You can use input data from various sources and create custom visualizations to suit your specific needs. You can use these as sources: requests, traces, failures, and more. You can either use built-in workbook templates or create your own from scratch. In Figure 3-12, you can see an example of a custom visualization created using data from traces, which shows how many of them were informational or critical.

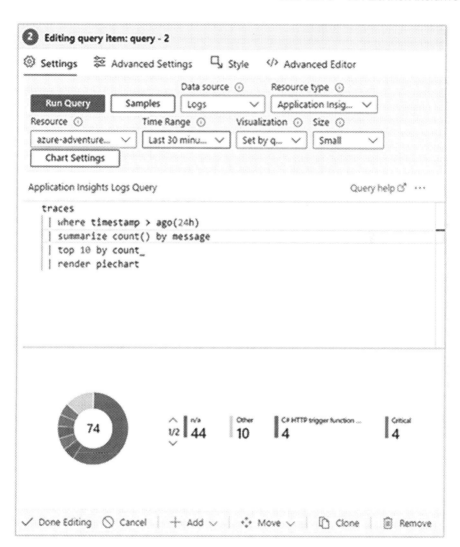

Figure 3-12. *Editing query for the workbook*

Application Map

You have the option to view the dependencies and relationships that exist between your function app and other services or components with the help of the application map. They may include storage accounts, databases, other application programming interfaces (APIs), or key vaults. Additionally, you are able to view the number of failures, request times, and performance of each dependence.

The screenshot in Figure 3-13 is showing the dependencies of an example Azure Function, calling the Storage Account for blob files. You can see on the arrow the number of calls and average time of request.

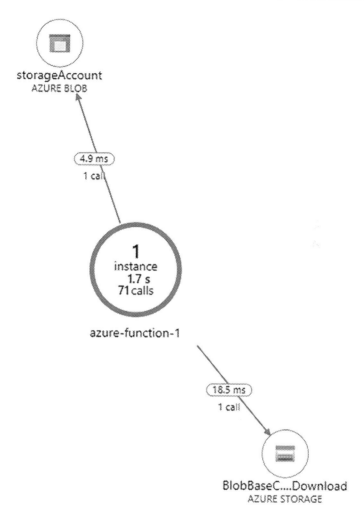

Figure 3-13. *Application map of Azure Function*

Alerts

Rules and action groups are two concepts related to Application Insights, a service that keeps an eye on the availability and performance of your applications. Rules are the conditions that trigger alerts when something goes wrong with your application, such as failures, exceptions, or slow requests. Action groups are sets of related actions that are performed when an alert is triggered, such as sending notifications, calling webhooks, or executing Azure functions.

Rules and action groups are created and managed in Azure Application Insights. You can create rules for different types of smart detection modules, which are features that automatically detect anomalies and issues in your application. You can also create action groups for these rules to enable multiple methods of taking actions or triggering notifications on new detections.

You can add a few action groups to an alert rule, and multiple alert rules can use the same action group. Action groups are executed concurrently, in no specific order. You can assign different types of actions to an action group such as email, SMS, voice call, webhook, Azure function, logic app, or automation runbook.

These instructions will help you in creating an example alert and notification when an exception happens while the program is being executed:

- Go to the Application Insights.

- Go to the Alert section.

- Click the Create button from the command bar and select the Create action group button.

- Fill in all required fields, the action group display name, and unique name, and choose your resource group, subscription where they are created, and a region like in Figure 3-14.

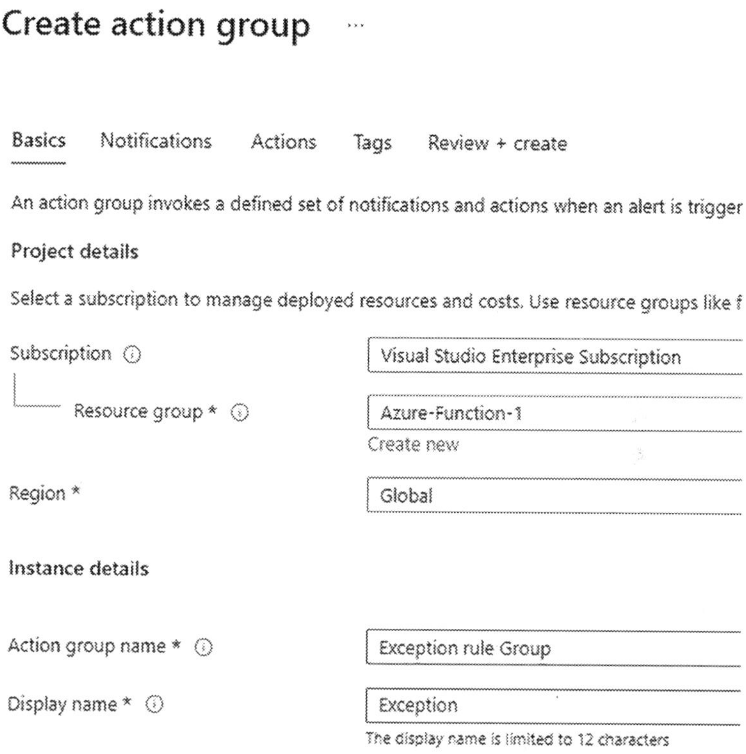

Create action group   ...

Basics   Notifications   Actions   Tags   Review + create

An action group invokes a defined set of notifications and actions when an alert is trigger

Project details

Select a subscription to manage deployed resources and costs. Use resource groups like f

Subscription ⓘ | Visual Studio Enterprise Subscription

    └──────   Resource group * ⓘ | Azure-Function-1
                                    Create new

Region * | Global

Instance details

Action group name * ⓘ | Exception rule Group

Display name * ⓘ | Exception
                   The display name is limited to 12 characters

Figure 3-14. *Basic tab of the Create action group step*

- Go to the Notification tab; if you select the Email/SMS/
  Push/Voice option (like in Figure 3-15), you can check
  and fill in the required text fields in the new pane (like
  in Figure 3-16).

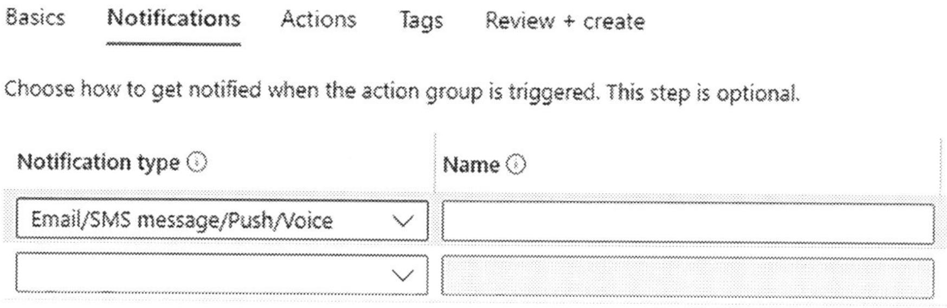

Basics   **Notifications**   Actions   Tags   Review + create

Choose how to get notified when the action group is triggered. This step is optional.

Notification type ⓘ | Name ⓘ

Email/SMS message/Push/Voice ∨ |

∨ |

Figure 3-15. *Notification tab of the Create action group*

137

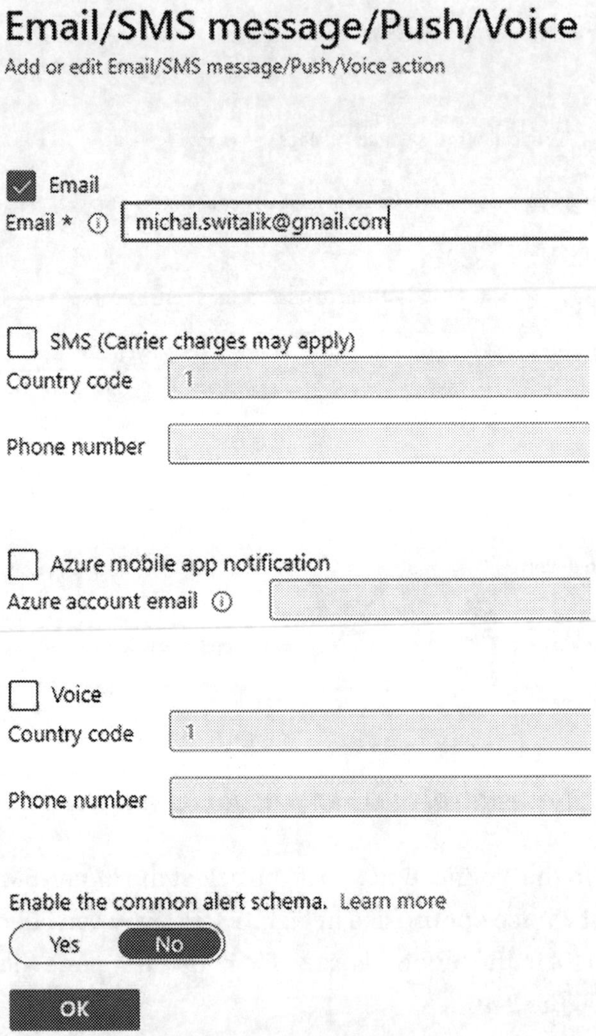

Email/SMS message/Push/Voice

Add or edit Email/SMS message/Push/Voice action

☑ Email

Email * ⓘ   michal.switalik@gmail.com

☐ SMS (Carrier charges may apply)

Country code   1

Phone number

☐ Azure mobile app notification

Azure account email ⓘ

☐ Voice

Country code   1

Phone number

Enable the common alert schema.   Learn more

(Yes   No)

OK

Figure 3-16. *Pane notification setup of the Create action group*

- In the Action tab, you can select a different action; currently, there are available options: Azure function, Automation Runbook, Event Hub, ITSM, Logic App, Secure Webhook, and Webhook.

Then we will create a rule to trigger the created action group:

- Go back to the Alert section.

- Click the Create button from the command bar and select the Create alert button.

- In the Scope tab, select the Application Insights for your Azure function.

- In the Condition, you can select various different conditions; all list is shown in Figure 3-17. We are selecting the Custom log search; in the text field, put this query: traces where severity >= 3. It will trigger an alert when an error or higher severity occurs.

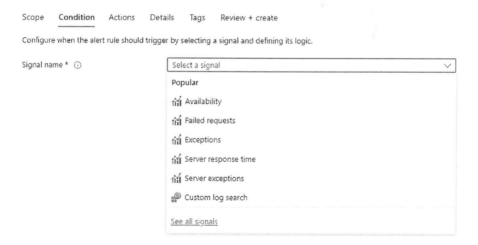

Figure 3-17. *Selecting condition for the alert*

- In the Actions section, select the previously created action group.

- In the Alert logic section, set the threshold value to 1, and set the rest of the options as it is in Figure 3-18.

Alert logic

ⓘ We have set the condition configuration automatically based on popular settings for this metric. Please review and make changes as needed.

Threshold ⓘ	⦿ Static ◯ Dynamic
Aggregation type ⓘ	Count ⌄
Operator ⓘ	Greater than ⌄
Unit ⓘ	Count ⌄
Threshold value * ⓘ	1 ⌄

Split by dimensions

Use dimensions to monitor specific time series and provide context to the fired alert. Dimensions can be either number or string columns. If you select more than one dimension value, each time series that results from the combination will trigger its own alert and will be charged separately. About monitoring multiple time series

Dimension name	Operator	Dimension values	Include all future values
Select dimension ⌄	= ⌄	0 selected ⌄ Add custom value	☐

When to evaluate

Check every ⓘ	1 minute ⌄
Lookback period ⓘ	5 minutes ⌄

╼ Add condition

Figure 3-18. *Setting up logic for the alert*

- Go to the next, Details tab, set the severity of the alert, and enter your alert name and short description.

- Finally, go to the Review + create section tab. You will
  see the price for this alert; in this case, it is only 0.10
  USD/month, as shown in Figure 3-19. Click the Create
  button to complete.

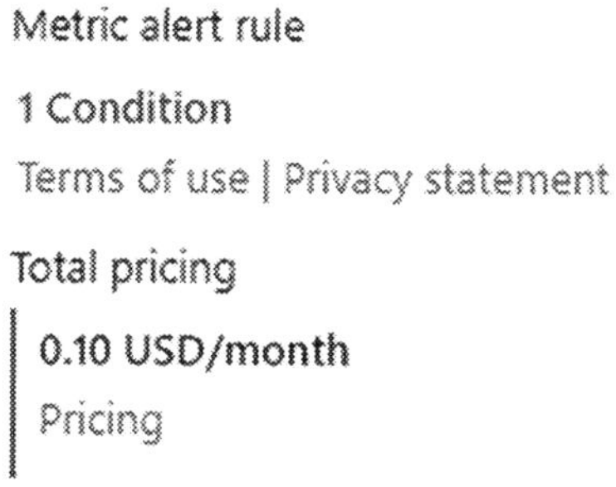

Metric alert rule

1 Condition
Terms of use | Privacy statement

Total pricing

0.10 USD/month
Pricing

-

Figure 3-19. *Pricing of the alert*

Summary

In this chapter, we have discovered the Application Insights service. It is
a service that provides monitoring features for performance and errors
in the Azure cloud. It collects data such as metrics, traces, and events,
allowing users to analyze and diagnose errors quickly. The App Insights
resource includes sections like logs, transactions, failures, metrics,
and alerts.

For the C# projects, the ILogger interface is being used. It is a service
that can be used to output information to the Application Insights. The
logger object can use methods like LogTrace, LogDebug, LogInformation,
LogWarning, LogError, LogCritical, and LogMetric to write messages to the
logs with different levels of severity.

Azure Application Insights provides various ways to read application logs, including checking live logs during function execution, searching through logs, and using the Kusto Query Language (KQL) to filter, aggregate, or sort logs. The Logs section displays the history of running functions, with a date and message. The KQL can be used to filter, aggregate, or sort logs, such as traces, where, requests, and exceptions. Transaction search allows users to find and explore all traces, exceptions, or other logs from the application, helping to trace and diagnose transactions. Transaction search is useful for debugging and troubleshooting web applications, providing end-to-end transaction details of requests or page views. Custom metrics can be used to measure the health, availability, and performance of your application.

Rules and action groups can be created and managed in Azure Application Insights, enabling users to create rules for smart detection modules and create action groups for multiple methods of taking actions or triggering notifications.

CHAPTER 4

Storage Account

An essential part of Azure that lets you store and manage various kinds of data is a storage account. This chapter will show you about the advantages and benefits of using a storage account, such as security, scalability, performance, and availability. Additionally, you will investigate the many storage services that a storage account can offer, including queues, tables, and blobs. You will be able to establish and configure a storage account for your very own needs and scenarios by reaching the end of this chapter.

A binary big object known as a blob is capable of storing any kind of data, including text files, photos, audio files, movies, documents, and more. Containers, which are logical collections of blobs with shared metadata and access controls, are where blobs are kept.

A data structure that fits to the First In, First Out (FIFO) principle is a queue. Messages that an application needs to process asynchronously are stored in queues. Queue services, which offer functions for adding, removing, and managing queues and messages, store queues.

Structured or semi-structured data can be stored in rows and columns in a table. Data that can be efficiently queried with a key or combination of keys is stored in tables. Table services, which offer functions for adding, removing, and managing tables and entities, store tables. Tables allow for a flexible schema, which allows for the customization of each entity's properties.

© Michał Świtalik 2024
M. Świtalik, *Azure Adventures with C#*, https://doi.org/10.1007/979-8-8688-0424-3_4

How to Deploy

You can deploy the storage account resource through the Azure Portal.
Log in to your account on the portal, look for the Storage Account type
resource, select all required fields (name and SKU level – LRS should be
enough), and select a subscription and resource group where it is going to
be created. Click the Review + Create button; to confirm, click Create.

Listing 4-1. Deployment of the storage account

```
resource storageAccount 'Microsoft.Storage/
storageAccounts@2023-01-01' = {
  name: 'azureadventureaccount'
  location: resourceGroup().location
  sku: {
    name: 'Standard_LRS'
  }
  kind:'StorageV2'
  properties: {
    supportsHttpsTrafficOnly: true
    encryption: {
      services: {
        blob: {
          enabled: true
        }
        queue: {
          enabled: true
        }
      }
    }
  }
```

```
    accessTier:'Hot'
    minimumTlsVersion:'TLS1_2'
  }
}
```

Listing 4-1 shows an example of a script with a storage account that can be used for deployment. There is a set name for azureadventureaccount; it should be a maximum of 24 characters, and lowercase letters and numbers are only allowed. It should be globally unique. The name will be used as part of the URL to access the storage account.

Then the SKU is set to standard LRS. All types of SKU are described in the first chapter, "Data Backup" section. The "kind" property setup a version of the storage account. Currently, the newest is version 2.

Then the HTTPS traffic only option is set to true, and for safety reasons, the encryption is enabled for blobs, queues, and tables. This ensures that the data stored in these entities is protected and secure.

The access tier is set to hot. It costs less when the blobs are highly accessed and changed. Another option is to set the access tier to cool. This option reduces the cost for blobs that are accessed less frequently. However, it may increase the retrieval time for those blobs.

The bicep script may include more features, like virtual network integration and RBAC setup.

Listing 4-2. Services of the storage account

```
resource queueService 'Microsoft.Storage/storageAccounts/
queueServices@2023-01-01' = {
  parent: storageAccount
  name: 'default'
  properties: {}
}
```

```
resource blobService 'Microsoft.Storage/storageAccounts/
blobServices@2023-01-01' = {
  parent: storageAccount
  name: 'default'
  properties: {}
}

resource azureAdventureQueue 'Microsoft.Storage/
storageAccounts/queueServices/queues@2023-01-01'  = {
  parent: queueService
  name: 'azure-adventure-queue'
  properties: {}
}

resource azureAdventureContainer 'Microsoft.Storage/
storageAccounts/blobServices/containers@2023-01-01' = {
  parent: blobService
  name: 'azure-adventure-reports'
  properties: {}
}

resource tableService 'Microsoft.Storage/storageAccounts/
tableServices@2023-01-01' = {
  parent: storageAccount
  name: 'default'
  properties: {}
}

resource azureAdventureTable 'Microsoft.Storage/
storageAccounts/tableServices/tables@2023-01-01' = {
  parent: tableService
  name: 'azure-adventure-table'
  properties: {}
}
```

The piece of script in Listing 4-2 is an example of how to create and configure various kinds of storage resources in Azure using the bicep language.

The first two lines of code create a queue service and a blob service under a storage account.

The next two lines of code create a queue and a container under the respective services. The queue is named "azure-adventure-queue," and it will be used to store messages. The container is named "azure-adventure-reports," and it will be used to store reports.

The last two lines of code create a table service and a table under the storage account. The table service allows to store structured data in tables, which can be queried using the OData protocol. The table is named "azure-adventure-table," and it will be used to store information.

This piece of code demonstrates how to use Bicep to create various types of storage resources in Azure in a concise and consistent way. It also shows how to use the parent property to specify the hierarchical relationship between the resources.

Azure Storage Explorer

In order to give you examples, firstly let's install the Azure Storage Explorer, which is a graphical user interface (GUI) application for managing and working with Azure storage accounts. This application provides an easier way to navigate and interact with your storage accounts.

Search for "Azure Storage Explorer" in your preferred search engine and follow the official download instructions. Once you have installed the application, run it. Figure 4-1 shows a list of all your storage accounts on the left-hand side. From here, you can easily manage and access your storage resources. Under each storage account, you will find containers, file shares, and queues that you can interact with.

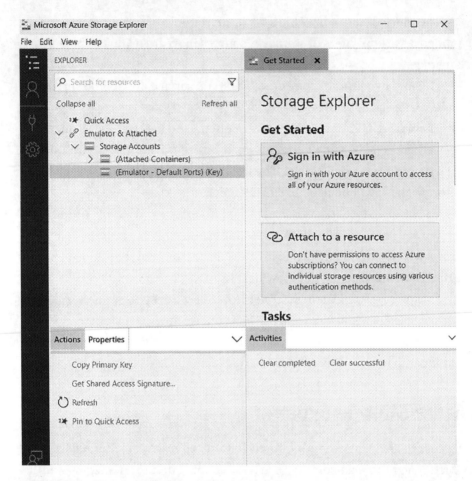

Figure 4-1. Azure Storage Explorer running

If you have chosen the Azurite option (shown in Figure 4-2) in the wizard when creating the Azure function, you should see logs as shown in Figure 4-3. These logs contain information about running the Azurite emulator in the background. After loading the solution, you can run the Azure Storage Explorer to access the Storage Account, create an example container or folder, and upload a file there.

Figure 4-2. *Use the Azurite emulator for the runtime*

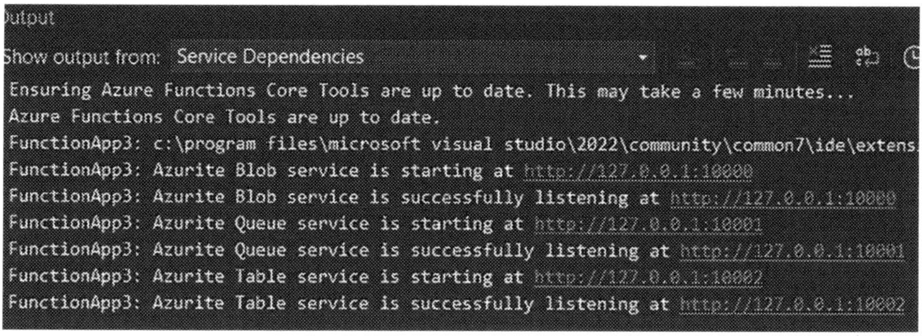

```
Output
Show output from:  Service Dependencies
Ensuring Azure Functions Core Tools are up to date. This may take a few minutes...
Azure Functions Core Tools are up to date.
FunctionApp3: c:\program files\microsoft visual studio\2022\community\common7\ide\extens
FunctionApp3: Azurite Blob service is starting at http://127.0.0.1:10000
FunctionApp3: Azurite Blob service is successfully listening at http://127.0.0.1:10000
FunctionApp3: Azurite Queue service is starting at http://127.0.0.1:10001
FunctionApp3: Azurite Queue service is successfully listening at http://127.0.0.1:10001
FunctionApp3: Azurite Table service is starting at http://127.0.0.1:10002
FunctionApp3: Azurite Table service is successfully listening at http://127.0.0.1:10002
```

Figure 4-3. *Visual Studio output logs*

Figure 4-4 is what the storage account will look like when you connect to it. I have created a container called "documents." Inside it, I have uploaded two documents and created a folder. For practice, try to do the same. The container name can have a maximum of 63 characters and must be lowercase letters or numbers. The directory inside can be a combination of lowercase and uppercase letters, numbers, and special characters.

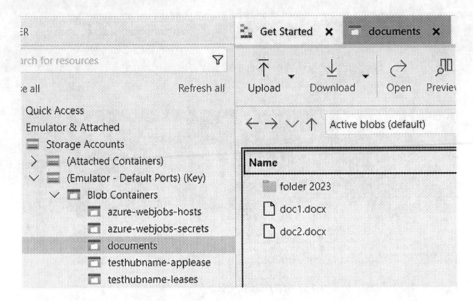

Figure 4-4. *Storage Account emulator with folder and documents*

In Figure 4-5, you can see the "Actions" menu. Besides the obvious actions like delete, open, or refresh, there are some other actions that can be performed, and they can be useful for managing the content or customizing the settings.

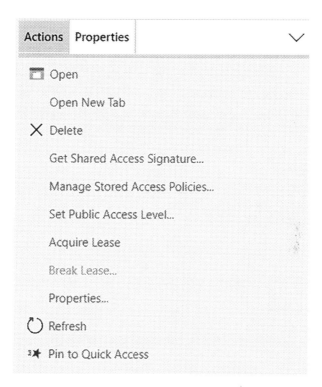

Figure 4-5. *Actions available for the container*

The "Set Publish Access Level" button allows you to change the settings of public access to the resources. There are three levels to choose from:

- No public access – It will be set to private access, and only authenticated users will have access.

- Public read access for container and blobs – All resources within the container and blob will be accessible to the public for reading.

- Public read access for blobs only – Every blob in the container will be readable by anybody with Internet access.

A special token that provides relatively short access to the container or blob can be generated by the "Get Shared Access Signature" method. Figure 4-6 shows all the options available for this token. You can select when the token will expire, when it will be working, and, most importantly, what permissions will be granted. You can optionally set the IP range or version.

Figure 4-6. *Creating shared access signature*

This is how an example URL with a SAS token may look like: http://127.0.0.1:10000/mydevaccount1/documents?sv=2018-03-28&st =2024-01-13T15%3A43%3A12Z&se=2024-01-14T15%3A43%3A12Z&sr= c&sp=rl&sig=Cg%2FLkEa1mu3Rn6muS7zmvB18Kb9MDqxW%2FwXAYx hY4s8%3D. There are parameters st which stands for start time, se which stands for end time, sr which stands for resource type, sp which stands for permissions, and sig which stands for signature.

You can use this token or URL and share it with other users who require short-term access to the resource. They can use it to view or download the resource; it depends on the given permissions associated with the token or URL. It can be a Word document, presentation, or some important agreement, and it needs to be securely shared and accessed by multiple individuals.

You can set the access policies by clicking "Manage Stored Access Policies." You can set the access policies to be read, add, create, write, or delete version for a specific time duration. You can use it while creating the SAS token.

The "Acquire Lease" button allows you to lock access to the specific container or blob for a specified period of time. This lock prevents any other operations from being performed during that time. You can still work on your task without worrying about interference from other users. When the specified time expires, the lock is automatically released, and other users can perform operations on the container or blob. It can help you to avoid situations when two or more users are trying to modify the same container or blob simultaneously and can overwrite their work. You can release the lock after pressing the "Break Lease" button.

Blobs

There are some solutions which requirements are to store, manage, or process files. Azure has a service to provide a resolution for this, and it is Azure Blob Storage. This is a reliable and secure choice for companies wishing to maximize their data storage capabilities. It offers high scalability and performance for keeping a lot of unstructured files and sending them back. It also provides advanced features such as data encryption and access control.

To save blobs, first you have to create a storage account; when you have it, then you can create a container within that account. Then you can either save the blobs directly to the container or create subdirectories within the container to organize your blobs.

Working with Blobs Through Azure Function

Blobs in your Azure storage account can be managed and modified with the help of the Azure Function. The Azure Function provides a convenient way to perform various operations on blobs, such as uploading, downloading, and deleting them. Additionally, you can also perform operations like copying and moving blobs using the Azure Function. The Azure Function simplifies blob management and allows for seamless integration with other Azure services.

To start working with blobs in the function, create a new project with the HTTP trigger type and select the "Use Azurite for runtime storage account" option when creating the Azure Function. Then install the "Azure.Storage.Blobs" package from the NuGet source using the Package Manager tool inside Visual Studio.

The "Access keys" section of the storage account on the Azure Portal with the Storage Account resource site contains the connection string you'll need to authenticate locally with the storage. To work with the local emulator, make sure you have the local.settings.json file created in

the project and its value set for the "AzureWebJobsStorage" key is set to
UseDevelopmentStorage=true. The file content should be like the code
snippet in Listing 4-3. During the local run, it will connect to the Azurite
emulator running in your Visual Studio.

Listing 4-3. The local settings file for the Azure Function

```
{
    "IsEncrypted": false,
    "Values": {
        "AzureWebJobsStorage": "UseDevelopmentStorage=true",
        "FUNCTIONS_WORKER_RUNTIME": "dotnet-isolated"
    }
}
```

To authenticate to the storage account, you will also need to acquire a
connection from the properties and copy it to the environment variables in
your Azure function resource. Follow these steps to do this:

- Go to your storage account.

- Find and click the Access Keys section.

- Copy the first value from the Connection string field, as
  shown in the screenshot in Figure 4-7.

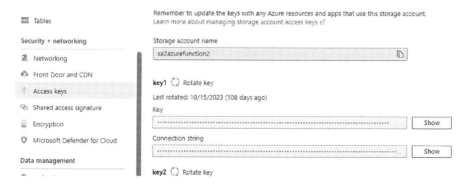

Figure 4-7. *Account storage access keys*

- Go to your Azure function.

- Go to the Configuration.

- You will see all application settings. Click the "New application setting" button.

- Enter the "AzureWebJobsStorage" string as a key and the connection string as a value, like in Figure 4-8.

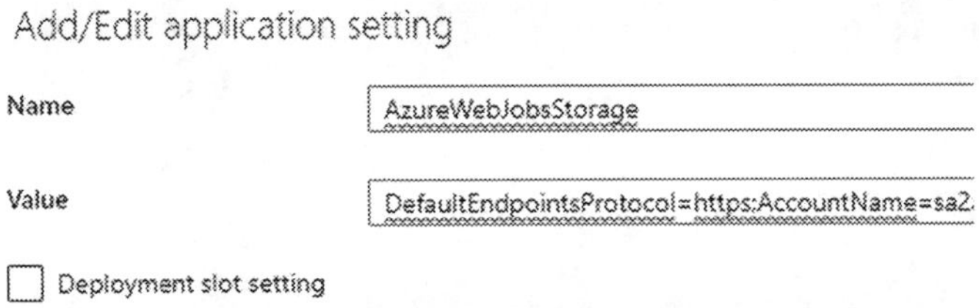

Add/Edit application setting

Name   AzureWebJobsStorage

Value   DefaultEndpointsProtocol=https;AccountName=sa2.

☐ Deployment slot setting

Figure 4-8. *Application setting*

The next step is to create an example blob service class. First, create an interface, like shown in Listing 4-4, that defines the methods for interacting with the blob service.

Listing 4-4. An interface for the blob service

```
public interface IBlobService
{
    string AcquireLeaseOnBlob(string blobName);
    BlobContainerClient CreateBlobContainer(string
    containerName = "reports");
    void DeleteBlob(string blobName);
    byte[] DownloadBlob(string blobName);
    string DownloadTextFile(string blobName);
    List<string> GetBlobsInFolder(string folderName);
    string GetSasTokenForBlob(string blobName);
    void ReleaseLeaseOnBlob(string leaseId, string blobName);
```

```
void UploadBlob(string blobName, Stream blobContent);
void UploadBlob(string blobName, Stream blobContent, string
leaseId);
}
```

Then implement this interface into a new service class, but we will do it step by step. First, create a class, a constructor, and the CreateBlobContainer method. Listing 4-5 has the first piece of a new service class. We define a new private read-only variable _configuration and initialize it using the IConfiguration interface in the constructor. This variable will be used to access the configuration settings. In the CreateBlobContainer method, we use the _configuration variable to retrieve the connection string from the configuration settings. This variable is directly added as a parameter to the BlobServiceClient constructor, allowing us to connect to the Blob storage solution. On the new instance, we call GetBlobContainerClient to get the BlobContainerClient type of instance. This client allows you to create, update, delete, or check if a container exists. It also allows you to delete, upload, or download blobs inside the container. We use the CreateIfNotExists method from the BlobServiceClient class to create the container if it hasn't been created yet. When the method is finished, we return a new instance of the container client to use in other methods.

Listing 4-5. Constructor and CreateBlobContainer method

```
public class BlobService : IBlobService
{
    private readonly IConfiguration _configuration;

    public BlobService(IConfiguration configuration)
    {
        _configuration = configuration;
    }
```

```
    public BlobContainerClient CreateBlobContainer(string
    containerName = "reports")
    {
        var blobServiceClient = new BlobServiceClient(_
        configuration.GetValue<string>("AzureWebJobsS
        torage"));
        BlobContainerClient containerClient =
        blobServiceClient.GetBlobContainerClient(conta
        inerName);
        containerClient.CreateIfNotExists();

        return containerClient;
    }
}
```

Listing 4-6 shows an UploadBlob method. It has a parameter blobName, a string type for the blob name, and a blobContent stream type for the file content. In the first line of the code, we use the previous CreateBlobContainer to get the container client instance, and then we use the GetBlobClient method to get the blob client instance for the given blob name. It allows you to manipulate blobs. The third line uploads the content of the stream to the blob and overwrites any existing content. In the second method of the upload, there is a third parameter for lease identification. When you upload a file, as the second parameter you pass the BlobUploadOptions and provide the Conditions parameter with a leaseId string. This way, we can upload a file if the lease is active on the blob.

Listing 4-6. UploadBlob method

```
public void UploadBlob(string blobName, Stream blobContent)
{
    var containerClient = CreateBlobContainer();
    BlobClient blobClient = containerClient.
    GetBlobClient(blobName);
    blobClient.Upload(blobContent, true);
}

public void UploadBlob(string blobName, Stream blobContent,
string leaseId)
{
    var containerClient = CreateBlobContainer();
    BlobClient blobClient = containerClient.
    GetBlobClient(blobName);

    blobClient.Upload(blobContent, new BlobUploadOptions
    {
        Conditions = new BlobRequestConditions
        {
            LeaseId = leaseId
        }
    });
}
```

Listing 4-7 shows a method that downloads a blob and returns it as an array of bytes. The name of the blob to download is specified as a string parameter that is passed to the method. It creates a blob client object that references the specific blob to download by its name. Then, it creates a memory stream object that will store the downloaded data in memory.

After that, it calls the DownloadTo method of the blob client object, which downloads the blob data to the memory stream. Finally, it calls the ToArray method of the memory stream object, which converts the data in the memory stream to an array of bytes and returns it.

Listing 4-7. Downloading blob

```
public byte[] DownloadBlob(string blobName)
{
    var containerClient = CreateBlobContainer();
    BlobClient blobClient = containerClient.
    GetBlobClient(blobName);

    MemoryStream ms = new MemoryStream();
    blobClient.DownloadTo(ms);
    return ms.ToArray();
}
```

Listing 4-8 shows a method that downloads a text file from a blob storage and returns its content as a string. It creates a BlobClient object by passing the blob name as a parameter to the GetBlobClient method. This object represents the blob that contains the text file. It calls the DownloadContent method of the blob client, which returns a Response<BlobDownloadResult> object that contains the content and metadata of the blob. Then we access the Content property of the Response<BlobDownloadResult> object, which gives a BinaryData object that is the content of the blob. Lastly, we invoke the BinaryData object's ToString method, which transforms the content into a string and returns it.

Listing 4-8. Download a blob as a text

```
public string DownloadTextFile(string blobName)
{
    var containerClient = CreateBlobContainer();
```

```
BlobClient blobClient = containerClient.
GetBlobClient(blobName);
var content = blobClient.DownloadContent();

return content.Value.Content.ToString();
}
```

Listing 4-9 shows a method that deletes a blob. It creates a BlobClient object by passing the blob name as a parameter to the DeleteBlob method of the container client. In the next line, we run the GetBlobClient to get the blob client instance. We call the DeleteIfExists method. It will delete the blob if it exists.

Listing 4-9. Delete a blob

```
public void DeleteBlob(string blobName)
{
    var containerClient = CreateBlobContainer();

    var blobClient = containerClient.GetBlobClient
    (blobName);
    blobClient.DeleteIfExists();
}
```

Listing 4-10 shows a method that lists all blobs inside the container and returns a list with their names. The parameter for this method is a folder name; it can be a prefix with a few subfolders, for example, reports/2024/01. Then the GetBlobs is getting all blobs with the specific prefix. In the last line of the code, the LINQ (Language INtegrated Query) Select method is used to generate a list with only blob names.

Listing 4-10. Get a list with the blob names

```
public List<string> GetBlobsInFolder(string folderName)
{
    var containerClient = CreateBlobContainer();
    var blobs = containerClient.GetBlobs(prefix: folderName);

    return blobs.Select(blob => blob.Name).ToList();
}
```

Listing 4-11 shows a method that generates and returns a SAS token for a specific blob. It creates a BlobClient object by passing the blob name as a parameter to the GetBlobClient method of the container client. Then we create a BlobSasBuilder object with the following parameters: BlobName, ResourceType, StartOn, and Expires. There are more available parameters, depending on the requirements for the solution. The resource type can be one of the following:

- b – If it is a blob, which provides access to the content and metadata of the blob

- c – If it is a container, which provides access to content and metadata of any blob within the container

Then we use the SetPermissions method to set the permissions; in this case, we set to read only. In the last line of the code, we call the GenerateSasUri on the blobClient instance to create the SAS token. Then we call the Query property to return only the access token. It is also possible to use the AbsoluteUri property to return the full URL with the access token if it is required and more convenient.

Listing 4-11. Generate a SAS token

```
public string GetSasTokenForBlob(string blobName)
{
    var containerClient = CreateBlobContainer();
```

```
BlobClient blobClient = containerClient.
GetBlobClient(blobName);

BlobSasBuilder sasBuilder = new BlobSasBuilder()
{
    BlobName = blobName,
    Resource = "b",
    StartsOn = DateTimeOffset.UtcNow,
    ExpiresOn = DateTimeOffset.UtcNow.AddHours(2),
};

sasBuilder.SetPermissions(BlobSasPermissions.Read);

return blobClient.GenerateSasUri(sasBuilder).Query;
}
```

The code in Listing 4-12 shows how to acquire and release a lease on a blob in Azure Blob Storage. A lease is a mechanism that prevents other clients from modifying or deleting a blob while it is being accessed by a specific client. To acquire a lease, the client needs to specify the name of the blob. The code is creating a BlobLeaseClient from the BlobClient instance. Then we call the Acquire method and set the duration of the lease to 60 seconds. The method AcquireLeaseOnBlob returns the lease ID, which is a unique identifier for the lease. To release a lease, the BlobLeaseClient needs to provide the lease ID. The Release method of the BlobLeaseClient class is called inside the ReleaseLeaseOnBlob method, which removes the lock on the blob and allows other clients to access it.

Listing 4-12. Create a lease on the blob and release

```
public string AcquireLeaseOnBlob(string blobName)
{
    var containerClient = CreateBlobContainer();
    BlobClient blobClient = containerClient.
    GetBlobClient(blobName);
```

```
    BlobLeaseClient blobLeaseClient = blobClient.
    GetBlobLeaseClient();

    BlobLease lease = blobLeaseClient.Acquire(duration:
    TimeSpan.FromSeconds(60));

    return lease.LeaseId;
}

public void ReleaseLeaseOnBlob(string leaseId, string blobName)
{
    var containerClient = CreateBlobContainer();
    BlobClient blobClient = containerClient.
    GetBlobClient(blobName);

    BlobLeaseClient blobLeaseClient = blobClient.
    GetBlobLeaseClient(leaseId);
    blobLeaseClient.Release();
}
```

The code in Listing 4-13 is an example usage of a method we have added to the blob service. After each method usage, we have a log information method used to trace the current flow of the program. The IBlobService which we have implemented earlier and ILogger interfaces are injected into the constructor and assigned to the private variables _logger and _blobService. When the function is started, the first method we call is a CreateBlobContainer to create a container to store new files or folders inside.

Then a content and a file name are created to simulate using a file, and then the variables are used to create a memory stream. This will simulate processing a file from an incoming HTTP request.

Then we are using the UploadBlob method to send the file to the container. If you put a break point after this method, you can check the container by using the Azure Storage Explorer to view the file. Then we download and display a file with the DownloadTextFile method.

Then we are using the AcquireLeaseOnBlob method to lock the file from modification by other clients. Then we are creating another fake file to simulate the upload of a new version. The UploadBlob method is inside the try catch closure because it will throw an exception. In the catch closure, we call the UploadBlob with the leaseId. Then it is downloaded and logged with the content again. In the final closure, the ReleaseLeaseOnBlob method is used to release the lock on the blob file.

The final lines are creating a URL with the SAS token, and finally, the file is deleted from the container.

Listing 4-13. HTTP function with an example of how to use a new service

```
public class Function1
{
    private readonly ILogger _logger;
    private readonly IBlobService _blobService;

    public Function1(ILoggerFactory loggerFactory, IBlobService
    blobService)
    {
        _logger = loggerFactory.CreateLogger<Function1>();
        _blobService = blobService;
    }

    [Function("Function1")]
    public async Task<HttpResponseData> RunAsync([Http
    Trigger(AuthorizationLevel.Anonymous, "get", "post")]
    HttpRequestData req)
    {
        _blobService.CreateBlobContainer();

        var fileContent = Encoding.UTF8.GetBytes("My finance
        report");
```

```
var fileContentStream = new MemoryStream(fileContent);
var fileName = "Finance.txt";

_blobService.UploadBlob(fileName, fileContentStream);

var leaseId = _blobService.AcquireLeaseOnBlob
(fileName);
_logger.LogInformation($"Lease is acquired with ID:
{leaseId}");

var content = _blobService.DownloadTextFile
(fileName);
_logger.LogInformation($"File Content: {content}");

var fileContent2 = Encoding.UTF8.GetBytes("My finance
report v2");
var fileContentStream2 = new
MemoryStream(fileContent2);
try
{
    _blobService.UploadBlob(fileName,
    fileContentStream2);
}
catch (RequestFailedException ex)
{
    _logger.LogError("Blob need a lease id.");
    fileContentStream2.Position = 0;
    _blobService.UploadBlob(fileName,
     fileContentStream2, leaseId);

    var content2 = _blobService.DownloadTextFile
    (fileName);
```

```
        _logger.LogInformation($"File Content with lease:
        {content2}");
    }
    finally
    {
        _logger.LogInformation("Releasing lease");
        _blobService.ReleaseLeaseOnBlob(leaseId, fileName);
    }

    var token = _blobService.GetSasTokenForBlob
    (fileName);
    _logger.LogInformation($"SAS token URL: {token}");

    _blobService.DeleteBlob(fileName);
    _logger.LogInformation("Blob is deleted");

    return req.CreateResponse(HttpStatusCode.OK);
    }
}
```

Queues

Storage account queues are an important service that allows for the reliable and scalable processing of messages. They provide a way to store and retrieve messages in a FIFO (First In, First Out) order. This order ensures that the messages are processed in the same sequence they were added to the queue. This service is essential for systems that require asynchronous communication between different components or services. It helps you to ensure that all messages are processed in the correct order and prevents any message from being skipped or lost. If the project requires an important message to be ensured to be processed, but the results do not need to be returned as soon as possible, this solution will fit this requirement.

Listing 4-14 shows an example QueuesService class with only one method. In the constructor, we inject the IConfiguration object and assign it to the private variable _configuration. In the SendMessage method, the message is added to the queue for processing. First, we retrieve the connection string from the environment, and then the QueueClient class instance is created using the connection string as the first parameter and the queue name as the second parameter. In the third parameter, QueueClientOptions are provided, which can be used for configuring additional options such as message handling and retry policies. We configure only the MessageEncoding property in the Base64 options. Finally, we use the SendMessage from the queueClient object to send it to the queue service. If you would like to send a class, you can serialize it into a string and pass it as a parameter.

Listing 4-14. Queue service class

```
using Azure.Storage.Queues;
using Microsoft.Extensions.Configuration;

namespace AzureAdventures4_Queues
{
    public class QueuesService : IQueuesService
    {
        private readonly IConfiguration _configuration;

        public QueuesService(IConfiguration configuration)
        {
            _configuration = configuration;
        }
        public void SendMessage(string message)
        {
            var connectionString = _configuration.GetValue<stri
            ng>("AzureWebJobsStorage");
```

```
        var queueClient = new QueueClient(connectionString,
        "incoming-reports", new QueueClientOptions
        {
            MessageEncoding = QueueMessageEncoding.Base64
        });

        queueClient.SendMessage(message);
    }
  }
}
```

The code in Listing 4-15 is a function where we inject the IQueueService interface created earlier and run the SendMessage method with example text in the HTTP trigger. This will create a new queue if it does not exist and will add a new message. After calling this method, you can go to the Azure Storage Explorer program and see the message in the new queue. In the program, go to Emulator & Attached in the Explorer window, then expand Storage Account, Emulator, and Queues, and there should be a visible new queue named incoming-reports with a new inserted message, as shown in Figure 4-9.

Listing 4-15. HTTP trigger with a QueueService

```
using System.Net;
using Microsoft.Azure.Functions.Worker;
using Microsoft.Azure.Functions.Worker.Http;

namespace AzureAdventures4_Queues
{
    public class QueueFunction
    {
        private readonly IQueuesService _queuesService;
```

```
    public QueueFunction(IQueuesService queuesService)
    {
        _queuesService = queuesService;
    }

    [Function("QueueFunction")]
    public HttpResponseData Run([HttpTrigger(AuthorizationL
    evel.Anonymous, "get", "post")] HttpRequestData req)
    {
        _queuesService.SendMessage("Test Message");
        return req.CreateResponse(HttpStatusCode.OK);
    }
  }
}
```

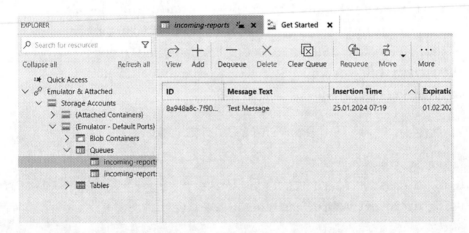

Figure 4-9. *A new queue with an incoming message*

In order to receive and process the message, we can create a new function with a queue trigger that will listen for incoming messages and automatically execute the desired actions. Listing 4-16 shows an example trigger that will display an example message on the console using the logger. The function also has a parameter called message, which is decorated with a QueueTrigger attribute. According to this property, the function will execute each time a new message is added to the incoming-reports queue. The method body contains a single statement that logs the message to the console using the _logger object, which is an instance of ILogger. In a real-world example, there might be additional logic within the method body, such as error handling or data processing.

Listing 4-16. Queue trigger

```
using Azure.Storage.Queues.Models;
using Microsoft.Azure.Functions.Worker;
using Microsoft.Extensions.Logging;

namespace AzureAdventures4_Queues
{
    public class Function1
    {
        private readonly ILogger<Function1> _logger;

        public Function1(ILogger<Function1> logger)
        {
            _logger = logger;
        }

        [Function(nameof(Function1))]
        public void Run([QueueTrigger("incoming-reports")]
        string message)
        {
            _logger.LogInformation($"New message in the queue:
            {message}");
        }
    }
}
```

Listing 4-17 shows an example of how to read a JSON object that can be represented as a C# class. This code snippet shows how to define a function that runs when a message is added to a queue named "incoming-reports". The function takes the message as a parameter, which is an object of type ReportModel. The ReportModel class has two properties, Id and Name, which store the identifier and the name of the report, respectively. The function uses a logger to write the name and the ID of the report to the console.

Listing 4-17. Queue trigger with a handle class model

```
[Function(nameof(Function1))]
public void Run([QueueTrigger("incoming-reports")]
ReportModel message)
{
    _logger.LogInformation($"Report Name: {message.Name},
    ID: {message.Id}");
}
}

public class ReportModel
{
    public string Id { get; set; }
    public string Name { get; set; }
}
```

To test this new trigger, we can use a new method in Listing 4-18. It takes a parameter ReportModel type, then serializes it to a string and passes it to the existing SendMessage method created before.

Listing 4-18. SendObjectMessage method

```
public void SendObjectMessage(ReportModel model)
{
    SendMessage(JsonConvert.SerializeObject(model));
}
```

Another way to test is to enter the message directly into the queue through the Azure Storage Explorer program. Go to your queue; at the top, there is a command with buttons to manage the messages, as shown in Figure 4-10. You can delete, add, or clear the queue. Click the Add button, and a new window will be shown. Enter an example JSON object from Listing 4-19. Leave the options as default and the encoding type as Base64.

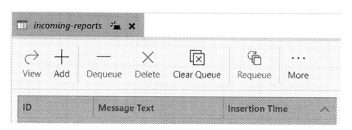

Figure 4-10. *Command bar of the incoming-reports queue*

Listing 4-19. Example JSON message

```
{
    "Id": "1",
    "Name": "New secret report"
}
```

When you run the program, the output of the queue trigger should be visible as shown in Figure 4-11.

```
Trigger Details: MessageId: d1f6f9c6-4548-48
00:00
Report Name: New secret report, ID: 1
Executed 'Functions.Function1' (Succeeded, I
```

Figure 4-11. *Screenshot of running the queue trigger*

Table

A table is a type of data storage service in Azure that is a great use for saving structured, non-relational data in a scalable and flexible way. Tables are ideal for storing large amounts of data that do not require complex queries or transactions.

Tables in Azure are designed to handle massive amounts of data and provide fast access to retrieve and update records. With tables, you can easily store and retrieve data by using a simple key-value structure. This makes them particularly suitable for scenarios where you need to store large datasets and access them quickly, such as IoT applications or logging and telemetry systems.

To deploy a table through the site, you need to follow these steps:

- Find and select Storage accounts from the left menu.

- Select or create a storage account where it is going to be created.

- In the overview page of the storage account, find and click Tables under the Services section.

- Click + Table to create a new table.

- Provide a name for the table and click OK.

The creation of the Table with the bicep is described at the beginning of this chapter.

To work with the Azure Table in C#, we need to install the Azure.Data. Tables NuGet package. First, create an interface with the methods that we are going to implement, like shown in Listing 4-20. There are methods to add, update, delete, get, and query entities.

Listing 4-20. IAdventureTable interface for service

```
public interface IAdventureTableService
{
    Task AddEntityAsync<T>(T entity) where T : ITableEntity;
    TableClient CreateTableClient(IConfiguration
    configuration);
    Task DeleteEntityAsync(string partitionKey, string rowKey);
    Task<T?> GetEntityAsync<T>(string partitionKey, string
    rowKey) where T : class, ITableEntity, new();
    List<T> Query<T>(string query) where T : class,
    ITableEntity, new();
    Task UpdateEntityAsync<T>(T entity) where T : ITableEntity;
}
```

Then change the Program.cs file to inject the class using the interface like in Listing 4-21.

Listing 4-21. Injecting a new interface

```
var host = new HostBuilder()
    .ConfigureFunctionsWorkerDefaults()
    .ConfigureServices(services =>
    {
        services.AddScoped<IAdventureTableService,
        AdventureTableService>();
    })
    .Build();
```

Listing 4-22 shows the constructor and the CreateTableClient method. We get the IConfiguration instance, then we call the CreateTableClient, where we get the connection string from the environment variables, and then we create a TableClient instance. This object can be used to create a new table, get, add, or get entities. This object is assigned to the private _tableClient variable and can be used in other methods.

Listing 4-22. Constructor in the AdventureTableService class

```
public class AdventureTableService : IAdventureTableService
{
    private readonly TableClient _tableClient;

    public AdventureTableService(IConfiguration
     configuration)
    {
        _tableClient = CreateTableClient(configuration);
    }

    public TableClient CreateTableClient(IConfiguration
    configuration)
    {
        var connectionString = configuration.GetValue<string>
        ("AzureWebJobsStorage");
        var tableClient = new TableClient(connectionString,
        "reports");

        tableClient.CreateIfNotExists();

        return tableClient;
    }
}
```

The code snippet in Listing 4-23 shows how to make basic actions on Azure Table using the Azure.Data.Tables library. The library provides methods for creating, updating, deleting, and querying entities in a table. The code assumes in every method that a TableClient object named _ tableClient has been initialized with the connection string and table name in the constructor.

The AddEntityAsync method takes an entity object that implements the ITableEntity interface and adds it to the table asynchronously. The entity object must have properties for the partition key and row key, which are used to distinguish the entity in the table in a unique way. The method returns a Task object that can be awaited or used to handle errors.

The parameters for the DeleteEntityAsync method are a partition key and a row key that identify an entity and deletes it from the table asynchronously.

The UpdateEntityAsync method takes an entity object that implements the ITableEntity interface and updates it in the table asynchronously. The entity object must have properties for the partition key and row key, as well as an ETag property that represents the version of the entity. The method also takes an ETag parameter that specifies the condition for updating the entity.

The GetEntityAsync method needs a partition key and a row key to search for an entity and returns it from the table asynchronously. The method also takes a generic type parameter that specifies the type of the entity object to return. The type must implement the ITableEntity interface. If the entity is not found, the method throws a RequestFailedException with a status code of 404 that is handled, and then we return null.

The Query method takes a query string that specifies the filter criteria for retrieving entities from the table. The method also takes a generic type parameter that specifies the type of the entity objects to return. The method returns a Pageable object that implements IEnumerable and allows iterating over the entities in pages. The method also supports using LINQ expressions to query entities.

177

Listing 4-23. Methods for the AdventureTableService class

```
public async Task AddEntityAsync<T>(T entity) where T :
ITableEntity
{
    await _tableClient.AddEntityAsync(entity);
}

public async Task DeleteEntityAsync(string partitionKey,
string rowKey)
{
    await _tableClient.DeleteEntityAsync(partitionKey, rowKey);
}

public async Task UpdateEntityAsync<T>(T entity) where T :
ITableEntity
{
    await _tableClient.UpdateEntityAsync(entity, ETag.All);
}

public async Task<T?> GetEntityAsync<T>(string partitionKey,
string rowKey) where T : class, ITableEntity, new()
{
    try
    {
        return await _tableClient.
        GetEntityAsync<T>(partitionKey, rowKey);
    }
    catch (RequestFailedException ex)
    {
        if (ex.Status == 404)
        {
            Console.WriteLine("Entity not found.");
        }
```

```
        return null;
    }
}

public List<T> Query<T>(string query) where T : class,
ITableEntity, new()
{
    Pageable<T> entities = _tableClient.Query<T>(query);

    return entities.ToList();
}
```

For testing purposes, we will create a ReportModel class as shown in Listing 4-24. It has all the required properties from the interface. The time stamp contains information about when the entity was last edited. The ETag property is for managing versions; it can be used to compare if we have the latest version and our entity needs to be updated. I have added an additional field named FileName as a string type.

Listing 4-24. ReportModel class

```
public class ReportModel : ITableEntity
{
    public string PartitionKey { get; set; }
    public string RowKey { get; set; }
    public DateTimeOffset? Timestamp { get; set; }
    public ETag ETag { get; set; }
    public string FileName { get; set; }
}
```

The use of our new service is demonstrated in Listing 4-25. The AdventureTableService is injected into the constructor and assigned to the private variable named tableService, the same way the _logger private variable is injected with the ILogger interface. In the RunAsync method,

179

we are creating a ReportModel class variable and assigning an example of simple properties. This model will be used to insert into the table in the next line. Then it is retrieved and assigned to the retrievedEntity variable using a simple where query to get items with a specific partition key. If it is not null, then we log information about this entity. In the next line, the file name property is updated, and we call the UpdateEntityAsync method with this model to update it, and information about it is logged. In the next line, we use an example query to retrieve it and log information about how many entities we have retrieved. Finally, the last method of deleting an entity is used to remove the row from the table.

Listing 4-25. HTTP trigger function

```
public class Function1
{
    private readonly ILogger _logger;
    private readonly IAdventureTableService _tableService;

    public Function1(ILoggerFactory loggerFactory,
    IAdventureTableService tableService)
    {
        _logger = loggerFactory.CreateLogger<Function1>();
        _tableService = tableService;
    }

    [Function("Function1")]
    public async Task<HttpResponseData> RunAsync([HttpTr
    igger(AuthorizationLevel.Anonymous, "get", "post")]
    HttpRequestData req)
    {
        var entity = new ReportModel()
        {
            PartitionKey = "partition1",
            RowKey = "row1",
```

```
    FileName = "SecretReport.xls",
};

await _tableService.AddEntityAsync(entity);

var retrievedEntity = await _tableService.GetEntityAsyn
c<ReportModel>("partition1", "row1");

if (retrievedEntity != null)
{
    .LogInformation($"Retrieved entity:
    PartitionKey={retrievedEntity.PartitionKey},
    RowKey={retrievedEntity.RowKey},
    FileName={retrievedEntity.FileName}");

    retrievedEntity.FileName = "IWillNeverGive
    YouUp.xls";
    await _tableService.UpdateEntityAsync(retriev
    edEntity);
    _logger.LogInformation($"Updated entity:
    PartitionKey={retrievedEntity.PartitionKey},
    RowKey={retrievedEntity.RowKey}, FileName=
    {retrievedEntity.FileName}");

    var entities = _tableService.Query<ReportModel>("Pa
    rtitionKey eq 'partition1'");
    _logger.LogInformation($"Queried entities:
    {entities.Count}");

    await _tableService.DeleteEntityAsync(
    "partition1", "row1");
    _logger.LogInformation("Deleted entity.");
}
```

```
        return req.CreateResponse(HttpStatusCode.OK);
    }
}
```

The screenshot in Figure 4-12 shows logs of the program execution from the example class in Listing 4-25. You can see that the entity was correctly added to the table, then retrieved, updated, queried, and finally deleted.

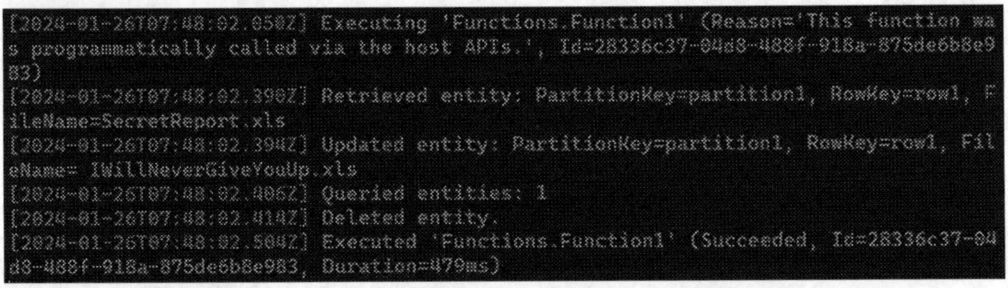

Figure 4-12. *Terminal with logs*

Summary

Azure storage accounts are crucial for managing various types of data, offering advantages such as security, scalability, performance, and availability. Storage accounts can be created through the Azure Portal. You can create and set up storage resources in Azure with Bicep, including queues, tables, and blobs.

You are familiar with the Azure Storage Explorer. It is a GUI tool for managing and working with storage accounts, providing an easier way to navigate and interact with them. By using this application, users can access and interact with storage accounts; create containers, tables, and queues; and manage their items.

Azure Blob Storage is a reliable and secure option for businesses looking to optimize their data storage capabilities. It offers high scalability, performance, data encryption, and access control. In this chapter, we have learned how to manage, create, and download blobs. We have learned what shared access signatures are, how to use them, and how they can be useful for the business case. This chapter also showed how to prevent overriding data with the lease.

Queues are essential services in Azure for storing and retrieving messages in a FIFO (First In, First Out) order. Queue triggers can listen for incoming messages and automatically execute desired actions.

Tables are data storage services in Azure that allow for structured, non-relational data storage in a scalable and flexible way. They are ideal for large datasets and provide fast access to retrieve and update records, making them suitable for scenarios like IoT applications or logging and telemetry systems. Tables allow for flexible schemas and can be customized for each entity's properties.

CHAPTER 5

Event Grid

Event Grid is good for real-time applications to route events from Azure services and not only to other apps. With Event Grid, developers can subscribe to specific events and receive notifications in real time, enabling them to take immediate action. This makes Event Grid particularly useful for scenarios such as IoT device monitoring, log processing, and workflow automation. Furthermore, Event Grid supports a wide range of Azure services and can seamlessly connect events between them, enabling developers to build robust and scalable event-driven solutions within the Azure ecosystem.

Event Grid is a push delivery mechanism that ensures that events are delivered reliably and efficiently, making it a reliable choice for real-time event processing.

Figure 5-1 illustrates the components and relationships of an Event Grid system, including topics, event sources, event subscriptions, event handlers, and filters.

© Michał Świtalik 2024
M. Świtalik, *Azure Adventures with C#*, https://doi.org/10.1007/979-8-8688-0424-3_5

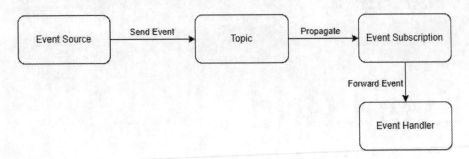

Figure 5-1. *Diagram with components and relationships in Event Grid*

Events are short messages that essential for enabling reactive and event-driven architectures, allowing developers to easily integrate and respond to events within their applications.

The event source is the origin of the events that developers can subscribe to and receive notifications from. These event sources can vary from Azure services such as Blob Storage, Azure Functions, and Azure Cosmos DB to custom applications and resources running outside of Azure.

The topic in the Event Grid is used to define the type or category of events that developers are interested in receiving notifications for. By defining a topic, developers can specify the specific events they want to subscribe to, ensuring they only receive relevant notifications. This enables developers to have more control over the events they are handling and allows for a more efficient and streamlined development process. Additionally, the Event Grid provides features such as filtering and routing.

Event Subscription is used to define the endpoint where developers want to receive notifications for a particular event. This could be an HTTP endpoint, a webhook, or a storage account. Developers can configure the Event Subscription to filter events based on specific criteria, ensuring they only receive notifications for events that meet their requirements.

The event handler is responsible for processing the received events and executing the necessary actions. It is the component that developers build to handle the events triggered by Event Grid. By implementing an event handler, developers can perform tasks such as data processing, sending notifications, and updating a database. This allows for custom logic to be executed based on the events received, providing flexibility and customization in the event handling process.

Azure storage blob change event can be a source for Azure Function CloudEvent or EventGridEvent – one key difference between CloudEvent and EventGridEvent is the level of detail they provide about the event. While CloudEvent provides a more generalized and abstract representation of the event, EventGridEvent offers more specific information, such as the event type and the resource it is associated with. Both events have a set of required and optional attributes, such as ID, source, type, data, subject, and time. The main difference between CloudEvent and EventGridEvent is that EventGridEvent has some additional attributes, such as dataVersion, topic, and dataVersion, that are specific to Event Grid.

One possible real-world example of the usage of the Azure Event Grid with the CloudEvent class as a trigger or EventGridEvent in the Azure Function is to create a serverless application that responds to events from an Event Grid source, such as a blob storage account. For example, you can use an Azure Function with an Event Grid trigger to run report statistics each time a new Excel file is added to a blob storage container. Another example is to propagate changes inside your application. For example, if a new user was created or the status of a task changed, other systems might want to know in order to sync and do their logic.

Figure 5-2 is an example of how the Event Grid propagates information about a new file (or its modification) in Azure Blob Storage to other systems. For example, when your application or user uploads a document to the Blob Storage, it is sending an event to the Event Grid. All connected event handlers will receive the information. It can be either an Azure function or a logic app. They can either download the file or send information about this event to other systems. The file can be uploaded to the SharePoint library, Amazon S3, or on-premises server, depending on the specific requirements of the organization.

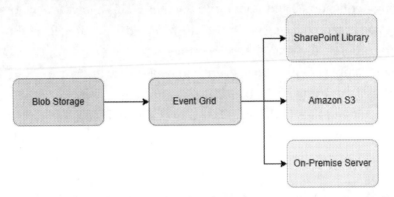

Figure 5-2. Example usage of the Event Grid

Creating an Event Grid

The Event Grid can be created through the Azure Portal or programmatically using the Azure SDK in Azure CLI or bicep. This allows for easy integration with various Azure services and custom applications, making it a versatile tool for event-driven architectures.

To create Event Grid, follow these steps:

- Go to your resource group.

- On the top command bar, click the Create button.

- Click the Create button under the Event Grid Topic tile, then click the Event Grid Topic button, as shown in Figure 5-3.

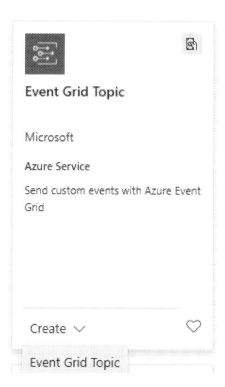

Figure 5-3. *Create Event Grid*

- On the form, fill in all the required fields as shown in
  Figure 5-4. Leave other fields on default values, then
  click the Review + create button.

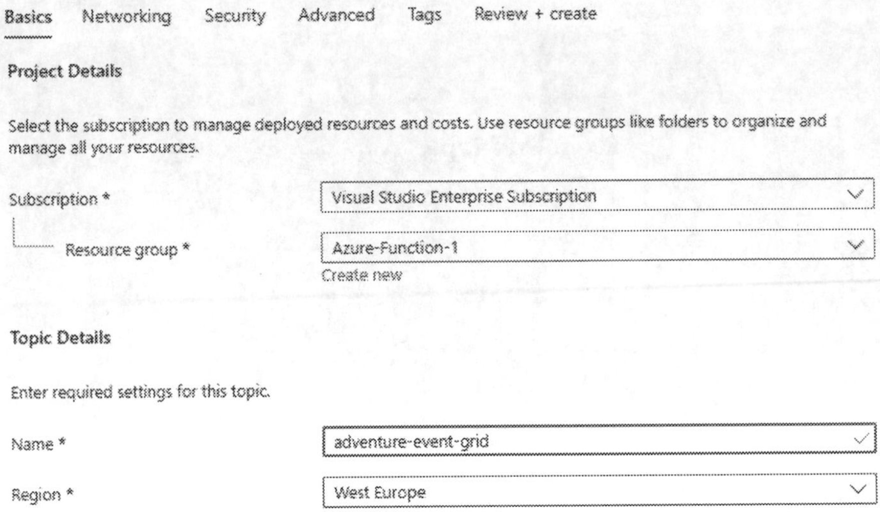

Basics   Networking   Security   Advanced   Tags   Review + create

Project Details

Select the subscription to manage deployed resources and costs. Use resource groups like folders to organize and manage all your resources.

Subscription *   Visual Studio Enterprise Subscription   ⌄

　　Resource group *   Azure-Function-1   ⌄
                        Create new

Topic Details

Enter required settings for this topic.

Name *   adventure-event-grid   ⌄

Region *   West Europe   ⌄

Figure 5-4. *Basic properties for Event Grid*

- Then click the Create button and wait until deployment is finished. It may take a few minutes to finish.

When it is created, go to the resource. Figure 5-5 is a screenshot from the Event Grid resource. These are new properties you can find on the first page. You have your topic endpoint for programs to send the custom event. Information about authentication, if it is enabled, you are required to use the SAS token or access key to be able to connect to the storage from a local PC. There are also pricing tiers and availability zone information.

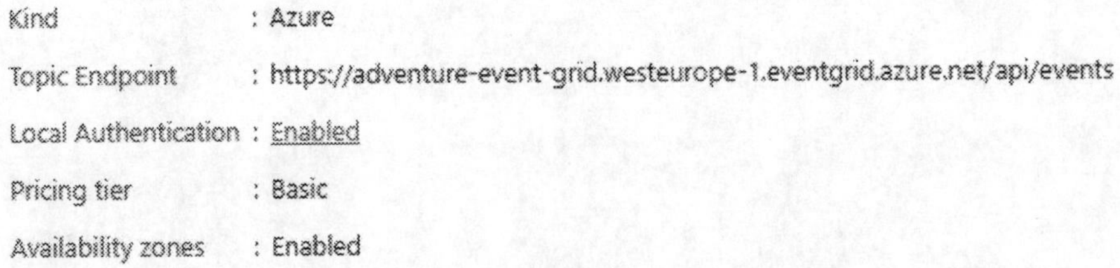

Kind   : Azure

Topic Endpoint   : https://adventure-event-grid.westeurope-1.eventgrid.azure.net/api/events

Local Authentication : Enabled

Pricing tier   : Basic

Availability zones   : Enabled

Figure 5-5. *New properties available for Event Grid service*

In the Access Keys section, you will see two access keys visible as in Figure 5-6. These keys can be used to authorize your requests to the Event Grid Topic when you send your events from the application.

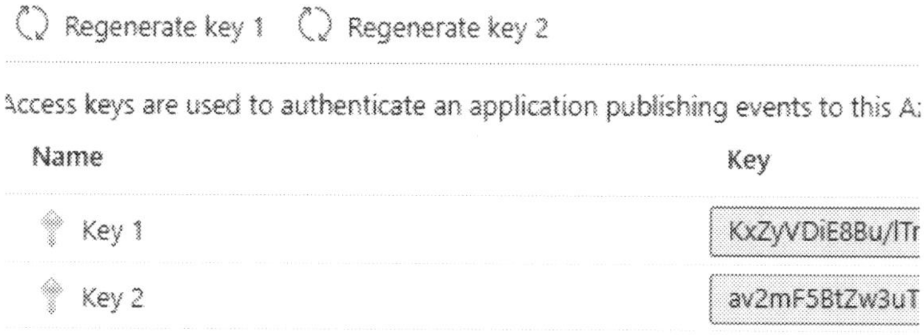

Figure 5-6. *Access keys for Event Grid*

In the Event Subscriptions section, you can view all active programs that are able to receive a new event from the topic. You can also create a new subscription from here.

Creating an Event Handler

Before creating a new subscription, we have to create a new Azure function with the Event Grid trigger to handle incoming events. It can also be a logic app or a queue in the storage account. It is required for a new subscription. It will require us to select an already existing handler to handle the events. This event handler will define how the incoming events will be processed and what actions will be taken based on them.

For the purpose of the demo, create a solution with an Azure Function and an Event Grid trigger. First, install an Azure.Messaging.EventGrid NuGet package. Then create an EventGridService class. Add the code from Listing 5-1 to the newly created class.

The code in Listing 5-1 is an example of how to use Azure Event Grid, a service that allows you to publish. The code consists of two classes: IEventGridService and EventGridService. The first one is an interface that defines a method called SendEventGridEventAsync, which is responsible for sending an event to the Event Grid endpoint. The second one is a class that implements the interface and provides the logic for the method.

The EventGridService class has a constructor that takes an ILogger parameter, which is used to log information and errors.

The SendEventGridEventAsync method initializes some variables, such as the endpoint URL, the topic key, and the credential for authentication. The SendEventGridEventAsync method creates an instance of the EventGridPublisherClient class, which is used to send events to the Event Grid endpoint. The method then calls the SendEventAsync method of the client, passing an EventGridEvent object as an argument. The EventGridEvent object contains information about the event, such as the topic, the subject, the ID, and the data. The data is an anonymous object that has two properties: Name and Time.

The method then logs a message indicating that the event was sent successfully. The method is asynchronous, meaning that it does not block the execution of the code until it finishes.

Listing 5-1. EventGridService class

```
using Azure;
using Azure.Messaging.EventGrid;
using Microsoft.Extensions.Logging;

namespace AzureAventure5_EventGrid
{
    public interface IEventGridService
    {
        Task SendEventGridEventAsync();
    }

    public class EventGridService : IEventGridService
    {
```

```
private readonly ILogger<EventGridService> _logger;

public EventGridService(ILogger<EventGridServi
ce> logger)
{
    _logger = logger;
}

public async Task SendEventGridEventAsync()
{
    _logger.LogInformation("Sending event");

    var endpoint = "https://adventure-event-grid.
    westeurope-1.eventgrid.azure.net/api/events";
    var topicKey = "yourtopickey";
    var credential = new AzureKeyCredential(topicKey);
    var client = new EventGridPublisherClient(new
    Uri(endpoint), credential);

    await client.SendEventAsync(new EventGridEvent
    ("MyResources", "NewResource", "1", new
    {
        Name = "Event Adventure",
        Time = DateTime.UtcNow
    }));

    _logger.LogInformation("Event sent");
    }
  }
}
```

To use the code, we have to add it to the Program.cs file in the services to inject it into the class. Listing 5-2 shows what it should look like.

Listing 5-2. Adding service to the services

```
services.AddScoped<IEventGridService, EventGridService>();
```

Listing 5-3 shows the modified function we have previously created. This class has two methods: EventTrigger and SendEventGridEvent. The EventTrigger method is decorated with the EventGridTrigger attribute, which means it will be invoked whenever an event is received from Event Grid. The method takes an EventGridEvent parameter, which represents the event data, and logs it using the ILogger interface. The SendEventGridEvent method is decorated with the HttpTrigger attribute, which means it will be invoked by an HTTP request. The method uses the IEventGridService interface, which is a custom service that encapsulates the logic for sending events to Event Grid. It uses the SendEventGridEventAsync method to send an event.

Listing 5-3. Functions with HTTP and Event triggers

```
using System.Text.Json;
using Azure.Messaging;
using Azure.Messaging.EventGrid;
using Microsoft.Azure.Functions.Worker;
using Microsoft.Azure.Functions.Worker.Http;
using Microsoft.Extensions.Logging;

namespace AzureAventure5_EventGrid
{
    public class Function1
    {
        private readonly ILogger<Function1> _logger;
        private readonly IEventGridService _eventGridService;
```

```
public Function1(ILogger<Function1> logger,
IEventGridService eventGridService)
{
    _logger = logger;
    _eventGridService = eventGridService;
}

[Function("EventGridTrigger")]
public void EventTrigger([EventGridTrigger]
EventGridEvent eventGridEvent)
{
    _logger.LogInformation($"{JsonSerializer.
    Serialize(eventGridEvent)}");
}

[Function("SendEventGridEvent")]
public async Task SendEventGridEvent([HttpTrigge
r(AuthorizationLevel.Anonymous, "get", "post")]
HttpRequestData req)
{
    await _eventGridService.SendEventGridEventAsync();
}
    }
}
```

Creating a Subscription

By creating a subscription in the existing Event Grid resource, you can ensure that the events sent by the SendEventGridEventAsync method are properly handled and processed. This subscription will allow you to define specific endpoints or actions to be taken when events are received from the Event Grid.

Publish your solution to the resource group; you can create a new one or use an already existing resource. When it is deployed, you will see functions in the list as shown in Figure 5-7.

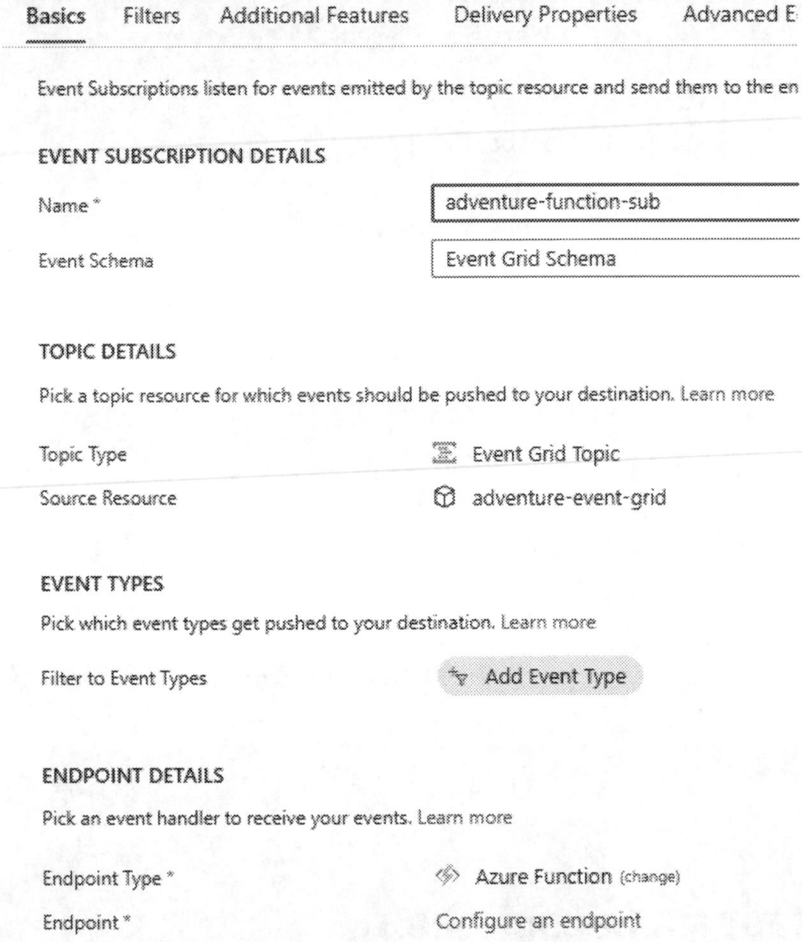

Basics   Filters   Additional Features   Delivery Properties   Advanced E

Event Subscriptions listen for events emitted by the topic resource and send them to the en

EVENT SUBSCRIPTION DETAILS

Name *	adventure-function-sub
Event Schema	Event Grid Schema

TOPIC DETAILS

Pick a topic resource for which events should be pushed to your destination. Learn more

Topic Type	🖵 Event Grid Topic
Source Resource	📦 adventure-event-grid

EVENT TYPES

Pick which event types get pushed to your destination. Learn more

Filter to Event Types	⬩ Add Event Type

ENDPOINT DETAILS

Pick an event handler to receive your events. Learn more

Endpoint Type *	✧ Azure Function (change)
Endpoint *	Configure an endpoint

Figure 5-7. *A form to create a new subscription*

By creating a subscription in the existing Event Grid resource, you can ensure that the events sent by the SendEventGridEventAsync method are properly handled and processed. This subscription will allow you to define specific endpoints or actions to be taken when events are received from the Event Grid.

- Go to the Event Grid resource.

- Click the New Subscription button.

- A new form will open, like in Figure 5-8. Provide a name, select schema to Event Grid Schema, and change the endpoint type to Azure Function.

Figure 5-8. *Selecting a function endpoint*

- In the pane, configure an endpoint, like in Figure 5-8. Select your resource group, deployed function, and function name.

197

In the filter tab (shown in Figure 5-9), you can select which events you want to receive for your endpoint. There are three options available:

- The subject starts with a provided value.

- The subject ends with a provided value.

- Turn on case sensitive if it is required to find a matching value.

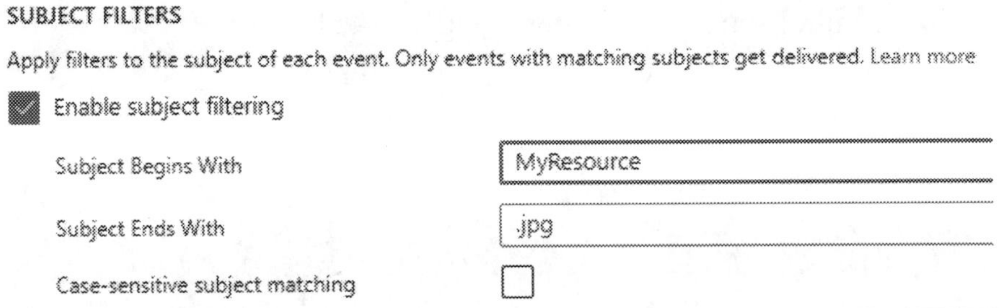

SUBJECT FILTERS

Apply filters to the subject of each event. Only events with matching subjects get delivered. Learn more

☑ Enable subject filtering

Subject Begins With	MyResource
Subject Ends With	.jpg
Case-sensitive subject matching	☐

Figure 5-9.   *Filters for the event*

Running the Event

In the previous steps, we configured the endpoint for the Azure Function in Event Grid. Now, we need to ensure that the event is running smoothly. By selecting the deployed resource and function name, we can monitor and receive specific events. This allows us to view the process and receive events.

Go to the deployed functions. Click the SendEventGridEvent function name. Go to the Monitor section, then click the Logs tab. This way, we will check if the application has started and received the message.

Then, go to the SendEventGridEvent function. Go to the Logs tab, like in the previous function. Then open in another window the Code + Test section. In Figure 5-10, you will see a way to run the function.

- Click the Run button.

- A new pane will open; there is no need to change any value there.

- Click the next Run button.

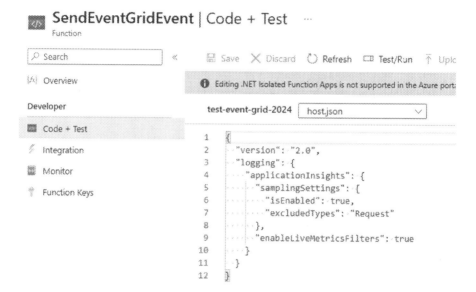

Figure 5-10. Code + Test section of the SendEventGridEvent function

You should see in the logs of the sender function if the message was sent, like in Figure 5-11.

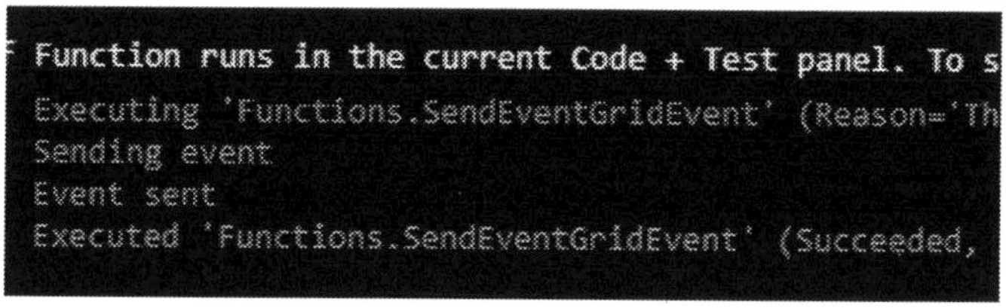

Figure 5-11. Running the sender function

In the logs of the trigger function, you should see the data of the received event in the format of a JSON object, as shown in Figure 5-12. By examining the logs of the trigger function, you can verify that the event was successfully received and processed. The JSON object format allows for easy identification and extraction of relevant data points such as the event ID, topic, subject, custom data, event type, event time, and data version. This detailed information can be crucial for troubleshooting and analyzing the flow of events within the system.

Figure 5-12. *Receiving of the event logs*

Receiving the Cloud Event

In this section, we will be receiving a cloud event with information on whether the blob was created or deleted. To use events on the Storage Account, we need to create a version 2 or upgrade it. This upgrade will allow us to receive cloud events with more detailed information, such as the type of operation performed on the blob and any associated metadata. By leveraging this upgraded version, we can enhance our ability to monitor and track changes within the Storage Account effectively.

To upgrade to version 2 of the Storage Account, go to your resource, go to the Configuration section, click the Upgrade button, and confirm it in a new pane. Remember that this action cannot be undone. Make sure all relevant stakeholders are informed of the upgrade to avoid any disruptions in monitoring and tracking processes.

A new button called Events will be visible on the left-side menu. Figure 5-13 shows what it looks like. You will see a list of existing subscriptions to the resource and a button to create a new one.

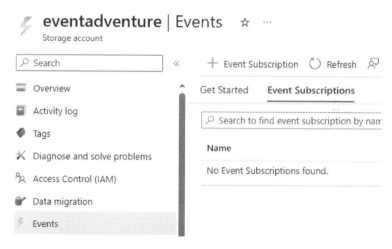

Figure 5-13. *Events of the resource*

Before creating a new subscription, first add a new function to our existing project with the code from Listing 5-4. It is a simple method that receives the CloudEvent parameter, serializes it, and displays all the information.

Listing 5-4. Cloud trigger function

```
[Function("CloudTrigger")]
public void CloudTrigger([EventGridTrigger] CloudEvent
cloudEvent)
{
 _logger.LogInformation($"{JsonSerializer.Serialize
 (cloudEvent)}");
}
```

Then go back to your resource and click the new Subscription button. The form is the same as the previous one for the standard event trigger. The only difference is that the source is the Storage Account, and you can choose the event type as shown in Figure 5-14. Build and publish your updated function. You should now see three functions in the resource.

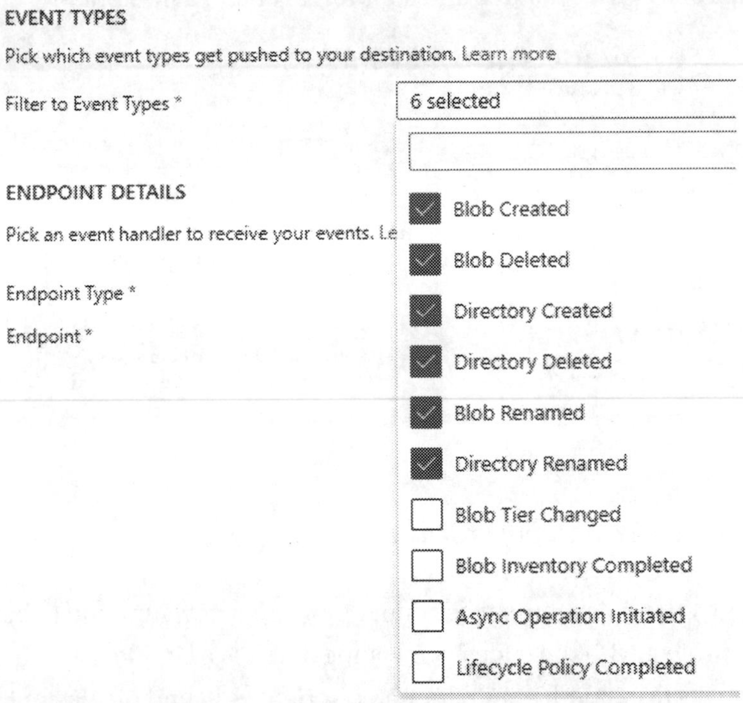

EVENT TYPES

Pick which event types get pushed to your destination. Learn more

Filter to Event Types *   6 selected

ENDPOINT DETAILS

Pick an event handler to receive your events. Le

Endpoint Type *   ☑ Blob Created

Endpoint *   ☑ Blob Deleted

                                             ☑ Directory Created

                                             ☑ Directory Deleted

                                             ☑ Blob Renamed

                                             ☑ Directory Renamed

                                             ☐ Blob Tier Changed

                                             ☐ Blob Inventory Completed

                                             ☐ Async Operation Initiated

                                             ☐ Lifecycle Policy Completed

Figure 5-14. *Event types for the resource*

When you create a new subscription to your function, go to the monitor and then logs of the new function to see a live stream of current processed messages. In a window, open your storage resource, create a new container, and upload a file. In the logs, you should see this new cloud event with all the data and type of action, like in Figure 5-15.

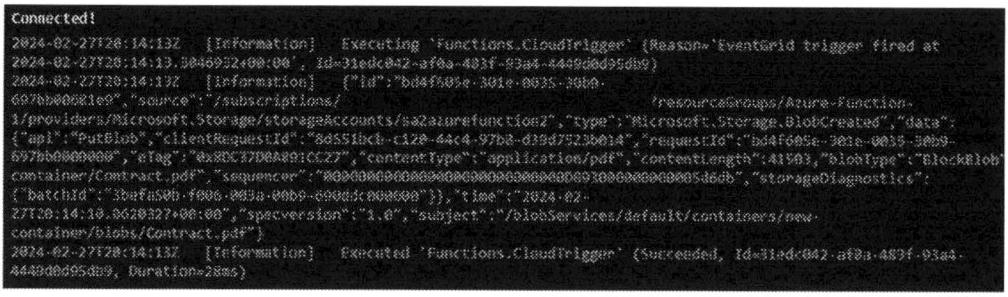

Connected!
2024-02-27T20:14:13Z   [Information]   Executing 'Functions.CloudTrigger' (Reason='EventGrid trigger fired at
2024-02-27T20:14:13.5846952+00:00', Id=31edc842-af0a-483f-93a4-4449d0d95db9)
2024-02-27T20:14:13Z   [Information]   {"id":"bd4f505e-301e-0035-30b9-
697b0006le9","source":"/subscriptions/   /resourceGroups/Azure-Function-
1/providers/Microsoft.Storage/storageAccounts/sa2azurefunction2","type":"Microsoft.Storage.BlobCreated","data":
{"api":"PutBlob","clientRequestId":"8d551bcb-c120-44c4-97b0-d39d7523b014","requestId":"bd4f605e-301e-0035-30b9-
697b00000000","eTag":"0x8DC37D8A891CC27","contentType":"application/pdf","contentLength":41503,"blobType":"BlockBlob"
container/Contract.pdf","sequencer":"00000000000000000000000000005d6db","storageDiagnostics":
{"batchId":"3befa50b-f006-003a-00b9-690d1c000000"}},"time":"2024-02-
27T20:14:10.9620327+00:00","specversion":"1.0","subject":"/blobServices/default/containers/new-
container/blobs/Contract.pdf"}
2024-02-27T20:14:13Z   [Information]   Executed 'Functions.CloudTrigger' (Succeeded, Id=31edc842-af0a-483f-93a4-
4449d0d95db9, Duration=28ms)

Figure 5-15. *Adding a new file event log*

Provisioning Event Grid with Bicep

To create it, you can use a bicep script. During the provisioning of the subscription, you need to ensure that your handler already exists and is deployed. This will help streamline the process and ensure consistency across different environments. Additionally, make sure to monitor the logs for any errors or issues during the provisioning process.

Listing 5-5. A bicep script to provision Event Grid

```
resource storageAccount 'Microsoft.Storage/
storageAccounts@2023-01-01' = {
  name: 'eventadventurestorage'
  location: resourceGroup().location
  sku: {
    name: 'Standard_LRS'
  }
  kind: 'StorageV2'
  properties: {
    accessTier: 'Hot'
  }
}
```

```
resource systemTopic 'Microsoft.EventGrid/
systemTopics@2022-06-15' = {
  name: 'eventadventuresystemtopic'
  location: resourceGroup().location
  properties: {
    source: storageAccount.id
    topicType: 'Microsoft.Storage.StorageAccounts'
  }
}

resource eventSubscription 'Microsoft.EventGrid/systemTopics/
eventSubscriptions@2022-06-15' = {
  parent: systemTopic
  name: 'eventadventureeventsubscription'
  properties: {
    destination: {
      properties: {
        endpointUrl: 'https://eventadventurefunction5.
        azurewebsites.net/runtime/webhooks/EventGrid?function
        Name=CloudTrigger&code=secretcode'
      }
      endpointType: 'WebHook'
    }
    filter: {
      includedEventTypes: [
        'Microsoft.Storage.BlobRenamed'
        'Microsoft.Storage.BlobCreated'
      ]
    }
  }
}
```

The code from Listing 5-5 is an example of a bicep script to create and configure resources for an event-driven application. The code consists of three main sections:

- The first section creates a storage account. There is a "name" property, "location" is set to the default value of the resource group. The "sku" property is set to "Standard_LRS", "accessTier" is set to "Hot" option, which is good for common operations on blobs and the kind is set to StorageV2. The last property is important to use; otherwise, there won't be events.

- The second section creates a system topic, which is a predefined topic that represents an event source in Azure. The system topic has a name, a location, a source, and a topic type. The name must be unique within the resource group, the location must match the resource group location, the source must be a valid resource ID of an event source, and the topic type must match the event source type.

- The third section creates an event subscription, which is a configuration that defines how events from a system topic are delivered to a destination. The event subscription has a parent, a name, and properties. The parent must be a valid system topic resource, the name must be unique within the system topic, and the properties include the destination, the filter, and other optional settings. The destination specifies where the events are sent, such as a webhook or an Azure function. The filter defines which events are included or excluded based on their types or subjects.

Summary

In this chapter, we have learned what Event Grid is and how to work with it. It can help you work with a real-time application to route events between components of a bigger solution. By using filters effectively, you can ensure that only relevant events are processed by your application. It can handle large volumes of events efficiently.

This service works in a push-based architecture and ensures minimal latency in event processing. When you provision the service, the handlers must already exist and be deployed.

At the end of the chapter, we have an example of how to use a bicep script for the automation process.

CHAPTER 6

Service Bus

Azure Service Bus is a robust cloud messaging service that supports the asynchronous exchange of data across various applications and services. By leveraging its robust message queuing and publish/subscribe capabilities, developers can build scalable and decoupled systems. It's particularly useful for integrating heterogeneous environments, simplifying complex communication patterns, and improving overall application resilience.

Compared to Event Grid, with Service Bus, you can control the load of the messages and have more advanced routing capabilities. This will help ensure that messages are delivered efficiently and reliably to the appropriate endpoints. It may happen that some of the systems will throttle if they receive too many at once. In these cases, Service Bus can help by managing the flow of messages to prevent throttling and optimize performance.

The Service Bus is delivering a high volume of messages efficiently and reliably to the appropriate endpoints. A message contains a payload of data that needs to be processed by the receiving system. The message can be either stored or will be required for further processing in another system. The Service Bus allows you to set up rules and filters to route messages based on certain criteria, such as message content or metadata. With Service Bus, you can also prioritize messages and schedule them for delivery at specific times or intervals. By utilizing these features, you can ensure that critical or time-sensitive messages are processed in a timely manner while preventing system overload. This efficient message delivery

M. Świtalik, *Azure Adventures with C#*, https://doi.org/10.1007/979-8-8688-0424-3_6

system helps streamline communication between different components of your architecture and enhances overall performance.

The Service Bus has a feature called AMQP (Advanced Message Queuing Protocol). This feature allows for faster, more reliable communication between applications and services by providing a standardized protocol for messaging. It is an open standard protocol that can be used across different programming languages and platforms.

This service can also detect duplication of messages and ensure that each message is processed only once. It can be helpful for the system design and future coding of the application to help avoid such issues and ensure efficient communication between components. It may also help the application to be more optimized because it will not be required to check if similar messages have already been processed or processed a second time. The application will be able to function more smoothly and effectively.

This service is a pull-based message broker that can significantly improve the overall performance of the application. It means that the application itself is able to retrieve messages from the broker when it is ready to process them. This type of architecture is particularly beneficial for applications with varying workloads. It is allowing the application to scale dynamically based on demand. By utilizing the resources when they are ready, it will optimize the costs.

Queues is a standard service provided by Service Bus to enable decoupling between components and allow them to communicate asynchronously.

Topics is another feature provided by Service Bus that allows for publish-subscribe messaging between components. It enables multiple subscribers to receive messages from a single sender. Topics can be used to scale out messaging in order to support large numbers of subscribers.

A publisher can send messages to a topic, and each subscriber can receive a copy of the message. Every subscriber must have a subscription. Subscription can be filtered based on specific criteria to ensure that subscribers only receive messages that are relevant to them.

An example usage of Service Bus can be a system for receiving orders from the shop application. Service Bus can be a system for receiving orders from the shop application to efficiently manage and process incoming requests. The diagram in Figure 6-1 shows an example system solution for such a process. The SPA application is connected to the Azure Function. The Azure Function is validating the order; if the product is available, the payment is processed correctly, and then it forwards the orders to the Service Bus for processing. The Service Bus then sends the processed orders to the back-end system for fulfillment, to the notification system to send emails, and to the courier service provider system to create a tracking number for the order. This system solution allows for seamless communication between different components, ensuring efficient order processing and customer satisfaction. There can be different courier systems, and the message may contain properties such as the type of order and chosen type of courier. The system can filter the message by properties in order to process only its own order.

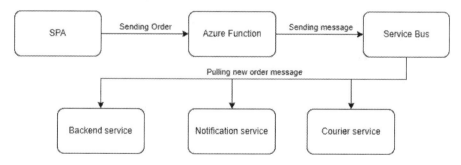

Figure 6-1. *A diagram of a shop with Service Bus*

Create Service Bus

Before we start working with queues and topics, we have to create a Service Bus resource. Once created, you can manage your Service Bus namespaces, queues, topics, and subscriptions through the Azure Portal

or programmatically via Azure SDKs. To create through the Azure Portal,
follow these steps:

- Go to the Azure resources.

- Search for Sevice Bus.

- Click the Create button and then the Service
  Bus button.

- Fill out the form with the required values as namespace
  name, location, pricing tier, subscription, and
  resource group. As shown in Figure 6-2, select the
  Standard tier.

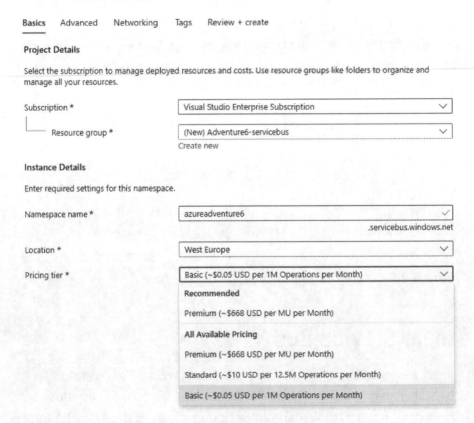

Figure 6-2. *Creating a Service Bus resource*

- Skip other tabs, as we don't require any additional changes from them.

When the resource is deployed, you will find useful data in the information table, including a hostname property with the URL that can be used to connect, fetch, or publish a message.

The Basic tier only has queues for usage. The Basic and Standard tiers have shared capacity with other Service Bus resources. The maximum message size is only 256KB. The Standard and Premium tiers also have topics available to choose from.

Only the Premium tier has dedicated capacity (which means it is separate from other resources like those in the lower tiers), the maximum message is increased to 100MB, and there is zone redundancy.

On the left side of the resource, you will see links that lead to the Topics and Queues. There will also be other features that are created for most of the resources, like access policies, costs, networks, and others.

Creating a Queue

Once we have created a resource on which we can work, first we will familiarize ourselves with the basic queue, which is available on the Service Bus.

On the top command bar, you have two buttons to create a new queue or a new topic.

When you click to create a new queue or topic, the pane will open as shown in Figure 6-3. Provide a name and leave other options on default values.

- Message time to live is the amount of time a message will be kept in the queue or topic before it expires.

- The lock duration of the message is locked when a receiver pulls the message for other receivers. This ensures that only one receiver can process the message at a time, preventing duplication. It is important to set appropriate values for both message time to live and lock duration based on the specific needs of your application.

- Enable duplicate detection to ensure that messages are not processed multiple times.

- Enabling partitioning can be used to distribute the workload and increase scalability.

- Enabling sessions can help you implement message sequence handling.

- Forwarding messages to queues or topics within the same Service Bus resource can simplify your architecture and reduce latency.

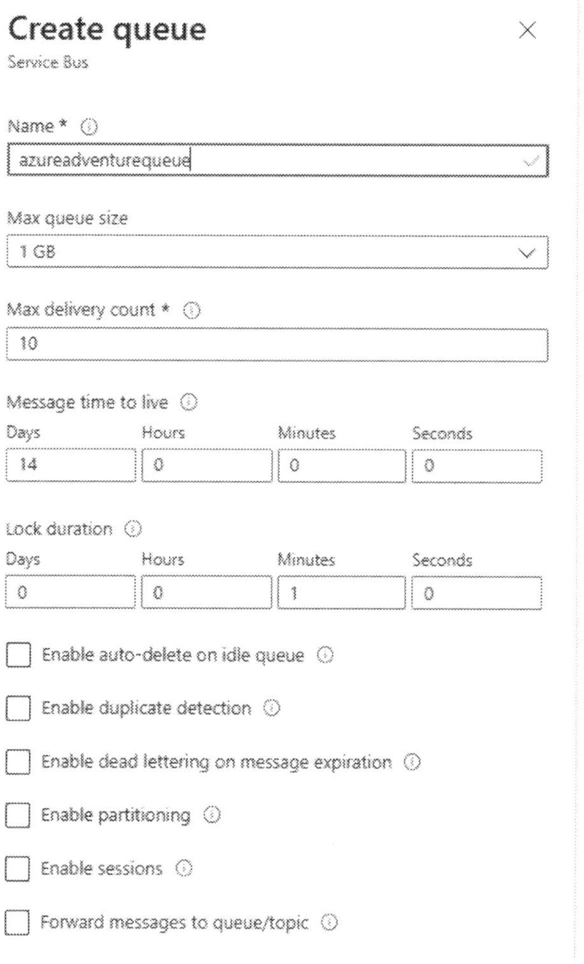

Figure 6-3. *Creating a new queue in the Service Bus*

Consume Queues with the Azure Function

In order to consume messages from the queue, we will have to create an Azure function with the queue trigger of the Service Bus that listens and processes messages as they arrive.

- Create a new Visual Studio 2022 project.

- Select the Azure Function template and click Next.

- Enter a new project name, then click Next.

- You can select the Service Bus queue trigger as the template; however, in this example, we select the HTTP trigger.

Then we need to add a connection string from the Service Bus. To find it, you can go to the shared access policies settings in the resource, and a new pane will open, as shown in Figure 6-3. You can copy the primary connection string and paste it into the configuration of the new project, as shown in Listing 6-1. We are also adding a new variable for a queue name.

Listing 6-1. Local setting values for the Service Bus project

```
{
  "IsEncrypted": false,
  "Values": {
    "AzureWebJobsStorage": "UseDevelopmentStorage=true",
    "FUNCTIONS_WORKER_RUNTIME": "dotnet-isolated",
    "serviceBusConnectionString": "{YourConnectionString}",
    "serviceBusQueueName": "azureadventure6queue"
  }
}
```

The project will use the Azure library Azure.Messaging.ServiceBus library to connect to the service and receive or send messages. Install it through the NuGet package manager for the project.

As a first step, let's create the ServiceBusService class with Listing 6-2. It has private variables _queueName, _connectionString, and _logger. In the constructor, we inject IConfiguration and set the values of queueName and _connectionString using the configuration passed in. We also inject and assign the logger object. In the method SendMessageAsync, we create a ServiceBusClient with the previously provided connection string and use it to create a ServiceBusSender with the queueName provided. With the client object, we can manage the queue or topic messages. After creating the ServiceBusSender, we can then send a message asynchronously using the client object. The message will be sent to the specified queue, and then a confirmation will be logged.

Listing 6-2. ServiceBusService class code

```
using Azure.Messaging.ServiceBus;
using Microsoft.Extensions.Configuration;

namespace AzureAventure6_ServiceBus
{
    public interface IServiceBusService
    {
        Task SendMessageAsync();
    }

    public class ServiceBusService : IServiceBusService
    {
        private readonly string _connectionString;
        private readonly string _queueName;

        public ServiceBusService(IConfiguration configuration)
        {
            _connectionString = configuration["serviceBusConnec
            tionString"];
            _queueName = configuration["serviceBusQueueName"];
        }

        public async Task SendMessageAsync()
        {
```

```
await using var client = new ServiceBusClient(_
connectionString);
ServiceBusSender sender = client.CreateSender(_
queueName);

ServiceBusMessage message = new ServiceBusMessage
("Azure Adventure!");
await sender.SendMessageAsync(message);
Console.WriteLine($"Sent a single message to the
queue: {_queueName}");
        }
    }
}
```

Add the new service to the DI like in Listing 6-3.

Listing 6-3. DI for ServiceBusService class

```
services.AddSingleton<IServiceBusService, ServiceBusService>();
```

Modify the QueueReceiver class to look like it is in Listing 6-4. At first, add and inject the IServiceBusService interface into the constructor and assign it to a private field. Then update the Run method; replace names with the configuration references to queue name and connection string. In the method, we log the body of the message received from the queue, and finally, we call the CompleteMessageAsync to complete the processing of the message and remove it from the queue. In the SendMessage method HTTP trigger type, we send a message to the specified queue using the SendMessageAsync method from the IServiceBusService.

Listing 6-4. QueueReceiver class with triggers

```
using System.Net;
using Azure.Messaging.ServiceBus;
using Microsoft.Azure.Functions.Worker;
```

```
using Microsoft.Azure.Functions.Worker.Http;
using Microsoft.Extensions.Logging;

namespace AzureAventure6_ServiceBus
{
    public class QueueReceiver
    {
        private readonly ILogger<QueueReceiver> _logger;
        private readonly IServiceBusService _serviceBusService;

        public QueueReceiver(ILogger<QueueReceiver> logger,
        IServiceBusService serviceBusService)
        {
            _logger = logger;
            _serviceBusService = serviceBusService;
        }

        [Function(nameof(QueueReceiver))]
        public async Task Run(
            [ServiceBusTrigger("%serviceBusQueueName%",
            Connection = "serviceBusConnectionString")]
            ServiceBusReceivedMessage message,
            ServiceBusMessageActions messageActions)
        {
            _logger.LogInformation($"Received message:
            {message.Body.ToString()}");
            await messageActions.CompleteMessageAsync(message);
        }

        [Function(nameof(SendMessage))]
        public async Task SendMessage([HttpTrigger(Authorizatio
        nLevel.Function, "get", "post")] HttpRequestData req)
```

```
    {
        await _serviceBusService.SendMessageAsync();

        var response = req.CreateResponse(HttpStatus
        Code.OK);
        response.Headers.Add("Content-Type", "text/plain;
        charset=utf-8");
        await response.WriteStringAsync("Message sent to
        queue");
    }
  }
}
```

If you are going to deploy it to the Azure function resource, you have to add these variables to the configuration.

Figure 6-4 is showing logs of the application. The first log is showing that the HTTP trigger is sending a message to the Service Bus queue and then it is processed and consumed by the queue trigger.

Figure 6-4. *Logs of sending and receiving messages*

In Figure 6-5, you can see a message on the site using the Service Bus Explorer. To access it, go to your resource, then click the queue name, and on the left-side menu, you will find the Service Bus Explorer.

Enqueued Time	Delivery Count	State	Body Size	Label/Subject	Message Text
Sun, Mar 10, 24, 03:54:08 PM GM...	0	Active	16 B		Azure Adventure!

Figure 6-5. *A new message in the Service Bus Explorer*

Create a Topic and Subscription

In this section, we will create a topic and subscribe a consumer to that topic. Once the topic is created, you can then add subscriptions for consumers to receive messages from the topic. To create a topic, follow these steps:

- Go to the resource.

- Click the + Topic button, and enter the topic name; leave other settings with default values as in Figure 6-6.

219

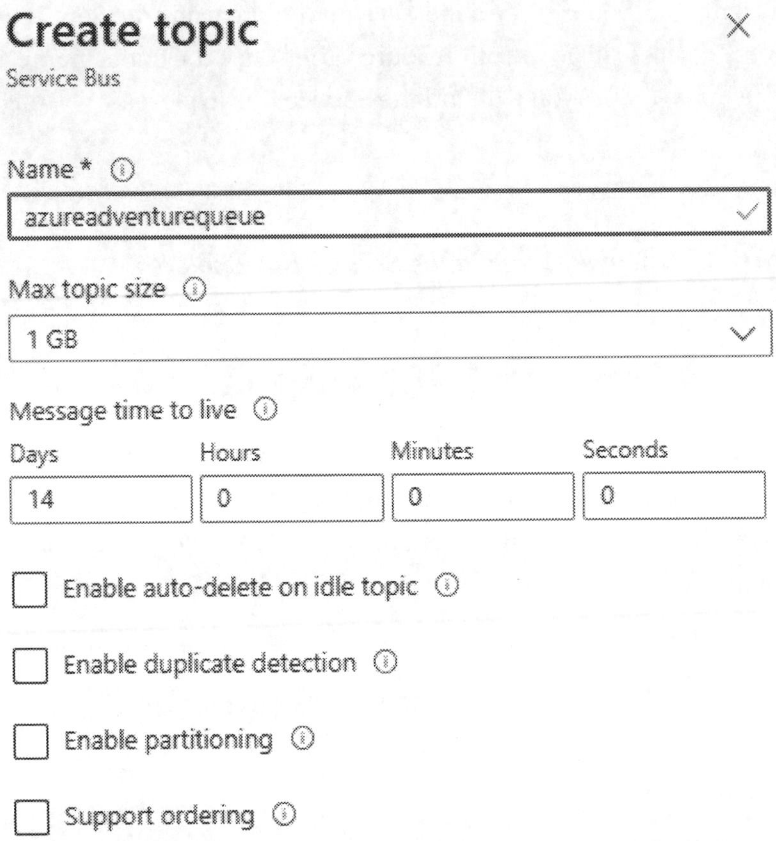

Create topic   ✕

Service Bus

Name *   ⓘ

azureadventurequeue   ✓

Max topic size   ⓘ

1 GB   ⌄

Message time to live   ⓘ

Days	Hours	Minutes	Seconds
14	0	0	0

☐ Enable auto-delete on idle topic   ⓘ

☐ Enable duplicate detection   ⓘ

☐ Enable partitioning   ⓘ

☐ Support ordering   ⓘ

Figure 6-6.   *Creating a new topic form*

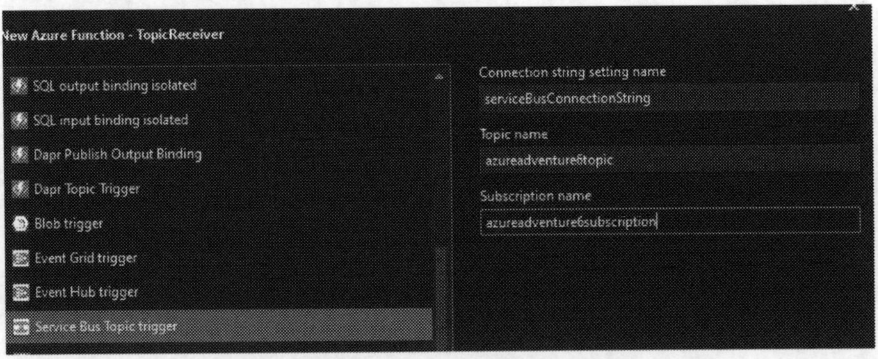

New Azure Function - TopicReceiver   ✕

SQL output binding isolated

SQL input binding isolated

Dapr Publish Output Binding

Dapr Topic Trigger

Blob trigger

Event Grid trigger

Event Hub trigger

Service Bus Topic trigger

Connection string setting name
serviceBusConnectionString

Topic name
azureadventure6topic

Subscription name
azureadventure6subscription

Figure 6-7.   *Creating a new trigger in Visual Studio 2022*

Then create a subscription in order to receive messages from the topic:

- Go to your topic.

- Click the + Subscription button.

- A new pane will open; enter azureadventure6subscription as the name, and leave other values on default.

- Then click Create.

Consume Topic with the Azure Function

We will use a previously created project to send and receive messages from the topic. Follow these steps to create a new function class in the project:

- Add a new Azure Function class and name it TopicReceiver.

- Select the Service Bus Topic trigger as a template.

- Enter a topic name, a subscription name, and a connection string as shown in Figure 6-7.

Modify the default code to process messages from the topic, like in Listing 6-5. We have the code to log the message to the console inside the Run method. We can further enhance the functionality by adding code to process the message or perform specific actions based on the message content. There is an additional method called SendMessageToTopic which is an HTTP trigger type. When it is called, it will send the message to a specific topic using the ServiceBusService class. We are using a settings reference in the ServiceBusTrigger function to access the topic name, connection string, and subscription name. If the message is sent without errors, the text "Message sent to topic" will be returned to the user.

Listing 6-5. The TopicReceiver class code

```
using Azure.Messaging.ServiceBus;
using Microsoft.Azure.Functions.Worker;
using Microsoft.Azure.Functions.Worker.Http;
using Microsoft.Extensions.Logging;
using System.Net;

namespace AzureAventure6_ServiceBus
{
    public class TopicReceiver
    {
        private readonly ILogger<TopicReceiver> _logger;
        private readonly IServiceBusService _serviceBusService;

        public TopicReceiver(ILogger<TopicReceiver> logger,
        IServiceBusService serviceBusService)
        {
            _logger = logger;
            _serviceBusService = serviceBusService;
        }

        [Function(nameof(TopicReceiver))]
        public async Task Run(
            [ServiceBusTrigger("%serviceBusTopic%",
            "%serviceBusSubscription%", Connection =
            "serviceBusConnectionString")]
            ServiceBusReceivedMessage message,
            ServiceBusMessageActions messageActions)
        {
            _logger.LogInformation($"Received message {message.
        Body}");
            await messageActions.CompleteMessageAsync(message);
        }
```

```
[Function(nameof(SendMessageToTopic))]
public async Task SendMessageToTopic([HttpTrigger(Autho
rizationLevel.Function, "get", "post")] HttpRequestData
req, FunctionContext context)
{
    await _serviceBusService.SendMessageToTopicWithProp
    ertiesAsync("Adventure");
    await _serviceBusService.SendMessageToTopicWithProp
    ertiesAsync("Walk");

    var response = req.CreateResponse(HttpStatus
    Code.OK);
    response.Headers.Add("Content-Type", "text/plain;
    charset=utf-8");
    await response.WriteStringAsync("Message sent to
    topic");
    }
  }
}
```

Add a new private variable to the service as shown in Listing 6-6 with the topic name and assign it in the constructor.

Listing 6-6. Adding a new private variable

```
// omitting code for clarity
private readonly string _topicName;

public ServiceBusService(IConfiguration configuration,
ILogger<ServiceBusService> logger)
{
    // ommiting code for clarity
    _topicName = configuration["serviceBusTopic"];
}
```

A new method from Listing 6-7 should be added to the service to handle sending messages to the specified topic. This method uses the _ topicName variable to determine which topic to send the message to. Like in the previous method, we create a sender with the topic name and send the message using that sender.

Listing 6-7. Send message to a topic method

```
public interface IServiceBusService
{
    Task SendMessageToTopicAsync();
}

public class ServiceBusService : IServiceBusService
{
    // ommiting code for clarity
    public async Task SendMessageToTopicAsync()
    {
        await using var client = new ServiceBusClient(_
        connectionString);
        ServiceBusSender sender = client.CreateSender(_
        topicName);

        ServiceBusMessage message = new
        ServiceBusMessage("Azure Adventure!");
        await sender.SendMessageAsync(message);
        _logger.LogInformation($"Sent a single message to the
        topic: topicName");
    }
}
```

Then add a missing setting with values to the local.settings.json file, as shown in Listing 6-8.

Listing 6-8. A new variable added to the settings

```
"serviceBusTopic": "azureadventure6topic",
"serviceBusSubscription": "azureadventure6subscription"
```

When you run the code, it will send a message to the specified topic. Then the Service Bus trigger will run and process the message that was sent to the topic. A screenshot in Figure 6-8 shows running a program locally will show the message being processed by the Service Bus trigger.

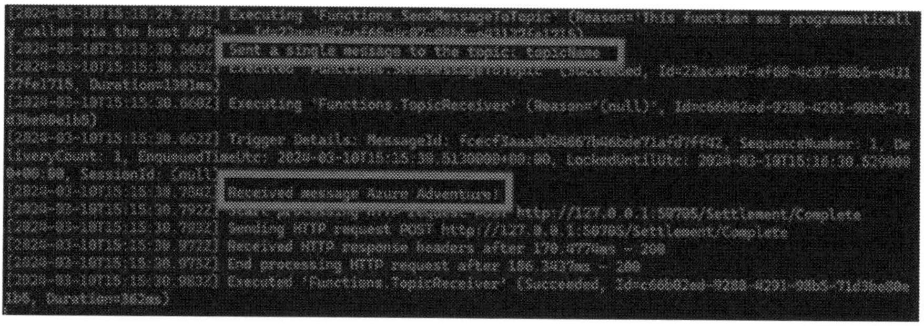

Figure 6-8. *Logs of running program*

Using the Filter on Topic

We can use the filter options on the topic to specify which messages should be processed by the trigger. This allows for more customization and control over the messages being handled.

The first step is to modify a subscription to include the desired filter criteria:

- Go to the Service Bus resource.

- Click the topic name.

- Click the subscriptions on the left menu.

- Click the name of your subscription.

- Edit the filters, as shown in Figure 6-9. Set the Filter
  Type to SQL Filter and put "Category = 'Adventure'" into
  the text field.

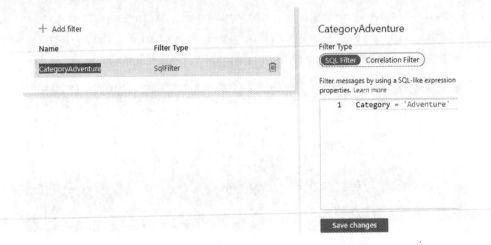

Figure 6-9. *Filter for the subscription*

- Click the Save Changes button.

We can use the SQL like command to filter the data even further. This
will help ensure you are only receiving the most relevant information
in your subscription. This specific SQL query will filter to allow only
messages with the property "Category" equal to "Adventure."

Then we add a new method SendMessageToTopicWithPropertiesAsync
to the ServiceBusService class as shown in Listing 6-9. This method
sends messages to a topic with specific properties asynchronously.
The properties are added to the ApplicationProperties property of the
ServiceBusMessage object.

Listing 6-9. A new method to the ServiceBusService

```
public interface IServiceBusService
{
    Task SendMessageToTopicWithPropertiesAsync(string category);
}

public class ServiceBusService : IServiceBusService
{
    public async Task SendMessageToTopicWithPropertiesAsync
    (string category)
    {
        await using var client = new ServiceBusClient
        (_connectionString);
        ServiceBusSender sender = client.CreateSender
        (_topicName);

        ServiceBusMessage message = new
        ServiceBusMessage($"Adventure from {category}
        category");
        message.ApplicationProperties.Add("Category",
        category);
        await sender.SendMessageAsync(message);
        _logger.LogInformation($"Sent a single message to the
        topic: {_topicName}");
    }
}
```

Now we are going to modify the SendMessageToTopic method
from the TopicReceiver class to send multiple messages using the
SendMessageToTopicWithPropertiesAsync from the ServiceBusService
class. The code in Listing 6-10 is showing changes for the class. We replace
the old SendMessageToTopicAsync method with a new one created. We
provide different values to have multiple messages in the topic.

Listing 6-10. Modified SendMessageToTopic method

```
public class TopicReceiver
{
    [Function(nameof(SendMessageToTopic))]
    public async Task SendMessageToTopic([HttpTrigger
    (AuthorizationLevel.Function, "get", "post")]
    HttpRequestData req, FunctionContext context)
    {
        await _serviceBusService.SendMessageToTopicWithProperti
        esAsync("Adventure");
        await _serviceBusService.SendMessageToTopicWithProperti
        esAsync("Walk");

    }
}
```

The screenshot from Figure 6-10 shows the logs of running the program with the triggered HTTP function to send the message. You can see that these two messages were sent, and the first message was received and processed before the second message was on the topic.

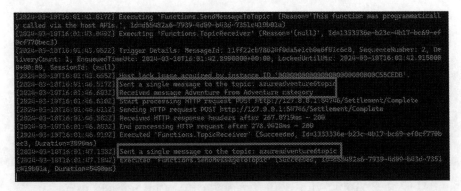

Figure 6-10. Screenshot with logs of running the program

Deploy Resources Using Bicep

To automate the deployment of the resource, you can use a bicep script. It will help you quickly and efficiently set up a new environment or roll out new configurations seamlessly without any manual intervention. Listing 6-11 has all resources in this chapter and can be easily deployed with the command from Listing 6-12.

The serviceBusNamespace resource defines a namespace called azureadventure6 in the same location as the resource group it belongs to. The namespace is set to use the Standard tier, which is a middle-tier offering that provides reliable messaging for a reasonable cost.

The queue resource specifies a queue within the defined namespace. The messages are saved until they are received and consumed by the application. The queue is named azureadventure6queue, indicating it is likely dedicated to a specific function or application within the azureadventure6 namespace.

The topic resource creates a topic named azureadventure6topic within the namespace. Topics are similar to queues but allow one-to-many communication. Multiple subscriptions can be associated with a single topic, each receiving a copy of the message sent to the topic.

The subscription resource establishes a subscription to the topic, named azureadventure6subscription. Subscriptions are used to receive messages published to a topic.

Finally, the sqlFilter resource sets up a rule named azureadventure6sqlfilter for the subscription. This rule uses a SQL-like expression to filter messages. In this case, only messages with the property Category equal to Adventure will be passed to the subscription.

Listing 6-11. The bicep script with Service Bus resources

```
resource serviceBusNamespace 'Microsoft.ServiceBus/
namespaces@2022-10-01-preview' = {
  name: 'azureadventure6'
  location: resourceGroup().location
  sku: {
    name: 'Standard'
    tier: 'Standard'
  }
}

resource queue 'Microsoft.ServiceBus/namespaces/
queues@2022-10-01-preview' = {
  parent: serviceBusNamespace
  name: 'azureadventure6queue'
}

resource topic 'Microsoft.ServiceBus/namespaces/
topics@2022-10-01-preview' = {
  parent: serviceBusNamespace
  name: 'azureadventure6topic'
}

resource subscription 'Microsoft.ServiceBus/namespaces/topics/
subscriptions@2022-10-01-preview' = {
  parent: topic
  name: 'azureadventure6subscription'
}

resource sqlFilter 'Microsoft.ServiceBus/namespaces/topics/
subscriptions/rules@2022-10-01-preview' = {
  parent: subscription
  name: 'azureadventure6sqlfilter'
```

```
  properties: {
    filterType: 'SqlFilter'
    sqlFilter: {
      sqlExpression: 'Category = \'Adventure\''
    }
  }
}
```

Listing 6-12. Command to deploy a bicep script

```
az deployment group create --resource-group Adventure6-
servicebus --template-file .\azureadventure6-servicebus.bicep
```

Summary

In this chapter, we have learned what an Azure Service Bus is. The main features of this service were presented. We have also learned how we can consume messages from the queue or topic and how to send them. This service is working in pull mode, where the receiver actively fetches messages from the queue or topic. So when we are creating an Azure function with a trigger, it is checking for a new message in the system at specified intervals.

It is also supporting the AMQP open standard for message queues and topics. It helps to ensure that the messages are delivered and that it is a reliable communication between the system components.

The Service Bus is providing us with many options during the creation of the topics, like specifying the message time to live, enabling duplicate detection, and defining custom message properties.

At the end of the chapter, we have learned how we can use a bicep script to automate the creation of resources with specific configurations.

CHAPTER 7

SQL Server

In this chapter, we will work with a SQL Server on Azure. It is recommended to have a basic understanding of SQL before proceeding. This database is a powerful system to store data with relational capabilities. SQL Server on Azure offers numerous benefits for businesses, such as scalability and high availability.

Every SQL Server can have multiple databases on the Azure platform. This chapter will guide you through setting up and utilizing SQL Server on Azure for your data storage needs. Understanding the basics of SQL will help you navigate and utilize the features of this powerful database system effectively.

SQL Server is hosted on Azure as a fully managed Platform as a Service (PaaS) offering. We don't manage the underlying infrastructure, but we can still adjust server configurations, like virtual networks, storage sizes, and performance levels, to meet our specific needs.

The SQL database can also be hosted on a virtual machine, then a user needs to provide a SQL Server license and manage the VM themselves. However, this option may require more technical expertise and maintenance.

Another proposal is to use SQL Managed Instance to simplify access management and authentication processes. This resource is ideal for users who want the benefits of a managed SQL database without the added complexity of managing a virtual machine. With SQL Managed

© Michał Świtalik 2024
M. Świtalik, *Azure Adventures with C#*, https://doi.org/10.1007/979-8-8688-0424-3_7

Instance, users can easily scale resources up or down based on their needs without having to worry about server configurations or maintenance tasks. All updates and maintenance are done automatically, without user involvement. This can save time and resources for the organization.

Create a SQL Server

In this section, we will create a SQL Server instance and configure it to make sure that it will work with our application. We will also set up user permissions and network rules. Follow these steps to create and configure a SQL Server:

- Click Create.

- Fill out the form as shown in Figure 7-1.

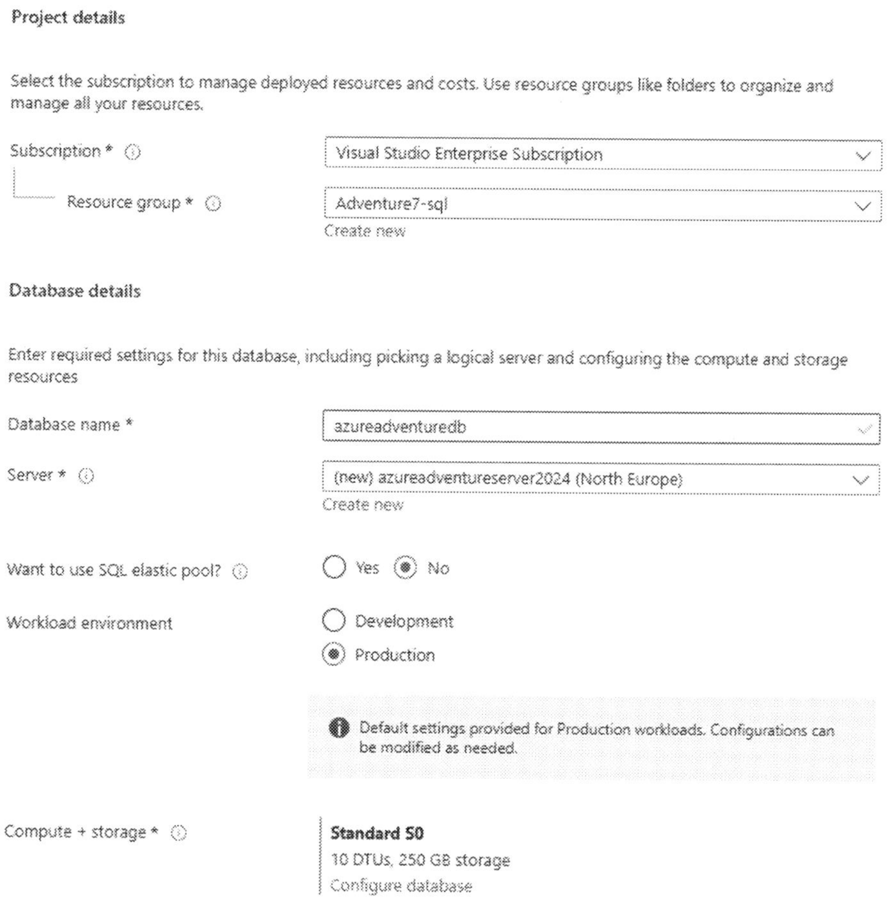

Project details

Select the subscription to manage deployed resources and costs. Use resource groups like folders to organize and manage all your resources.

Subscription * ⓘ

| Visual Studio Enterprise Subscription | ⌄ |

Resource group * ⓘ

| Adventure7-sql | ⌄ |
Create new

Database details

Enter required settings for this database, including picking a logical server and configuring the compute and storage resources

Database name *

| azureadventuredb | ⌄ |

Server * ⓘ

| (new) azureadventureserver2024 (North Europe) | ⌄ |
Create new

Want to use SQL elastic pool? ⓘ   ◯ Yes   ⦿ No

Workload environment   ◯ Development

⦿ Production

ⓘ Default settings provided for Production workloads. Configurations can be modified as needed.

Compute + storage * ⓘ

Standard S0
10 DTUs, 250 GB storage
Configure database

Figure 7-1. *A SQL database form*

- Click the Create New button to create and configure a server as shown in Figure 7-2.

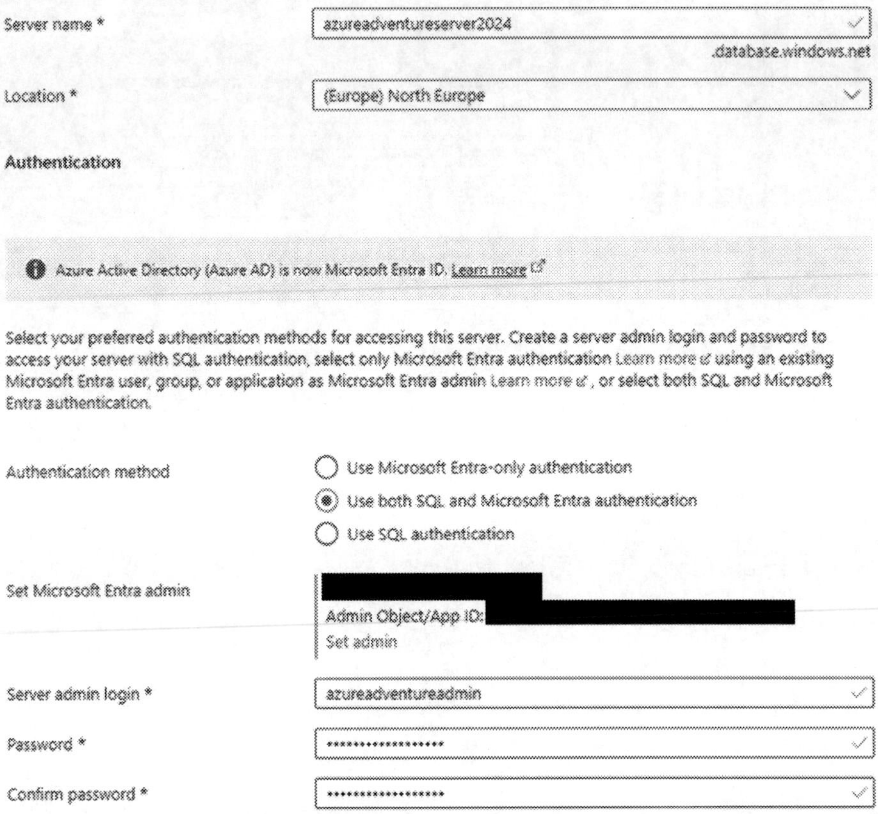

| Server name * | azureadventureserver2024 | ✓ |

.database.windows.net

| Location * | (Europe) North Europe | ⌄ |

Authentication

ℹ️ Azure Active Directory (Azure AD) is now Microsoft Entra ID. Learn more ⌐

Select your preferred authentication methods for accessing this server. Create a server admin login and password to access your server with SQL authentication, select only Microsoft Entra authentication Learn more ⌐ using an existing Microsoft Entra user, group, or application as Microsoft Entra admin Learn more ⌐ , or select both SQL and Microsoft Entra authentication.

Authentication method	◯ Use Microsoft Entra-only authentication
	⦿ Use both SQL and Microsoft Entra authentication
	◯ Use SQL authentication

Set Microsoft Entra admin	███████████████
	Admin Object/App ID: ████████████████
	Set admin

| Server admin login * | azureadventureadmin | ✓ |

| Password * | ••••••••••••••••• | ✓ |

| Confirm password * | ••••••••••••••••• | ✓ |

Figure 7-2. *Creating a SQL Server*

- Go to the service and compute tier. The screenshot in Figure 7-3 shows the available options and recommendations for the development environment.

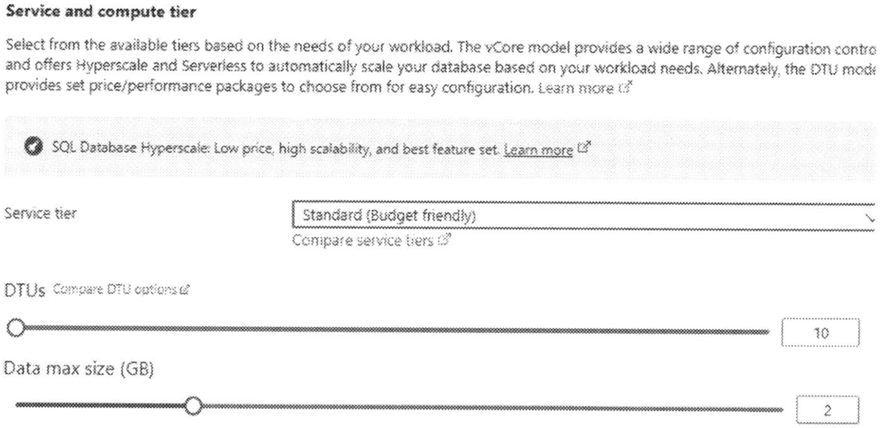
Service and compute tier
Select from the available tiers based on the needs of your workload. The vCore model provides a wide range of configuration contro and offers Hyperscale and Serverless to automatically scale your database based on your workload needs. Alternately, the DTU mode provides set price/performance packages to choose from for easy configuration. Learn more
SQL Database Hyperscale: Low price, high scalability, and best feature set. Learn more
Service tier
Standard (Budget friendly)
Compare service tiers
DTUs Compare DTU options
10
Data max size (GB)
2

***Figure 7-3.** Screenshot of the compute tier and configuration*

- In the Networking tab, choose the public endpoint so we can connect to the database from a local computer.
- Also, check to add the current client IP address and allow Azure services to connect to the server; otherwise, you will be blocked, and you can't connect to the database. The options are visible in Figure 7-4.

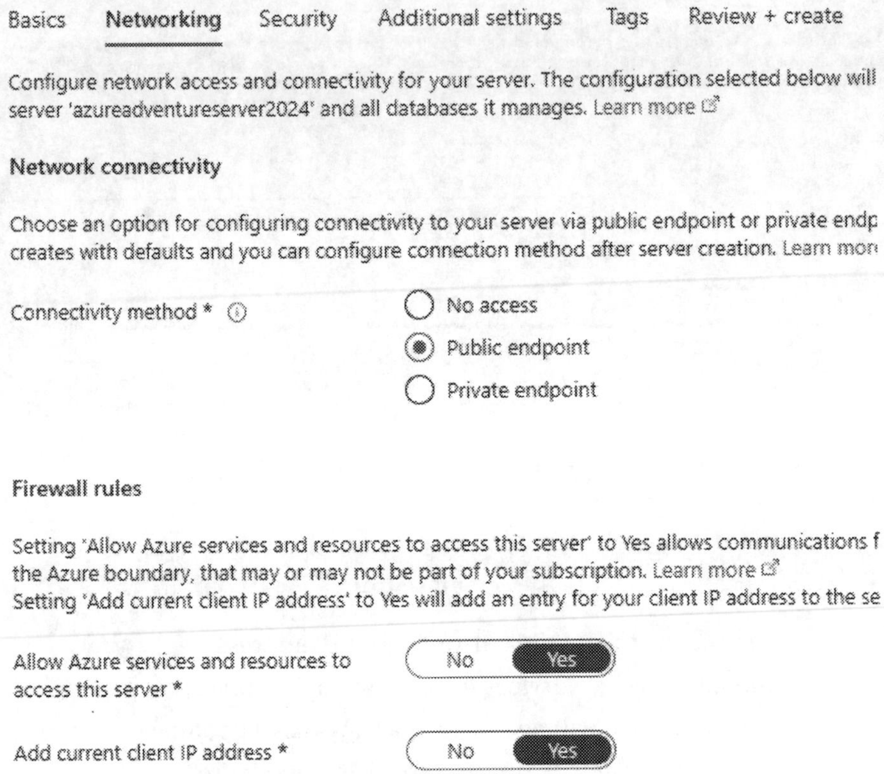

Basics **Networking** Security Additional settings Tags Review + create

Configure network access and connectivity for your server. The configuration selected below will
server 'azureadventureserver2024' and all databases it manages. Learn more ⬀

Network connectivity

Choose an option for configuring connectivity to your server via public endpoint or private endp
creates with defaults and you can configure connection method after server creation. Learn more

Connectivity method * ⓘ

○ No access

◉ Public endpoint

○ Private endpoint

Firewall rules

Setting 'Allow Azure services and resources to access this server' to Yes allows communications f
the Azure boundary, that may or may not be part of your subscription. Learn more ⬀
Setting 'Add current client IP address' to Yes will add an entry for your client IP address to the se

Allow Azure services and resources to
access this server *   No   **Yes**

Add current client IP address *   No   **Yes**

Figure 7-4. *Network options for a server*

- Click the Review and Create button, then wait for
  deployment to complete.

When the resources are deployed, go to the SQL Server resource. In
the Information section, as shown in Figure 7-5, you can see the server
name, which is a URL, if there is an elastic pool, what the price tier is,
information about the last restoration point, and a link to the database
connection string.

Server name   : azureadventureserver2024.database.windows.net

Elastic pool   : No elastic pool

Connection strings   : Show database connection strings

Pricing tier   : Standard S0: 10 DTUs

Earliest restore point : No restore point available 📋

Figure 7-5. *Information section for SQL Server*

The DTU acts as a measure of the resources that it is capable of providing. DTU consists of CPU, memory, and read/write operations. The DTU level can be adjusted to meet the needs of the application. The DTU is also crucial for the business to determine the cost of the Azure SQL Database service. Adjusting the DTU level can help optimize performance and cost efficiency for your application running on the Azure SQL Database.

To change or remove the Entra admin, go to the Microsoft Entra ID settings like in Figure 7-6, click Set admin to change or add an admin, or click the Remove admin button to remove an admin. If you want to, you can use only Entra ID accounts to connect to the server, including the application. This will be discussed more in Chapter 9.

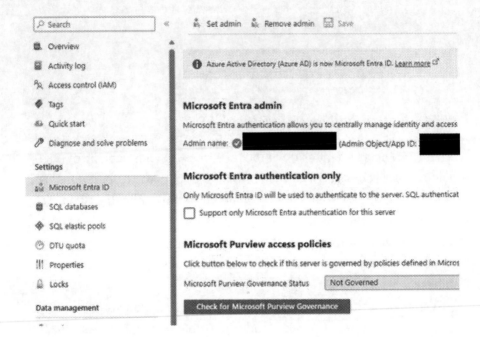

Figure 7-6. *Microsoft Entra admin access for SQL Server*

To add more IPs or remove old ones, go to the network settings. You will see the Firewall rules as shown in Figure 7-7. You can use the button labeled "Add a firewall rule" to add a new IP or range of IPs or remove an existing one. It will also suggest adding your current IP to the rules.

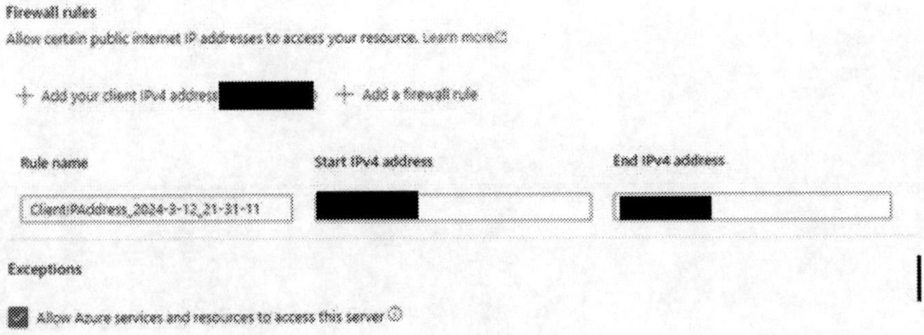

Figure 7-7. *Changing firewall rules*

By default, the server is disabled for the public. This is why you have to add your IP, virtual network, or other IPs to give access to the server.

In the resource group view, you will see a list of all the resources within that group, as shown in Figure 7-8. There will be a server with the name listed, as well as all databases with the name of the server inside the braces.

Name ↑	Type ↑↓
▦ azureadventuredb (azureadventureserver2024/azureadventuredb)	SQL database
▦ azureadventureserver2024	SQL server

Figure 7-8. *Resource group view with SQL Server and database*

Prepare Data

To prepare data, we will log in using the SQL Editor through the Azure Portal. It is a query editor in the portal that allows us to write and execute queries on our databases. Go to the database resource, and on the left-side menu, click the SQL Editor option. Use the script from Listing 7-1 to create a new table. The table name is Book; it has columns Id as the primary key and Title as a varchar with a 255 limit. Figure 7-9 shows how the running of the script will look like in the SQL query.

Listing 7-1. Script to create a table

```
CREATE TABLE Book (
    ID INT IDentity(1,1) PRIMARY KEY,
    Title VARCHAR(255)
);
```

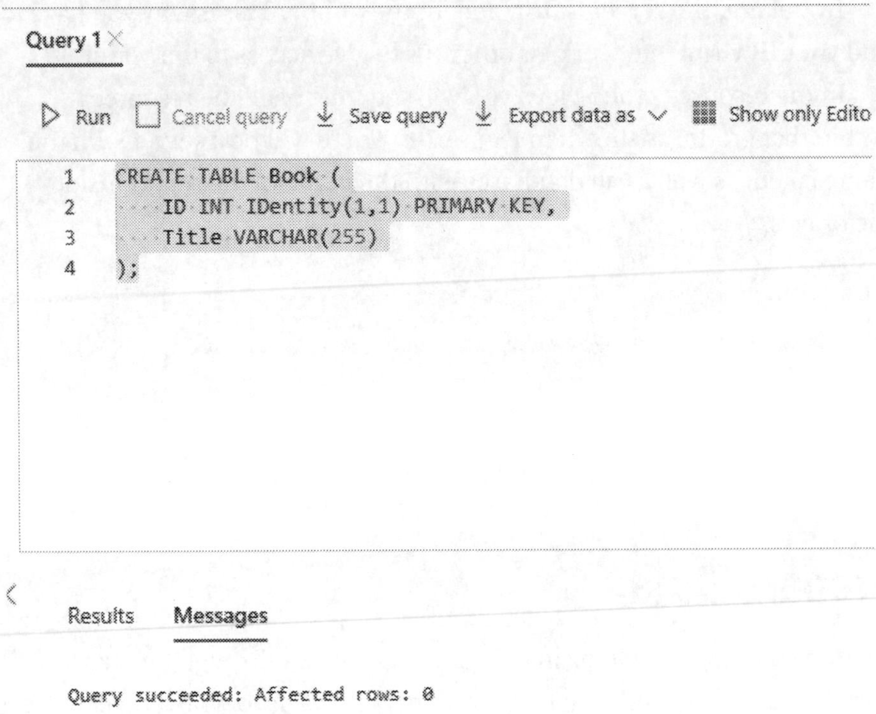

Query 1 ✕

▷ Run ☐ Cancel query ↓ Save query ↓ Export data as ∨ ▦ Show only Edito

```
1  CREATE TABLE Book (
2      ID INT IDentity(1,1) PRIMARY KEY,
3      Title VARCHAR(255)
4  );
```

‹   Results   **Messages**

```
Query succeeded: Affected rows: 0
```

Figure 7-9. *Script running on the SQL Editor*

You can now run any SQL query like SELECT * FROM [dbo].[Book] to list all rows of the table.

Figure 7-10 shows the table to view and select to query data from the Book table in the SQL Editor available through the portal.

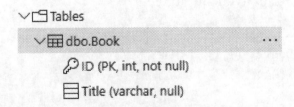

∨◻ Tables
  ∨▦ dbo.Book   ...
      🔑 ID (PK, int, not null)
      ▤ Title (varchar, null)

Figure 7-10. *Tables screenshot in the SQL Editor*

Create a Function to Connect

We will create a function with an HTTP trigger type to connect to the SQL database and add and retrieve data from the book table. Create a function with the name AzureAventure7_SQLDatabase and a function name SayHiSql.

Firstly, add a Microsoft.Data.SqlClient NuGet package to the project. Then we will create a SQLService class, from Listing 7-2, will handle all the database operations. In the constructor, we inject the ILogger interface and assign it to the private variable, and the IConfiguration interface is used to get the connection string from the environment settings.

We have the AddBook method, which will take in a string as a parameter and insert the data into the Book table.

First, we create a SqlConnection object with the OpenAsync method to open a SQL connection. Then, we create a SqlCommand object with the query to insert a book title, then use the AddWithValue method to add a property; the first parameter is a property name, and the second parameter is a value. Then we run the ExecuteNonQueryAsync method to execute the SQL query. And finally, we log the information that the book title was added.

We also have a GetBooks method that retrieves all the book titles from the table, joins them, and returns them as a single string. We create a SQL command with the retrieve query. The ExecuteReaderAsync method returns an object on which we use the Read to read to the last row. Every title is appended to the StringBuilder object, and then it is returned at the end of the method.

Listing 7-2. SQLService class

```
using Microsoft.Data.SqlClient;
using Microsoft.Extensions.Configuration;
using Microsoft.Extensions.Logging;
```

```
using System.Text;

namespace AzureAventure7_SQLDatabase
{
    public interface ISqlService
    {
        Task AddBook(string title);
        Task<string> GetBooks();
    }

    public class SqlService : ISqlService
    {
        private readonly string _connectionString;
        private readonly ILogger<SqlService> _logger;

        public SqlService(IConfiguration configuration,
        ILogger<SqlService> logger)
        {
            _connectionString = configuration.GetValue<string>(
            "SQLConnectionString");
            _logger = logger;
        }

        public async Task AddBook(string title)
        {
            using var connection = new SqlConnection(_
            connectionString);
            await connection.OpenAsync();

            var command = new SqlCommand("INSERT INTO Book
            (Title) VALUES (@title)", connection);
            command.Parameters.AddWithValue("@title", title);

            await command.ExecuteNonQueryAsync();
```

```
        _logger.LogInformation("Added book to the
        database");
    }

    public async Task<string> GetBooks()
    {
        using var connection = new SqlConnection(_
        connectionString);
        await connection.OpenAsync();

        var command = new SqlCommand("SELECT Title FROM
        Book", connection);
        var stringBuilder = new StringBuilder();
        var reader = await command.ExecuteReaderAsync();

        while (reader.Read())
        {
            stringBuilder.Append(reader["Title"]);
            stringBuilder.Append(", ");
        }

        return stringBuilder.ToString();
    }
  }
}
```

The code from Listing 7-3 is a C# function to manage the SQL database. It is interacting with a SQL database using a service interface named ISqlService. The function is triggered by HTTP requests, as indicated by the HttpTrigger attribute, which allows both GET and POST methods and does not require authentication.

When the function is invoked, it performs two operations on the SQL database through the ISqlService using the AddBook method: it adds two new books with the titles "Azure Adventure" and "History of hello worlds."

After adding these books, it retrieves a list of all books in the database with the GetBooks method. The function then sends an HTTP response with the status code OK, indicating that the operation was successful.

Listing 7-3. SQL function

```
using Microsoft.Azure.Functions.Worker;
using Microsoft.Azure.Functions.Worker.Http;
using Microsoft.Extensions.Logging;
using System.Net;

namespace AzureAventure7_SQLDatabase
{
    public class SayHiSql
    {
        private readonly ISqlService _sqlService;

        public SayHiSql(ISqlService sqlService)
        {
            _sqlService = sqlService;
        }

        [Function(nameof(SayHiSql)]
        public async Task<HttpResponseData> Run([HttpTrig
ger(AuthorizationLevel.Anonymous, "get", "post")]
HttpRequestData req)
        {
            await _sqlService.AddBook("Azure Adventure");
            await _sqlService.AddBook("History of hello
            worlds");

            var books = await _sqlService.GetBooks();

            return req.CreateResponse(HttpStatusCode.OK);
```

```
        }
    }
}
```

Deploy Function

To test the function, we are going to deploy it to the Azure Portal. Before running it, we need to set up the necessary environment variable. Copy the connection from the SQL database, go to your database resource, find and click "Show database connection strings," then copy and paste it into the configuration with the name of the SQLConnectionString variable.

To test it, go to your function, then Test and Run; click the Test button. When the program runs, you will see the output in the Logs tab, as shown in Figure 7-11. After this, you can go back to the SQL Editor and query the database to verify the data.

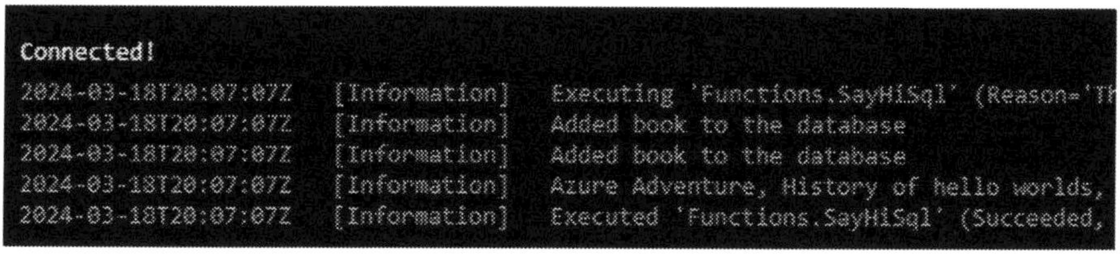

Figure 7-11. *Running SayHiSql function logs*

Summary

In this chapter, we have covered a SQL database on Azure, how to create it, and other options available for it. We have also discussed how to create a simple function to manage data within the database and how to manage a network in the SQL Server to provide access to our application. In the next chapter, we will learn how to hide connection strings in the key vault, use managed identities for authorization, and use a virtual network to enhance security.

CHAPTER 8

Key Vault

When we are working with multiple systems, we need to ensure that they are all properly integrated and communicating with each other effectively. This is crucial for ensuring seamless operation and avoiding any potential issues. Another issue is security. To increase it, we must use, for example, secrets, certificates, or other methods to authenticate components or systems between them. These strings or files are very important and need to be protected and prevented from unauthorized access. This is when a Key Vault can be useful.

Azure Key Vault is a cloud-based service that offers a protected storage for confidential information. It provides a safe way to store and oversee confidential data, such as passwords, certificates, and encryption keys. This service allows you to manage access to these confidential information by implementing access restrictions and auditing to guarantee compliance to regulations. Additionally, it provides the capability to monitor and receive notifications regarding any unauthorized access to your stored confidential information.

Keys are utilized for cryptographic operations such as encryption, decryption, as well as signing and verification processes.

A secret can be used to authorize other systems or services. Secrets should be stored securely and only accessed by authorized users. A secret can be a random string, a connection string, or a verified token.

A certificate can be used as a secret for authentication and authorization purposes.

© Michał Świtalik 2024
M. Świtalik, *Azure Adventures with C#*, https://doi.org/10.1007/979-8-8688-0424-3_8

Overall, Azure Key Vault provides a secure service for managing keys, secrets, and certificates. By utilizing its features effectively, you can enhance the security of your applications and data.

Creating Key Vault

To create a Key Vault, we can use either the Azure Portal or Bicep template:

- Search for Key Vault.

- Click the Create button.

- Fill in the name value and leave other values on default, as shown in Figure 8-1. Change the resource group to your destination.

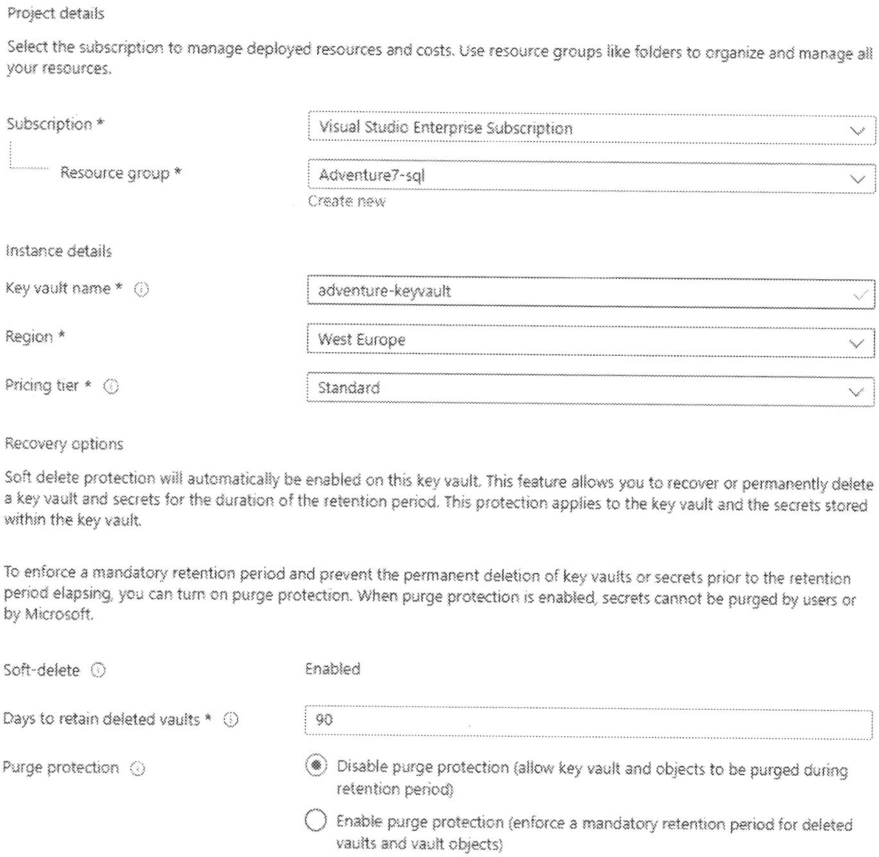

Project details

Select the subscription to manage deployed resources and costs. Use resource groups like folders to organize and manage all your resources.

Subscription * | Visual Studio Enterprise Subscription   ⌄ |

        Resource group * | Adventure7-sql   ⌄ |
                            Create new

Instance details

Key vault name * ⓘ | adventure-keyvault   ⌄ |

Region * | West Europe   ⌄ |

Pricing tier * ⓘ | Standard   ⌄ |

Recovery options

Soft delete protection will automatically be enabled on this key vault. This feature allows you to recover or permanently delete a key vault and secrets for the duration of the retention period. This protection applies to the key vault and the secrets stored within the key vault.

To enforce a mandatory retention period and prevent the permanent deletion of key vaults or secrets prior to the retention period elapsing, you can turn on purge protection. When purge protection is enabled, secrets cannot be purged by users or by Microsoft.

Soft-delete ⓘ   Enabled

Days to retain deleted vaults * ⓘ | 90 |

Purge protection ⓘ   ◉ Disable purge protection (allow key vault and objects to be purged during retention period)

                        ◯ Enable purge protection (enforce a mandatory retention period for deleted vaults and vault objects)

Figure 8-1. *Form for creating a Key Vault*

- In the Access Configuration, change the vault access policy, as shown in Figure 8-2. Role-based access control will be discussed in the next chapter.

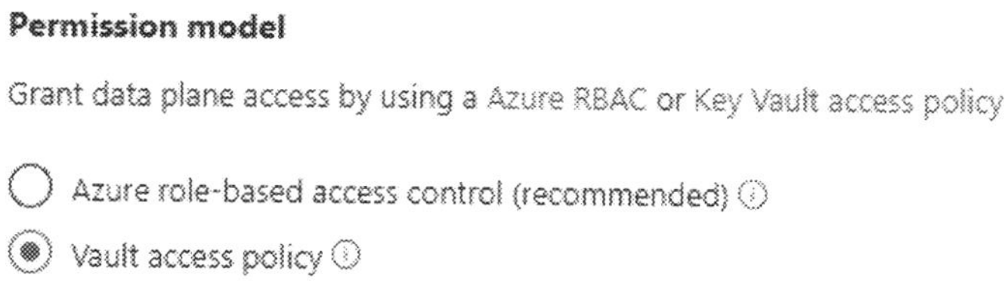

Permission model

Grant data plane access by using a Azure RBAC or Key Vault access policy

◯ Azure role-based access control (recommended) ⓘ

◉ Vault access policy ⓘ

Figure 8-2. *Permissions for Key Vault*

- By default, your account will be added to the access list with all permissions to manage the keys, secrets, and certificate resources.

- In the networking and tags tabs, leave the default option. Ensure that public access is enabled.

- Click the Review + Create button, and finally click the Create button to create your key vault.

After the deployment of the resource, you will receive the vault URI. That you can use in order to connect to the resource from the application. In the information section, you will see the Sku/pricing tier and information if the soft-delete or purge protection is enabled.

Soft-delete means that deleted resources are retained for a period of time before being permanently deleted, allowing for easier recovery if needed.

Purge protection prevents the accidental deletion of resources that are critical to your infrastructure. It will enforce to retain keys in the recycle bin for some period of time.

Create a Secret

Before working with secrets in the application with C# and SDK, let's create a secret in the key vault:

- Go to the key vault and select Secrets on the left menu.

- Click the Generate/Import button.

- A new form will open, like in Figure 8-3. Enter a name and the secret value, which will be masked with a series of asterisks for security purposes. Leave other values on default.

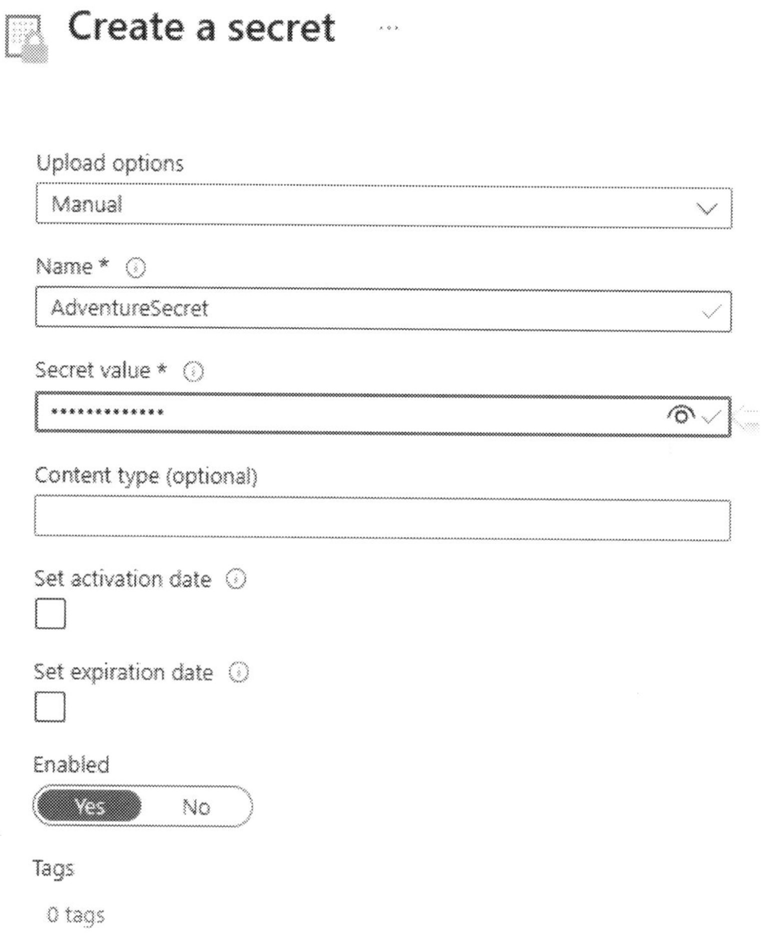

Create a secret ...

Upload options

> Manual   ⌄

Name * ⓘ

> AdventureSecret   ✓

Secret value * ⓘ

> ••••••••••••   👁 ✓

Content type (optional)

>

Set activation date ⓘ

☐

Set expiration date ⓘ

☐

Enabled

(**Yes**   No)

Tags

0 tags

Figure 8-3. *Form to create a secret*

- Then click the Create button to add the secret.

There are also other available options. You can set the activation and expiration dates if you want to work with a time limit for the secret value or even add tags to categorize and organize your secrets.

253

Create a Function

The most common operation in the application is to retrieve the secret value. In this section, we will learn how to retrieve, delete, and create secrets using the C# code to replace them if they require an update.

When you create an HTTP trigger type function, install these packages from the NuGet gallery:

- Azure.Security.KeyVault.Secrets – It contains an object to manage secrets in the key vault.

- Azure.Identity – It can be used in order to authenticate to the key vault from the code.

Get your key vault URI from the information resource and create a variable in the local.settings.json to look like the code in Listing 8-1.

Listing 8-1. Key vault variable

```
"KeyVaultUri": "YourKeyVaultUri"
```

Let's create a VaultService class. Use the code from Listing 8-2. It contains a private read-only field _keyVaultUri, which stores the URI of the Key Vault. This URI is obtained from the application's configuration. The constructor of VaultService accepts an IConfiguration object and uses it to initialize the _keyVaultUri field. The GetSecretAsync method in the VaultService class creates a SecretClient object, which is part of the Azure SDK and is responsible for communicating with the Key Vault. The SecretClient is initialized with the Key Vault URI and a DefaultAzureCredential object, which handles the authentication with Azure services. The method then calls GetSecretAsync on the SecretClient, passing in the secretName. The result of this call is awaited, and the value of the secret is extracted and returned.

Listing 8-2. VaultService class

```
using Azure.Identity;
using Azure.Security.KeyVault.Secrets;
using Microsoft.Extensions.Configuration;

namespace AzureAventure8_KeyVault
{
    public interface IVaultService
    {
        Task<string> GetSecretAsync(string secretName);
    }

    public class VaultService : IVaultService
    {
        private readonly string _keyVaultUri;

        public VaultService(IConfiguration configuration)
        {
            _keyVaultUri = configuration["KeyVaultUri"];
        }

        public async Task<string> GetSecretAsync(string
        secretName)
        {
            var keyVaultClient = new SecretClient(new Uri
            (_keyVaultUri), new DefaultAzureCredential());

            return (await keyVaultClient.GetSecretAsync
            (secretName)).Value.Value;
        }
    }
}
```

Then, change the HTTP function to look like the code in Listing 8-3. We inject the IVaultService into the constructor, and then we can access the secret value using the GetSecretAsync method in the method, and then the value is displayed in the logs of the function.

Listing 8-3. Function code calling the vault service for the secret

```
using Microsoft.AspNetCore.Http;
using Microsoft.AspNetCore.Mvc;
using Microsoft.Azure.Functions.Worker;
using Microsoft.Extensions.Logging;

namespace AzureAventure8_KeyVault
{
    public class VaultFunction
    {
        private readonly ILogger<VaultFunction> _logger;
        private readonly IVaultService _vaultService;

        public VaultFunction(ILogger<VaultFunction> logger,
        IVaultService vaultService)
        {
            _logger = logger;
            _vaultService = vaultService;
        }

        [Function(nameof(ReadSecret))]
        public async Task<IActionResult> ReadSecret([Http
        Trigger(AuthorizationLevel.Anonymous, "get", "post")]
        HttpRequest req)
        {
            var secretName = "AdventureSecret";
            var secret = await _vaultService.GetSecretAsync
            (secretName);
```

```
        _logger.LogInformation($"Secret: {secret}");

        return new OkResult();
    }
  }
}
```

Ensure that you have added to the DI a new service to the collection of services as shown in Listing 8-4.

Listing 8-4. Setting the DI for VaultService

```
services.AddSingleton<IVaultService, VaultService>();
```

Ensure you are logged in to the Azure cloud in Visual Studio before running the function. Follow these steps to ensure this:

- Go to Tools.

- Then select the Options.

- Type in the search bar the Azure word, then select the Azure Service Authentication option, as shown in Figure 8-4.

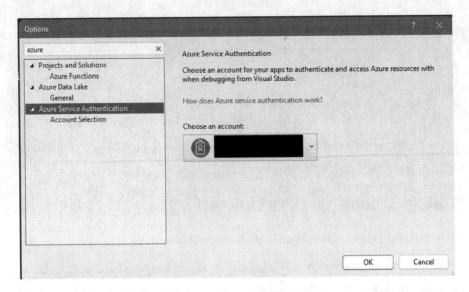

Figure 8-4. *Authentication for Azure in Visual Studio*

- If your account is not appearing or there is an error, then enter your credentials to authenticate your account.

If you run the program and request the API, you will be automatically authenticated using your Azure account. Then you should see the secret displayed in the log console. For future security, do not log the secrets, keys, or certificate thumbprints in the logs.

Let's add two new methods to the service class from Listing 8-5: delete and update secrets. In both, we have created a SecretClient object with the URI and a DefaultAzureCredential object. Then we use the StartDeleteSecretAsync method to start the process of deleting a secret or the SetSecretAsync method to update a secret.

Add these methods as well to the interface.

Listing 8-5. New methods for the VaultService class

```
public async Task DeleteSecretAsync(string secretName)
{
    var keyVaultClient = new SecretClient(new Uri
    (_keyVaultUri), new DefaultAzureCredential());

    await keyVaultClient.StartDeleteSecretAsync(secretName);
}

public async Task UpdateSecretAsync(string secretName, string
secretValue)
{
    var keyVaultClient = new SecretClient(new Uri
    (_keyVaultUri), new DefaultAzureCredential());

    await keyVaultClient.SetSecretAsync(secretName,
    secretValue);
}
```

Change the code of the function to look like in Listing 8-6 to create a flow to manage secrets. The process begins with updating a secret using the UpdateSecretAsync method, where secretName is the identifier for the secret and "Adventure" is the new value being assigned. Following the update, the GetSecretAsync method retrieves the updated secret to confirm the change, and the result is logged using LogInformation.

Subsequently, the code attempts to delete the secret with DeleteSecretAsync. After deletion, it tries to retrieve the deleted secret to ensure it has been removed. If the secret is still retrievable, it logs the information. However, if the secret is not found, which is the expected outcome after deletion, an error is logged using LogError. This error handling is crucial, as it confirms the secret's deletion and ensures that sensitive information is not left accessible.

Listing 8-6. New code flow for the HTTP function

```
await _vaultService.UpdateSecretAsync(secretName, "Adventure");
var secretUpdated = await _vaultService.
GetSecretAsync(secretName);
_logger.LogInformation($"Secret updated with {secretUpdated}");

await _vaultService.DeleteSecretAsync(secretName);
try
{
    var secretDeleted = await _vaultService.
    GetSecretAsync(secretName);
    _logger.LogInformation($"Secret deleted: {secretDeleted}");
} catch
{
    _logger.LogError("Secret not found");
}
```

Adding the Application Permissions

Now we are going to apply permissions to access the Key Vault. Adding the application permissions will allow the code to securely access and manage secrets within the Key Vault. This step is essential for maintaining data security and preventing unauthorized access to sensitive information.

Before adding Azure Function access to the Key Vault, you need to enable the identity. It will be discussed more in the next chapter about Managed Identity.

- Go to your Azure Function.

- Go to the Identity setting.

- Switch the button to On, as shown in Figure 8-5.

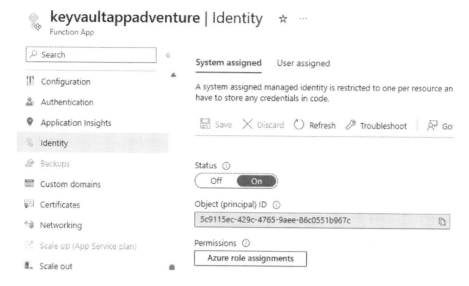

Figure 8-5. Identity enabled for Azure Function

Now in the Entra ID, a new app will be registered; you can go there and search for it and check its properties.

In order to grant access to the service, follow these steps:

- Go to the key vault service.

- Click the access policies.

- Click the Create button.

- You can select a configuration from the template. However, it is good advice to limit permissions. Now select permissions as shown in Figure 8-6.

261

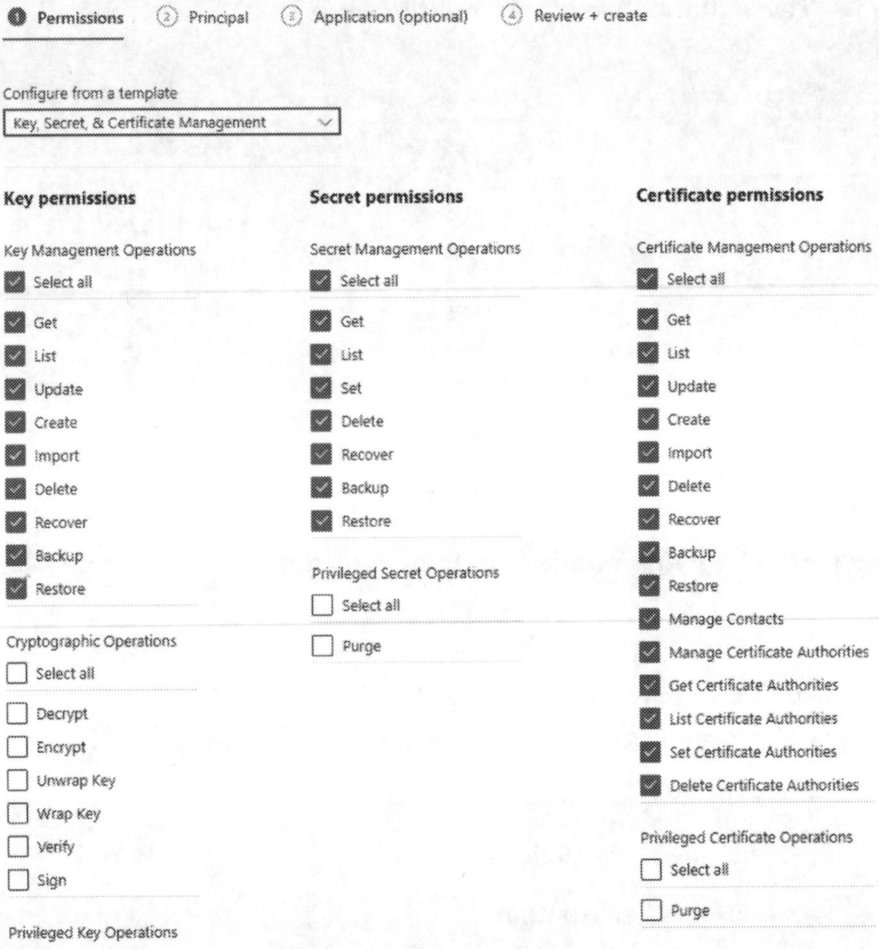

① Permissions   ② Principal   ③ Application (optional)   ④ Review + create

Configure from a template

Key, Secret, & Certificate Management   ⌄

Key permissions

Key Management Operations

☑ Select all

☑ Get
☑ List
☑ Update
☑ Create
☑ Import
☑ Delete
☑ Recover
☑ Backup
☑ Restore

Cryptographic Operations

☐ Select all

☐ Decrypt
☐ Encrypt
☐ Unwrap Key
☐ Wrap Key
☐ Verify
☐ Sign

Privileged Key Operations

Secret permissions

Secret Management Operations

☑ Select all

☑ Get
☑ List
☑ Set
☑ Delete
☑ Recover
☑ Backup
☑ Restore

Privileged Secret Operations

☐ Select all

☐ Purge

Certificate permissions

Certificate Management Operations

☑ Select all

☑ Get
☑ List
☑ Update
☑ Create
☑ Import
☑ Delete
☑ Recover
☑ Backup
☑ Restore
☑ Manage Contacts
☑ Manage Certificate Authorities
☑ Get Certificate Authorities
☑ List Certificate Authorities
☑ Set Certificate Authorities
☑ Delete Certificate Authorities

Privileged Certificate Operations

☐ Select all

☐ Purge

Figure 8-6. *Permissions for Key Vault*

- In the Principal tab, select your account.

- In the Application tab, search for your app registration, as shown in Figure 8-7.

Create an access policy   ...

adventure-keyvault

Permissions   ✓ Principal   ③ **Application (optional)**

Authorizes this application to perform the specified permissions on the U:
Use the new embedded experience to select an application. The previous

🔍   keyvaultappadventur

keyvaultappadventure
0e11d88f-aaa4-4598-8333-dcc2481f4662

Figure 8-7. *Searching for the application*

- Click Next and click the Create button to finish.

If you deploy your application and run the program, you should see the logs as shown in Figure 8-8. The message indicates if the secret was read, updated, or deleted correctly and it fails on reading.

Figure 8-8. *Logs of running program*

Recovering a Secret

In order to recover the secret, you can do it by UI, as shown in Figure 8-9.
Go to the secrets in your key vault, then click the Recover button. Now you
can select deleted secrets and click the Recover button to move them back.
An alternative for this is to use the StartRecoverDeletedSecret method
from the SecretClient object.

Figure 8-9. *Recovering a deleted secret*

Create a Certificate

Let's see how easy it is to generate or import a certificate in the Azure Key Vault:

- Go to the service.

- Go to the Certificates section.

- Click the Import/Generate button.

- In Figure 8-10, you can see how to fill in fields in order to generate a new certificate. Set the "Lifetime action type" field to automatically renew it before it expires. Then click "Create" to generate the new certificate.

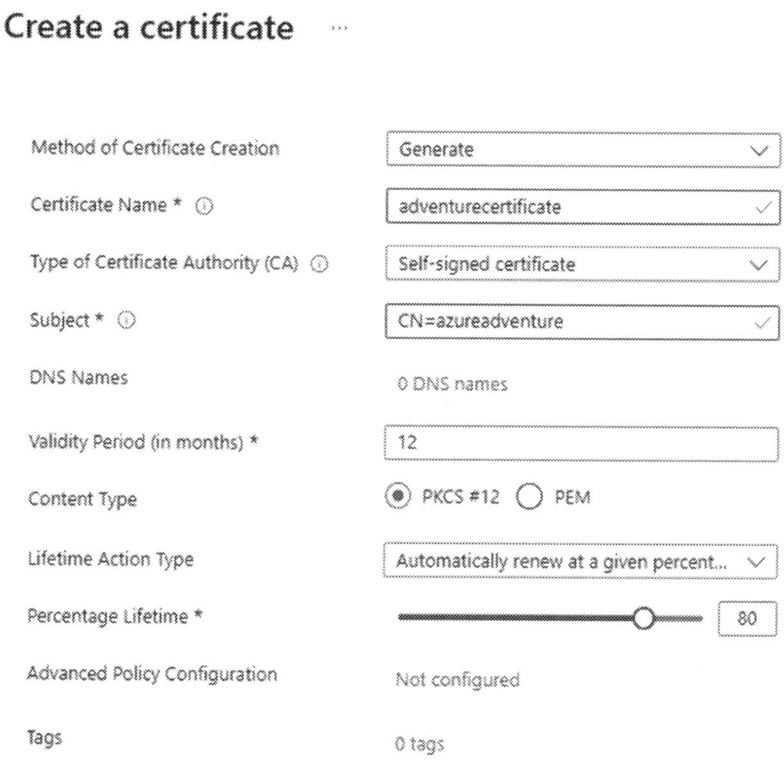

Create a certificate

Method of Certificate Creation	Generate
Certificate Name *	adventurecertificate
Type of Certificate Authority (CA)	Self-signed certificate
Subject *	CN=azureadventure
DNS Names	0 DNS names
Validity Period (in months) *	12
Content Type	⦿ PKCS #12 ◯ PEM
Lifetime Action Type	Automatically renew at a given percent...
Percentage Lifetime *	80
Advanced Policy Configuration	Not configured
Tags	0 tags

Figure 8-10. *Generating a certificate*

In the advanced policy configuration, you can set additional options if it's required, and we will set the default values. You can as well set the tags to group certificates together for easier management.

After creating a certificate, it should be visible in the Certificates list. Install the Azure.Security.KeyVault.Certificates package to the project for operations on certificates in the Azure Key Vault. Once the package is installed, you can start managing certificates securely.

We are adding two methods from Listing 8-7. GetSecretCertificateAsync is a method that retrieves a secret certificate from the Key Vault using the specified name and returns it as X509Certificate2. Inside, it creates a SecretClient. When we use the GetSecretAsync method to get the base64 of the certificate, it is converted to a string with the FromBase64String method, so we can create a new X509Certificate2 object with this string. This new object can then be used for authentication purposes. The GetCertificateAsync method returns a KeyVaultCertificateWithPolicy type object that contains the certificate along with its policy details. In this method, we create the CertificateClient object, then use the GetCertificateAsync method of the CertificateClient object to retrieve the certificate information.

Listing 8-7. Methods to manage a certificate

```
public async Task<X509Certificate2> GetSecretCertificateAsync
(string certificateName)
{
    var keyVaultClient = new SecretClient(new Uri
    (_keyVaultUri), new DefaultAzureCredential());

    var secret = await keyVaultClient.GetSecretAsync
    (certificateName);

    return new X509Certificate2(Convert.
    FromBase64String(secret.Value.Value));
}
```

```
public async Task<KeyVaultCertificateWithPolicy>
GetCertificateAsync(string certificateName)
{
    var keyVaultClient = new CertificateClient(new Uri
    (_keyVaultUri), new DefaultAzureCredential());

    var certificate = await keyVaultClient.GetCertificateAsync
    (certificateName);

    return certificate.Value;
}
```

Listing 8-8 has a process for retrieving and logging information about a digital certificate from a secure vault service using previously created methods. Initially, a variable certificateName is declared with the value "adventurecertificate," which is presumably the identifier for the certificate we wish to retrieve. The code then asynchronously calls a method GetCertificateAsync from an object _vaultService, passing the certificate name as a parameter. This method call returns a certificate object, which contains various properties about the certificate, such as its name and the date before which it is not valid (NotBefore).

Listing 8-8. New flow to use the methods

```
var certificateName = "adventurecertificate";
var certificate = await _vaultService.GetCertificateAsync
(certificateName);
_logger.LogInformation($"Certificate name {certificate.Name},
expiry date {certificate.Properties.NotBefore}");

var certificateDownloaded = await _vaultService.Download
CertificateAsync(certificateName);
_logger.LogInformation($"Certificate2: {certificateDownloaded.
Thumbprint}");
```

Figure 8-11 shows logs of the running program with the flow we have previously created. You can see that it displays the certificate object with the properties we wanted it to show us.

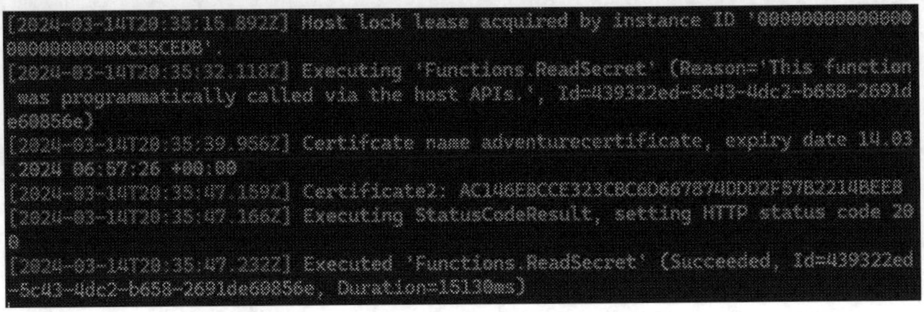

Figure 8-11. *Logging of retrieving the certificate*

Bicep Script for Deployment

Listing 8-9 is a script that helps automate the deployment of the Key Vault resource with a Standard tier and with the provided name in the object. The "Standard" tier encrypts only using a software key. To have HSM (hardware security module), you have to use a Premium tier. The property name is set to "adventure-keyvault"; this is how our resource will be named globally. The script is using your default selected subscription, tenant, and resource group.

Listing 8-9. A bicep script to deploy Key Vault service

```
resource keyVault 'Microsoft.KeyVault/vaults@2023-07-01' = {
  name: 'adventure-keyvault'
  location: resourceGroup().location
  properties: {
    tenantId: subscription().tenantId
```

```
    sku: {
      family: 'A'
      name: 'Standard'
    }
  }
}
```

Summary

Azure Key Vault is a very useful service for storing and managing sensitive information such as secrets, certificates, and connection strings. After this chapter, you should know how to create a secret or generate a certificate with an automatic renewal option. We have provided example code listings on how to use them in the function and also examples of bicep script to automate deployment.

It is a good practice to limit access to the Key Vault to authorized and trusted users only to manage sensitive data. This way, we can limit chances of leaking information that can be used to get access to internal systems.

CHAPTER 9

Managed Identity and RBAC

When working on many services in Azure, we usually use secrets or connection strings in order to connect and authenticate. This way, we have security. What if we could give up connection strings and just call for data? This is when the Managed Identity comes in handy. Managed Identity allows services to authenticate to Azure services without the need for secrets or connection strings. This is a much more secure and convenient option for accessing data from Azure services. This is especially useful for applications running in Azure that need to access other Azure resources securely. This eliminates the need to store sensitive information within the codebase or in the Key Vault.

The process is straightforward: when a resource with Managed Identity attempts to access another service, it requests a token from Entra ID. Entra ID then validates the identity and returns a token, which the resource can use to prove its identity to the service it's trying to access. This token-based approach is a secure method of authentication and authorization, ensuring that credentials are not stored in code or configuration files, thereby reducing the risk of credential leaks.

System-Assigned Identity is created only for one resource, so it can't be shared between multiple services. It automatically creates an identity in Entra ID. It is deleted when a resource is deleted. This is a con because then you have to set up permissions to access other resources again.

M. Świtalik, *Azure Adventures with C#*, https://doi.org/10.1007/979-8-8688-0424-3_9

User-Assigned Identity is created for multiple resources. It can be assigned to multiple resources in Azure. One resource can also be assigned multiple identities.

Managed Identity also simplifies the management of permissions and access control. By using Azure's role-based access control (RBAC), you can define what resources the identity can access and at what level. This granular control allows for a more secure and manageable environment, as permissions can be adjusted without changing the application code. This helps to reduce the risk of unauthorized access and potential security breaches.

Managed Identity in Azure Function

In this chapter, we will explore how Managed Identity can be used in Azure Functions to securely access Azure resources without the need for credentials in the code. We will also show how to call other functions securely without using an API key or other secrets.

Firstly, create an Azure function by following the steps outlined in Chapter 2. Then turn on the identity in the function with the following steps:

- Go to the Azure Function resource.

- On the left menu, select "Identity."

- Change the switch to "On" and click the Save button.

It will automatically create an identity for this function in the Entra ID. Then create another function with app authentication as shown in Chapter 2.

If the application is authenticated with an Azure Application Registration, then it's possible to use this identity for authentication and authorization in the application.

To allow the app to acquire an access token from the authentication application, we have to create a role and add the caller app registration to the authentication application.

The first step is to create a "Customer" role in the authentication app registration.

- Go to the Entra ID; find it in the app registration using either the name or ID.

- Go to the Roles settings.

- Click the "Create app role" button.

- Enter Consumer as the value as shown in Figure 9-1.

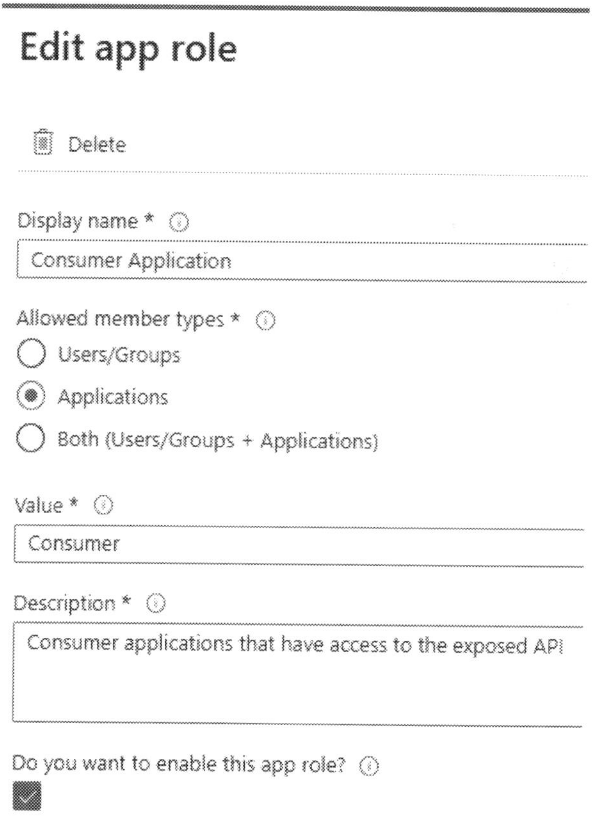

Figure 9-1. *Adding a new application role*

When it is done, copy the identity of the authentication app and get the identity of the consumer role. To assign the caller app registration to the authentication app registration, use the script from Listing 9-1. Before running it, install the Azure PowerShell package with the Azure AD module. This will allow you to successfully assign the caller app registration to the authentication app registration. The script's first command will open a browser to log in to Azure. Then we provide the function name to get its app registration. Then we get the service principal of the authentication application. Finally, we assign the caller app registration to the authentication app registration using the consumer role.

Listing 9-1. PowerShell script to assign a consumer role

```
Connect-AzureAD
$clientAppReg = Get-AzureADServicePrincipal -SearchString
'adventure-caller'
$authenticationAppRegistration = Get-AzureADServicePrincipal
-ObjectId {enter-auth-app-object-id}
$consumerRoleId = '{enter-consumer-role-id}'
New-AzureADServiceAppRoleAssignment -ObjectId $clientAppReg.
ObjectId -PrincipalId $clientAppReg.ObjectId -ResourceId
$authenticationAppRegistration.ObjectId -id $consumerRoleId
```

Create a Visual Studio function project; change the default HTTP trigger class to have a simple return object as shown in Listing 9-2.

Listing 9-2. Hello function code

```
using Microsoft.AspNetCore.Http;
using Microsoft.AspNetCore.Mvc;
using Microsoft.Azure.Functions.Worker;

namespace AzureAdventure8_Identity
{
```

```
public class HelloFunctionHttpTrigger
{
    [Function("HelloFunction")]
    public IActionResult HelloFunction([HttpTrigger(Authori
    zationLevel.Anonymous, "get", "post")] HttpRequest req)
    {
        return new OkObjectResult("Hello from the other
        side!");
    }
}
}
```

In the second function, we are returning the message "Hello from the other side!" as an OkObjectResult.

Let's create the second function to call the API. Then add the Azure.Identity NuGet package to the project. This package is helping programmers authenticate with Azure services easily and securely. We will add the GetDataService service class, which has the logic to get access from the identity and then calls the function to get the data. Listing 9-3 has the class of this service. The GetDataAsync method handles the API call asynchronously. Inside the method, we use the private method GetAccessToken to retrieve the access token for the API call, which utilizes Azure's DefaultAzureCredential class to simplify authentication against various Azure services. Once the token is obtained, it creates an HttpClient instance to send an HTTP GET request to a specified URL (httpFunctionApiUrl). If the request is successful, it reads the response content as a string and logs the information. In the event of failure, it logs an error with the status code.

The GetAccessToken method is particularly interesting as it demonstrates how to obtain an Azure Entra ID token for a specific resource, which in this case is represented by a placeholder <function-api-guid>. This token is then used to authenticate the HTTP request made by the HttpClient. The token is passed in the Authorization header of the request to ensure proper authentication and authorization. The <function-api-guid> placeholder is a guid from the identity settings of the application.

Listing 9-3. GetDataService class code

```
using Azure.Core;
using Azure.Identity;
using Microsoft.Extensions.Logging;

namespace AzureAdventure8_Caller
{
    public interface IGetDataService
    {
        Task<string> GetDataAsync();
    }

    public class GetDataService : IGetDataService
    {
        private readonly ILogger<GetDataService> _logger;

        public GetDataService(ILogger<GetDataService> logger)
        {
            _logger = logger;
        }

        public async Task<string> GetDataAsync()
        {
            try
            {
                var token = GetAccessToken();

                using var httpClient = new HttpClient();
```

```csharp
        httpClient.DefaultRequestHeaders.
        Add("Authorization", $"Bearer {token}");

        var response = await httpClient.GetAsync
        ("httpFunctionApiUrl");
        if (response.IsSuccessStatusCode)
        {
            var content = await response.Content.
            ReadAsStringAsync();
            _logger.LogInformation($"Function response:
            {content}");
        }
        else
        {
            _logger.LogError($"Error calling the
            function. Status code: {response.
            StatusCode}");
        }
    }
    catch (Exception ex)
    {
        _logger.LogError($"Error: {ex.Message}");
    }

    return "";
}

private string GetAccessToken()
{
    var credential = new DefaultAzureCredential();

    var resource = "api://<function-api-guid>/.default";
```

```
        var token = credential.GetToken(new
        TokenRequestContext(new[] { resource }));

        return token.Token;
    }
  }
}
```

Add the service injection to the HTTP trigger function as shown in Listing 9-4 and call the GetDataAsync method to get the data from the other API. Don't forget to add the service to the injection services in the Program class, as shown in Listing 9-5.

Listing 9-4. Using the class to get the data in the function

```
using Microsoft.AspNetCore.Http;
using Microsoft.Azure.Functions.Worker;

namespace AzureAdventure8_Caller
{
    public class CallerFunctionHttpTrigger
    {
        private readonly IGetDataService _getDataService;

        public CallerFunctionHttpTrigger(IGetDataService
        getDataService)
        {
            _getDataService = getDataService;
        }

        [Function("Caller")]
        public async Task Caller([HttpTrigger(Authorization
        Level.Anonymous, "get", "post")] HttpRequest req)
```

```
    {
        await _getDataService.GetDataAsync();
    }
  }
}
```

Listing 9-5. Adding the service class to injection configuration

```
services.AddScoped<IGetDataService, GetDataService>();
```

To test it, we need to deploy both functions to their respective resources. Then go to the monitor and use the test and run function to ensure that the integration is functioning correctly. In the logs, you should see the output from the function indicating that the integration was successful.

Storage with Managed Identity

By enabling a Managed Identity for your Azure function, you can grant it permissions to access and manage storage resources directly, eliminating the need to manage storage keys or connection strings. In this chapter, we will give an example of how to use it to access storage resources within your Azure function.

There are many roles that can be used for the storage account; the most important for us to use are as follows:

- Storage Blob Data Contributor – Allowing read, write, and delete access to storage containers and blobs

- Storage Blob Data Owner – Allowing full control over storage containers and blobs, including assigning roles

- Storage Blob Data Reader – Allowing read-only access to storage containers and blobs

- Storage Queue Data Contributor – Allowing read, add, and update access to storage queues

- Storage Queue Data Message Processor – Allowing read, add, update, and delete access to storage queues

- Storage Queue Data Message Sender – Allowing read, add, and send access to storage queues

- Storage Queue Data Reader – Allowing read access to storage queues

- Storage Table Data Contributor – Allowing read, write, and delete access to storage tables

- Storage Table Data Reader – Allowing read access to storage tables

To assign a role to the application, we must first turn on identity in the settings. Then you can assign the appropriate role based on the desired level of access needed for the application. Go to the resource, find and go to Access Control (IAM), click "Add role assignment," select the role, and choose the application.

To authenticate, use the code from Listing 9-6. In the provided code snippet, Azure.Identity is a namespace that contains classes for managing authentication across Azure services. The DefaultAzureCredential class is part of this namespace and is used to simplify the authentication process when interacting with Azure services. It provides a seamless authentication experience by attempting multiple authentication methods in a specific order, catering to a variety of development environments, from local development to deployment in Azure.

The code defines an interface, IStorageService, which outlines three methods for accessing different Azure storage services: blobs, tables, and queues. The StorageService class implements this interface, providing concrete methods to retrieve clients for these services. By using DefaultAzureCredential, the code automatically selects the best authentication method based on the environment. All created clients will have different permissions depending on the assigned role for the application in the resource.

Listing 9-6. Creating clients with Managed Identity

```
using Azure.Data.Tables;
using Azure.Identity;
using Azure.Storage.Blobs;
using Azure.Storage.Queues;

namespace AzureAdventure8_Storage
{
    public interface IStorageService
    {
        BlobContainerClient GetBlobContainerClient();
        TableClient GetCloudTableClient();
        QueueClient GetQueueClient();
    }

    public class StorageService : IStorageService    {
        public BlobContainerClient GetBlobContainerClient()
        {
            var blobServiceClient = new BlobServiceClient(new
            Uri("https://storageName.blob.core.windows.net"),
                new DefaultAzureCredential());

            return blobServiceClient.GetBlobContainerClient
            ("container");
        }

        public QueueClient GetQueueClient()
        {
```

```
        return new QueueClient(new Uri("https://
        storageAccountName.queue.core.windows.net/
        queueName"), new DefaultAzureCredential());
    }

    public TableClient GetCloudTableClient()
    {
        return new TableClient(new Uri("https://
        accountName.table.core.windows.net/"), "tableName",
        new DefaultAzureCredential());
    }
  }
}
```

In order to use Managed Identity with triggers, you have to set up variables with the following patterns:

- AdventureConnection_blobServiceUri – For example,
  `https://adventurestorage.blob.core.windows.net`

- AdventureConnection_queueServiceUri – For example,
  `https://adventurestorage.queue.core.windows.net`

Then, in the function queue trigger attribute, set the name for the Connection string. This will be a prefix with the same value as the variable name, as shown in Listing 9-7.

Listing 9-7. Queue trigger with connection

```
public void Run([QueueTrigger("incoming-reports", Connection =
"AzureAdventure")] string message)
```

Service Bus with Managed Identity

The Managed Identity can also be used with the Service Bus with the following roles:

- Service Bus Data Owner – Allowing full access to topics, queues, and messages

- Service Bus Data Sender – Allowing to send messages to queues and topics

- Service Bus Data Receiver – Allowing to receive messages from queues and topics

Listing 9-8 has the GetClient method, which returns the ServiceBusClient object instance to interact with Azure Service Bus. It is using the DefaultAzureCredential to authenticate the client.

Listing 9-8. ServiceBusService class

```
using Azure.Identity;
using Azure.Messaging.ServiceBus;

namespace AzureAdventure8_ServiceBus
{
    public interface IServiceBusService
    {
        ServiceBusClient GetClient();
    }

    public class ServiceBusService : IServiceBusService
    {
        public ServiceBusClient GetClient()
        {
```

```
            return new ServiceBusClient("busname.servicebus.
            windows.net", new DefaultAzureCredential());
        }
    }
}
```

Key Vault with Managed Identity

By default, we can't connect to the Key Vault using connection strings or secrets. We need to use Azure Managed Identity to connect to the Key Vault. As in previous examples, we use the DefaultAzureCredential class to easily authenticate the client. Code using the default credentials is presented in Listing 9-9. To change using the RBAC, go to the Access Configuration settings, then choose "Azure role-based access control" and click the Save button.

Listing 9-10 presents how we can add a reference in the Configuration settings to the Key Vault to securely store sensitive information such as connection strings or API secrets. This can help ensure that only authorized users have access to these sensitive pieces of information, because they can't see the value itself. Then, in the application, we don't have to use the SecretClient class. Instead, we can use the IConfiguration interface and read a variable from the environment. We have to remember to always add the role to the application.

Listing 9-9. KeyVaultService

```
using Azure.Identity;
using Azure.Security.KeyVault.Secrets;

namespace AzureAdventure8_KeyVault
{
```

```
public interface IKeyVaultService
{
    SecretClient GetSecretClient();
}

public class KeyVaultService : IKeyVaultService
{
    public SecretClient GetSecretClient()
    {
        return new SecretClient(new Uri
        ("https://adventurevault.vault.azure.net/"), new
        DefaultAzureCredential());
    }
}
}
```

Listing 9-10. Key Vault variable reference in the Azure Function configuration

```
@Microsoft.KeyVault(SecretUri=https://adventurevault.vault.
azure.net/secrets/mysecret/)
```

These are useful roles to use in the Key Vault and assign to other applications or users:

- Key Vault Administrator – Allowing access to and managing secrets, keys, and certificates

- Key Vault Reader – Granting read-only permissions to secrets, keys, and certificates

- Key Vault Certificates Officer – Allowing to manage certificates

- Key Vault Certificate User – Granting only permissions to use certificates

- Key Vault Secrets Officer – Allowing to manage secrets

- Key Vault Secrets User – Granting only permissions to use secrets

Summary

In this chapter, we have presented examples of how to use managed identities in order to have much more secure resources without using secrets or connection strings. The examples demonstrated the importance of utilizing managed identities to enhance security measures within applications. We have also discussed the commonly used roles, which we can use to grant different levels of access to resources within our applications or to users.

CHAPTER 10

Virtual Network

In this chapter, we will add a virtual network as an additional layer of security for our resources. This will help ensure that only authorized traffic can access our resources. Additionally, setting up a virtual network will help prevent unauthorized access and protect sensitive data. By creating boundaries and rules for communication between resources, we can control the flow of traffic more effectively.

A virtual network is not a physical network but rather a software-defined network that allows for greater flexibility and security measures. This added layer of security will provide peace of mind knowing that our resources are better protected from potential threats. It is essentially a representation of one's own network in the cloud, complete with a range of IP addresses, subnets, and associated network devices such as network security groups (NSGs). Virtual networks provide safe communication between resources, the Internet, and on-premises networks.

The network security group contains rules to allow or block traffic either from specific IP addresses, ports, or virtual networks. Each rule has its own priority. The higher it is set, the higher the precedence it takes over other rules.

Figure 10-1 displays how we connect a Storage Account and Azure Function with a virtual network. They are connected with the use of service endpoints. They are the entry points for communication in and out of the virtual network. Now they can securely communicate with each other without needing to traverse the public Internet. However, services are still visible to resources outside of the virtual network.

© Michał Świtalik 2024
M. Świtalik, *Azure Adventures with C#*, https://doi.org/10.1007/979-8-8688-0424-3_10

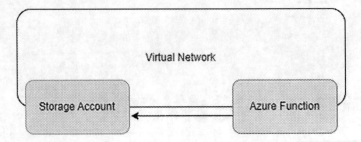

Figure 10-1. *Virtual network with service endpoint*

Figure 10-2 shows a visual representation of the communication flow between the private endpoints within the virtual network. In this case, the private endpoints are able to securely exchange data without exposure to the public Internet. The transmitted data is sent through an encrypted tunnel to ensure privacy and security. This solution is ideal for organizations that require strict data security measures. However, it is more resource-intensive and may require more maintenance than other solutions.

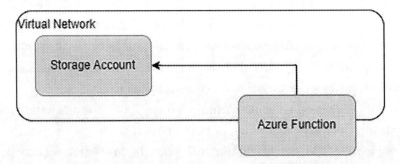

Figure 10-2. *Virtual network with private endpoint*

Deploying Virtual Network with Bicep

In the ARM template from Listing 10-1, the "networkSecurityGroup" resource is defined with the name 'adventure-nsg' and an empty array of "securityRules," indicating that no specific traffic rules have been set at this point. The "location" property typically refers to the Azure region where the NSG will be deployed, and it is assumed to be defined elsewhere in the template.

The "vnet" resource is named 'adventure-vnet' and is also assigned a "location." The "addressSpace" property defines the IP range that the virtual network will use. The "subnets" array consists of a solitary subnet called 'adventure-subnet', which employs the identical address prefix as the vnet. The network subnet is linked to the previously specified network security group (NSG) via the "networkSecurityGroup" field, which contains the ID of the NSG. Additionally, a "serviceEndpoints" is set up for several service endpoints, allowing them to use the subnet.

Listing 10-1. Virtual network script

```
param location string = resourceGroup().location

resource networkSecurityGroup 'Microsoft.Network/
networkSecurityGroups@2023-09-01' = {
  name: 'adventure-nsg'
  location: location
  properties: {
    securityRules: []
  }
}

resource vnet 'Microsoft.Network/
virtualNetworks@2023-09-01' = {
  name: 'adventure-vnet'
  location: location
  properties: {
    addressSpace: {
      addressPrefixes: [
        '10.0.0.0/24'
```

```
      ]
    }
    subnets: [
      {
        name: 'adventure-subnet'
        properties: {
          addressPrefix: '10.0.0.0/24'
          networkSecurityGroup: {
            id: networkSecurityGroup.id
          }
          serviceEndpoints: [
            {
              service: 'Microsoft.AzureActiveDirectory'
              locations: [
                '*'

              ]
            }
            {
              service: 'Microsoft.Sql'
              locations: [
                *
              ]
            }
            {
              service: 'Microsoft.KeyVault'
              locations: [
                '*'
              ]
            }
            {
              service: 'Microsoft.Storage'
```

```
      locations: [
        '*'
      ]
    }
    {
      service: 'Microsoft.Web'
      locations: [
        '*'
      ]
    }
  ]
  delegations: [
    {
      name: 'Microsoft.Web.serverFarms'
      properties: {
        serviceName: 'Microsoft.Web/serverFarms'
      }
    }
  ]
}
    }
  ]
}
}
```

Connecting Azure Function

Listing 10-2 is a continuation of the previous script for virtual networks. This illustrates the method of connecting a virtual network to an Azure function. Such integration allows the Azure Function to securely communicate with other Azure services within the same network. It is done in the "properties" settings, where we provide the subnet ID from the previously created vnet object.

Listing 10-2. Virtual network for function

```
resource functionApp 'Microsoft.Web/sites@2023-01-01' = {
  name: 'adventure-network'
  kind: 'functionapp'
  location: location
  properties: {
    virtualNetworkSubnetId: vnet.properties.subnets[0].id
  }
  // other properties are omitted for brevity
}
```

Connecting Key Vault

Listing 10-3 shows how to integrate the virtual network with the key vault resource. It is done in the "networkAcls" property. We set the default action to deny all network traffic and then specified the virtualNetworkRules property with a subnet ID to bypass this rule. If you are going to access the vault through the portal, remember to add your current public IP in the script or add it in the Network tab in the resource.

Listing 10-3. Key Vault resource with the virtual network

```
resource keyVault 'Microsoft.KeyVault/vaults@2023-07-01' = {
  name: 'adventure-kv'
  location: location
  properties: {
    tenantId: subscription().tenantId
    sku: {
```

```
    family: 'A'
    name: 'standard'
  }
  networkAcls: {
    bypass: 'None'
    defaultAction: 'Deny'
    ipRules: []
    virtualNetworkRules: [
      {
        id: vnet.properties.subnets[0].id
        ignoreMissingVnetServiceEndpoint: false
      }
    ]
  }
  accessPolicies: []
}
}
```

Connecting Storage Account

Listing 10-4 shows how to ingrate with the storage account. We set the "allowBlobPublicAccess" flag to false so that only authorized users can access the blobs. In the "networkAcls" object property, we deny all actions, and in the "virtualNetworkRules" property, we add a virtual network rule to allow access only from specific virtual networks.

Listing 10-4. Virtual network for storage account

```
resource storageAccount 'Microsoft.Storage/
storageAccounts@2023-01-01' = {
  name: 'adventurestorage'
  location: location
```

```
sku: {
  name: 'Standard_LRS'
}
kind:'StorageV2'
properties: {
  supportsHttpsTrafficOnly: true
  allowBlobPublicAccess: false
  networkAcls: {
    bypass: 'None'
    virtualNetworkRules: [
      {
        id: vnet.properties.subnets[0].id
        action: 'Allow'
      }
    ]
    defaultAction: 'Deny'
  }
  minimumTlsVersion: 'TLS1_2'
}
// other properties are omitted for brevity
}
```

Connecting SQL Server

By default, SQL Server is disabled from public access, and you need to turn on the option to enable Azure service connection to the server. This can be improved by creating and adding it to the virtual network.

Finally, in Listing 10-5, we integrate the virtual network with the SQL Server. In the "property" object, we set the "virtualNetworkSubnetId" property to the virtual network subnet ID. In this example, we use the resourceId function to concatenate the resource ID.

Listing 10-5. Virtual network for SQL Server

```
resource server 'Microsoft.Sql/servers@2020-11-01-preview' = {
  name: 'adventure-server'
  location: location
  // other properties are omitted for brevity
}

resource serverName_subnet 'Microsoft.Sql/servers/
virtualNetworkRules@2021-02-01-preview' = {
  parent: server
  name: 'adventure-subnet'
  properties: {
    virtualNetworkSubnetId: resourceId('Microsoft.
    Network/virtualNetworks/subnets', 'adventure-vnet',
    'adventure-subnet')
    ignoreMissingVnetServiceEndpoint: false
  }
}
```

When the script is deployed, you can go to the Network tab in the Azure Portal to view the virtual network configuration. Every resource can have a different set of available options to view and modify. In the Key Vault and SQL Server resources, you have to add your IP address to the firewall rules for them to be accessible.

Manually Creating and Configuring

The creation of the virtual network can also be done through the user interface. To create a virtual network, follow these steps:

- Search for Virtual Network in the Marketplace.

- Click the "Create" button.

- Enter the required values, like the name, region,
  subscription, and resource group, as shown in
  Figure 10-3.

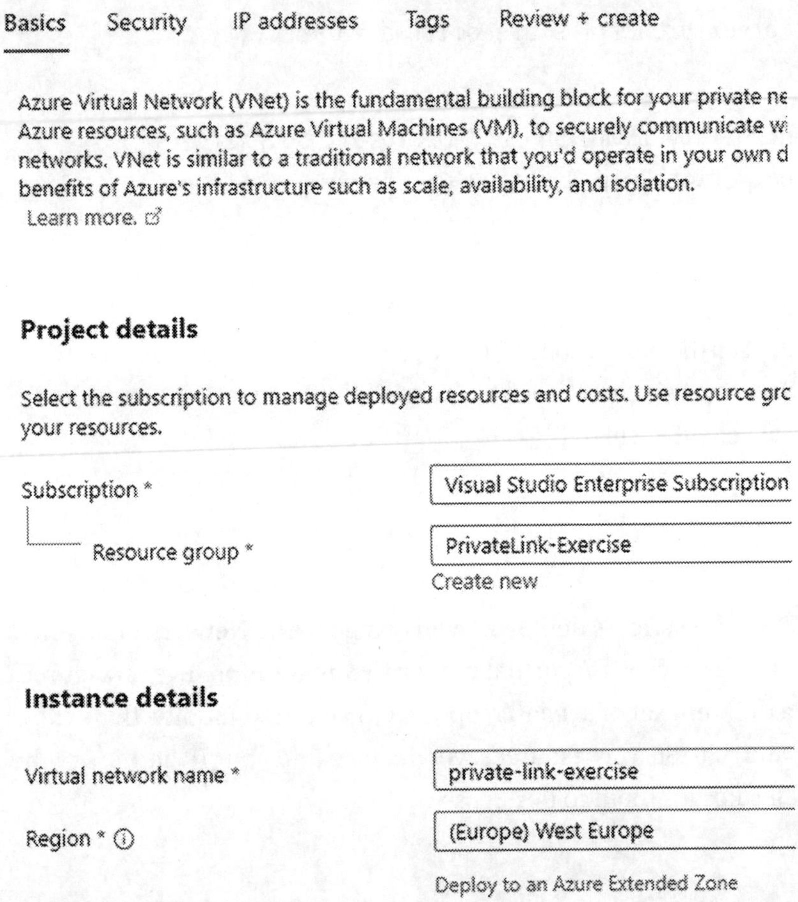

Basics   Security   IP addresses   Tags   Review + create

Azure Virtual Network (VNet) is the fundamental building block for your private ne
Azure resources, such as Azure Virtual Machines (VM), to securely communicate w:
networks. VNet is similar to a traditional network that you'd operate in your own d
benefits of Azure's infrastructure such as scale, availability, and isolation.
Learn more. ☐

Project details

Select the subscription to manage deployed resources and costs. Use resource grc
your resources.

Subscription * | Visual Studio Enterprise Subscription |

     Resource group * | PrivateLink-Exercise |
            Create new

Instance details

Virtual network name * | private-link-exercise |

Region * ⓘ | (Europe) West Europe |

Deploy to an Azure Extended Zone

Figure 10-3. *Creation of the virtual network*

- Go to Review + Create, then click the Create button.

Now we have to connect your virtual network with the Azure Function:

- Go to your Azure Function resource.

- Go to "Networking" in the "Settings" section.

- Click the "Not configured" next to "Virtual network integration" as shown in Figure 10-4.

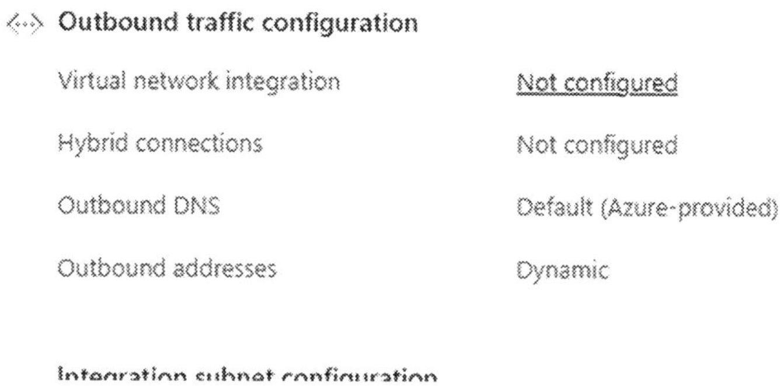

⟨··⟩ **Outbound traffic configuration**

Virtual network integration	<u>Not configured</u>
Hybrid connections	Not configured
Outbound DNS	Default (Azure-provided)
Outbound addresses	Dynamic

Integration subnet configuration

***Figure 10-4.** Outbound configuration for Azure function*

- Click the "Add" button.

- Select your virtual network as shown in Figure 10-5 and save.

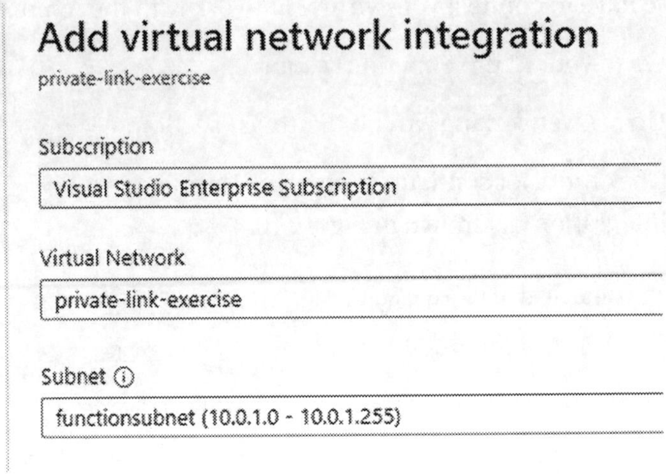

Add virtual network integration

private-link-exercise

Subscription

Visual Studio Enterprise Subscription

Virtual Network

private-link-exercise

Subnet ⓘ

functionsubnet (10.0.1.0 - 10.0.1.255)

Figure 10-5. *Adding a virtual network to the Azure function*

To connect the virtual network to your Storage Account:

- Go to the resource.

- Go to the "Networking" tab.

- Select option "Enable public access from selected virtual networks and IP addresses."

- Click the "Add" button, select your virtual network, and save.

Now your Storage Account is disabled from access to the public Internet, but still can be used by your Azure Function.

Configuring the Network with Other Services

The virtual network topic is a broad and complex subject that requires careful attention to detail. It is important to follow the proper steps outlined in the documentation to ensure successful integration. Most of the resources available in PaaS are easily integrated with the virtual network.

If you are going to use a private link (with private endpoints), you will also have to use other Azure services to provide Internet access to your Azure function. For more complex solutions, like integrating with the on-premises network, you may want to use Express Route. You can use an Azure VPN solution to limit access to only specific IP addresses, but this will require installing software on the customers' PCs.

Summary

After this chapter, you will have a clear understanding of how to manage and secure resources in a virtual network configuration. You can use this additional layer for increased security and control over access to your resources. You have also learned how to implement and enforce proper firewall rules for them to be accessible. You can always search for more advanced solutions on Microsoft official documentation.

Index

A

AcquireLeaseOnBlob method, 165

Application insights

App Service Environment
     (ASE), 78

Azure

Azure function